# Peking University

## Chinese Scholarship and Intellectuals, 1898–1937



Xiaoqing Diana Lin

STATE UNIVERSITY OF NEW YORK PRESS

Published by
State University of New York Press, Albany



Printed in the United States of America



For information, address State University of New York Press,
90 State Street, Suite 700, Albany, NY 12207

Production by Judith Block
Marketing by Susan Petrie

Library of Congress Cataloging in Publication Date

Lin, Xiaoqing Diana, 1963–
Peking University : Chinese scholarship and intellectuals, 1898–1937 / Xiaoqing Diana Lin.
p. cm. — (SUNY series in Chinese philosophy and culture)
Includes bibliographical references and index.
ISBN 0-7914-6321-4 (alk. paper) — ISBN 0-7914-6322-2 (pbk. : alk. paper)
1. Beijing da xue—History—20th century. 2. China—Intellectual life—20th century. I. Title. II. Series.
LG51.P28L55 2004
378.51'156—dc22

2004042993

10 9 8 7 6 5 4 3 2 1

# *Peking University*

SUNY series in Chinese Philosophy and Culture

Roger T. Ames, editor

To Kevin

# Contents

# Acknowledgments

Growing up in Beijing, China, I was always intrigued by the post-1952 campus of Peking University: its beautiful and serene scenery, built with a synthesis of traditional Chinese and modern Western architectural styles, its association with history, and its pride that went beyond the Communist era—the English letterhead of campus stationary has defiantly remained "Peking University," a spelling that goes against the *pinyin* system popularized in the 1970s that would render the university's English spelling to "Beijing University." Even the most radical Communist revolutionaries at Peking University would uphold "Peking University" because that name evokes an era beyond the short Communist history, an era associated with the May 4th movement, the chancellorship of Cai Yuanpei, the spread of New Culture, and the enormous influence the university faculty and students exerted on Chinese culture and society in the first half of the twentieth century. In this book I have followed the spelling "Peking University" rather than its pinyin spelling "Beijing University" because I think the name itself allows us a glimpse of how the university perceived itself, and its relationship to history. I have also decided to use the Chinese calligraphy for Peking University by Communist Party Chairman Mao Tse-tung—hung above the university gates and engraved on university student badges—on the book cover, again suggesting continuity: the continued political and intellectual importance of Peking University today. I thank Professor Akira Iriye for admitting me into the University of Chicago and giving me the opportunity for greater intellectual enrichment that I had ever thought possible. Professor Iriye's own scholarly integrity, great intellectual capabilities, and high expectations of his students were a great source of inspiration. I thank my dissertation advisers at the History Department of the University of Chicago, Guy Alitto, Akira Iriye, Prasenjit Duara, and Michael Geyer, for their insight, rigorous scholarship, and academic standards that helped me to develop the study of Peking University from an impressionistic idea to a detailed scholarly exploration.

Over the years, while the dissertation was being revised into a book I have also incurred much debt to many friends and colleagues. In particular, I thank

Yung-chen Chiang, Q. Edward Wang, Lung-Kee Sun, Charles Hayford, and Denise Chen for reading through chapters and giving me helpful suggestions. I thank Peter Zarrow for his exhaustive and insightful comments on the entire manuscript. I also thank Leo Oufan Lee, Theodore Huters, Irving Epstein, James Lane, Roberta Wollons, Ed Kenar, Paul Kern, and the late Rhiman Rotz for reading and commenting on portions or the entire manuscript. I want to thank the late Qiyi Xing, professor of chemistry at Peking University, for introducing me to a conversation with Deng Guangming, Hu Shi's student and later secretary. I also want to thank H. H. Wu. renowned historian of modern China, who tirelessly advised me at the manuscript stage and generously pointed me to many historical materials. Thanks also go to Guo Jianrong, historian of Peking University whose help with archival research at Peking University in 1998 greatly enriched this manuscript and who contributed part of the photographs included in this book. Wang Shiru, professor emeritus and librarian at Peking University whose kind invitation for me to attend the international conference commemmorating Cai Yuanpei in 1998 at Peking University gave me the chance to revisit the Peking University campus and further my research there; and Lui Shusen, who provided great help in securing a number of books by Peking University faculty not available in U.S. libraries. A library travel grant fron the University of Michigan in 1994 enabled me to browse the large collection of modern Chinese intellectual history at Ann Arbor. An associate membership at the University of Chicago East Asian Studies Center over the past six years has allowed me unlimited use of the libraries there and tremendously helped my research. I also thank Indiana University for several grants, including three summer fellowships and two international research grants, which have greatly facilitated the research and writing of the manuscript. Chapter 6 is based on a revision of an article published in Modern China "Historicizing Subjective Reality: Rewriting History in Early Republican China," (v.25, no.1, 1999). Chapter 7 partially draws on an article published in Chinese Science "Social Science and Social Control: the Case of Peking University, 1910s–1920s," (v.14, 1997). I thank *Modern China* and *Modern Science* for permission to use parts of these two articles here. I thank the two anonymous readers for SUNY Press for their helpful comments. I thank my editors at SUNY Press Nancy Ellegate for her judicious editorial review; Judith Block for her production skills, general editing, and donation of photographs of the contemporary Peking University campus, taken by Professor Eric Block; Debra Soled for copyediting; and Susan Petrie for marketing. Of course, all arguments here represent my own views, and I am solely responsible for any errors in this book.

I thank my mother Ching Tsien for her love and support through the years and my late father Tianlin Chen who had probably never thought his daughter would ever write a book in English when he exhorted me painstakingly to study English in my early teens. Over the long years the dissertation was written and then revised into a manuscript, my husband Kevin has exemplified great patience, forbearance, love, and belief in me, without which completion of this manuscript would be inconceivable. I also thank our children David and Lisa for refreshing me each day with their questions and challenges and most of all, with so much love.

# Introduction

Peking University, founded in 1898 as the Imperial Peking University, was China's first modern state university and was at the center of the country's major intellectual movements in the twentieth century: the introduction of Western learning, a revived interest in Buddhism, and a reinterpretation of Confucian and other branches of Chinese learning. Buddhism, with its metaphysical approach and long period of assimilation into the Chinese society, often became the stepping-stone to an understanding of metaphysical Western ideas, while Western philosophy was incorporated into the reinterpretation of Confucian learning. This book explores how the development of intellectual culture, especially in the areas of the introduction of Western learning and reinterpretation of Confucian and other branches of Chinese learning, was influenced by the operations of the modern university through an examination of development at Peking University (1898–1937) of seven academic disciplines: history, Chinese language and literature, philosophy, education, psychology, law, and political science. As such, it is a cross between educational/institutional history and intellectual history. Although administrative decisions and the curriculum at Peking University often reflected intellectual trends of the day, the university also provided a unique setting for the development and systematization of many discrete strands of thought, Chinese and Western, traditional and modern, that contributed to modern Chinese culture.

Western learning had a profound impact on the transformation of Chinese culture in the twentieth century. As an agent of change, the modern Chinese educational system—based on Japanese and Western educational systems—developed out of a pragmatism that first introduced Western learning for its potential practical effects, which, however, led to more subtle and metaphysical changes in Chinese society.

By fostering a new relationship between Chinese and Western, traditional and modern, learning, the modern university played a critical role in bringing about change in Chinese society and culture. The university certainly was not alone in helping create a new intellectual milieu in China; social and political forces as well as cultural forces outside the university played important roles, too. Because of the rise of the city and the emergence of modern cultural institutions such as the mass media, modern schools and universities, and various other middle-class professions independent of the state, the educated gained autonomy from the state with respect to both access to public communication and financial independence.

This book examines the role the university played in the formation of a new Chinese intellectual culture. The establishment of Imperial Peking University in 1898 was a direct consequence of the Sino-Japanese War of 1895, in which the modern Japanese navy annihilated the Chinese navy, and Japan took Korea and Taiwan as colonies. The university was founded on the traditional Chinese principle of making education serve the state. Japan's victory showed many Chinese that Western learning could strengthen an Asian state and made many Chinese realize that what they needed was not only incremental changes in guns and battleships, but technological advances bolstered by a new sociopolitical reality. They thus started to search for Western principles that guided the development of Western society and politics. Although established as a part of the state bureaucracy, the university gradually drifted away from its association with the state, as a result of the abolition of the imperial examination system and the decision to establish a civil service examination system similar to that in the West; the association was formally dissolved in the summer of 1911, not long before the downfall of the empire in the autumn of that year.

Thereafter, the history of Peking University is one of carving out its own identity as an independent center of culture and knowledge production, through its administrative policies, curriculum, and various other activities. One consistent theme in this history—from Zhang Zhidong's curriculum for the university in 1903 to Cai Yuanpei and Jiang Menglin's curricula from the 1910s to the 1930s—was a redefinition of Chinese learning, an introduction to Western learning, and the creation of a synthesis of Chinese and Western learning. Zhang Zhidong continued his lingering attempts to rebuild a moral framework of Chinese learning, but by Cai Yuanpei's arrival, a more universal framework for Chinese learning had already become the norm in China. This change was due to individual initiatives and state policies that separated education from officialdom. The content of knowledge, in the humanities, came to be distinguished with an emphasis on historicism, evolution, and scientific methods, often in an eclectic combination with textual exegesis, the popular approach to scholarship in the Qing dynasty (1644–1911), and European metaphysics. Historicism made possible this eclectic blend of approaches.

The historical approach, new to China and to Peking University campus in the early twentieth century, was similar to Western historicism as both the result of the latter's direct influence and a similarity of circumstances. As the failure of the French Revolution led to the renunciation of a natural harmony between individuals and social values that guided societies as championed by the Enlightenment historians in nineteenth century Europe, it was a disjuncture in social values and practices that led the Chinese historians to accept change as essential to historical development. In both cases, historicism developed in the wake of the disintegration of an established authority or challenge to traditional authority, which led to challenges to rules that used to be perceived as unchangeable. It focuses on the concrete and individual, pinning the meaning of historical events to their specific contexts.[1] The practice of historical writings was for rejecting a Confucian interpretation of the past and discovery of new, hitherto unknown elements of the past.

As chancellor of the university from 1917 to 1926, Cai Yuanpei left the most indelible impact on the university of any of its administrators. Cai tried to fashion a university culture distinct from politics, and this culture had a tremendous impact on the contours of twentieth-century Chinese intellectual culture generally, not only in the policy of *jianrong bingbao* (all subjects of learning would be tolerated and included), but also in the many ramifications of such policy. Cai was the first university administrator to advocate a university culture separate from purely utilitarian concerns, most notably, immediate relevance to national salvation. This policy allowed an evenhanded blend of science and metaphysics, textual exegetical and evolutionary linear approaches to Chinese learning, although scientific approaches to learning outweighed the more traditional ones. This newly founded university culture mirrored the national culture, but not without difficulty. For one thing, the university's relationship to society was never properly defined, which complicated the objective of those disciplines such as education and psychology, subjects that were premised on social service. For another, Western learning was often used as an agent of social transformation, rather than of values; the practice of law and politics made this especially clear.

Despite these problems, Peking University contributed to the transformation of Chinese national culture, in particular, a relegation of Confucian culture to largely the private realm and a blend of Chinese and Western culture. Such a transformation was also the result of a change in the social milieu. With the abolition of the imperial examination system in 1905, a decision the Chinese government made to encourage the development of the modern educational system, scholars no longer meddled in local administration. Living more and more in urban centers instead of rural areas, they relied on newspapers, associations, and schools for their life and propagation of ideas, and were immediately responsible to their audience through the mass media. Because of these changes, the emphasis on rituals and social hierarchy in Confucian learning was the most rapid to go. On the one hand, Confucian learning, especially with respect to ethical education, has had a stronger hold on Chinese intellectuals.[2] On the other hand, many Chinese intellectuals began at an early age to live independently and in big cities, so they found it easy to accept Western values. They came to equate common sense with Western science, whereas in the past common sense was associated with Confucian social and ritual practices.[3] In that sense, Cai Yuanpei's curriculum reflected a national trend, so it gained popularity and had a lasting impact.

This book consists of eight chapters. Chapters 1 to 3 deal with the founding and academic development of the university: the visions of Zhang Zhidong, Cai Yuanpei, and Jiang Menglin, among others, who were major contributors to the university's curriculum and administrative structure from the founding of the university until 1937. Chapters 4 to 6 discuss the transformation of Chinese learning (primarily in the humanities) through the teaching and research of these disciplines. Chapters 7 and 8 cover the social science disciplines and how their viability was influenced by both the social milieu and university culture. The conclusion evaluates the changes in Chinese intellectual culture as it relates to the transformation of learning in the university.

# 1

# From *Gewu zhizhi* to Building a New Moral Universe?

## The Development of the Imperial Peking University Curriculum (1898–1911)

Modern Chinese education developed out of contact with Western learning. The decision to learn from the West stemmed first from Chinese defeats in battles with Western countries and Japan in the latter part of the nineteenth century. From that very practical decision to make weapons and ships comparable to those in the West, the Chinese gradually came to accept many other Western concepts. Western practices and subjects of learning expanded Chinese views of the universe, leading to, among other things, more accurate mapmaking, knowledge of foreign customs and practices, and scientific explanations of the universe. As Benjamin Schwartz described it:

> What truly struck figures such as Yan Fu, Liang Qichao, and Kang Youwei as new was not so much the bare abstract idea of progress as what was perceived as the fact that the West had actually attained the realization of entirely new human possibilities in such realms as technology, science, and even social and political organization. It is thus no wonder that Western ideologies which promise a total historical redemption in an ideal order—whether these ideologies take the form of Marxism-Leninism, "modernization theory," or even the technological redemptionism of a Toffler—should continue to exercise such an extraordinary hold on the minds of so many modern Chinese.[1]

Western learning as introduced by missionaries from the Society of Jesus (Jesuits) started to challenge Confucian cosmology as early as the seventeenth century.[2] Western influence, however, was limited to the imperial calendar and the writings of a few scholars. In twentieth century China, many Chinese, recognizing the unbridgeable gap between their ideals and the Chinese socio-political reality as a result of Western intrusion, embarked on the search for a new reality. After the Second Opium War (1858–60), numerous Chinese scholars talked about "unprecedented changes" conveyed through an array of Chinese terms, including *bianju* (changed scene), *qibian* (dramatic change), *qiju* (dramatic changed scene), *chuangju* (unprecedented change), *shibian* (world change), and *dabian* (tremendous change). An estimate is that no fewer than eighty-one Chinese government officials used these terms in writing between 1840–1902, especially from 1884 to 1902. In the latter period alone China saw three wars with Europe, Japan, and the U.S. This pervasive mood of change was also fed by the writings of Western residents in China such as Sir Thomas Wade, the British envoy to China in the 1860s. These ideas often contained a tinge of Darwinism as they sought to develop a new worldview based on pro-active change for the purpose of helping China to help itself, a process that came to be known as self-strengthening.[3]

The borrowing of Western ideologies that "promise a total historical redemption," was not immediate. Initially, many Chinese reformers wanted to fit their new discoveries of the outside world neatly into the rubric of the Confucian moral universe. A pattern of reasoning was developed by the neo-Confucians of the Cheng-Zhu school of the Song dynasty (960–1279) that combined elements of Buddhism and Daoism in its interpretation of Confucian studies and envisioned a more metaphysical level of heavenly rules than previous Confucian scholars from preceding dynasties. They emphasized that understanding of the metaphysical rules would be achieved only after studying the minute rules in the specific relationships of things, which could be achieved through reading Confucian classics. As one major leader of that school, Zhu Xi put it, "investigation of things" through study (*gewu*) was needed to link the minute rules governing specific phenomena with the unifying Confucian rules (*zhizhi*). The Chinese reformers sought to treat the new discoveries as myriad things governed by rules that ultimately would be linked to the metaphysical rules of Confucian learning. The earliest schools offering Western education were meant to explore these specific rules. They included those that trained interpreters, such as the Jiangnan Arsenal where "engineering and technical subjects were taught in addition to languages, and considerable work in the translation of Western texts of science and technology was undertaken." An official institution in the south, the Fuzhou Navy Yard School, which focused on naval technology, had both English and French divisions. Private individuals, including provincial gentry and scholars, also established schools, such as Beiyang gongxue (North Sea Public School) in Tianjin in 1895 and Nanyang gongxue (South Sea Public School) in Shanghai in 1896.[4]

The Chinese state initiated its own institutions of higher education in the Western style in the 1890s, primarily to consolidate a traditional linkage between education and politics.[5] In contrast to the Christian missionaries, who opened numerous modern schools, Chinese individuals established few modern schools at the middle-school level or above in the nineteenth century, for the moment ceding the task to the state. The initial state development of Western schools, however, was very unbalanced with its focus on higher education which ignored primary and secondary education, suggesting the government lacked a unified vision of how Western learning could benefit China.[6] Far from being a centrally driven phenomenon, the schools were largely the work of reformist governors in their own provinces. Even the Imperial Peking University lacked primary and secondary schools as feeder institutions; in its first twelve years of operation, it had to focus on preparatory schools to prepare students for a university education, and after the university proper was opened in 1910, its preparatory school continued into the late 1920s because of the absence of a sufficiently established modern primary and secondary school system. This tendency to place a priority on higher education, at the expense of the lower levels, seemed a carryover of the imperial examination system, where scholars were expected to have studied the classical texts largely through private tutelage. One possible explanation for this is that the state did not have the resources and was not prepared to build a nationwide educational system in 1898, but went ahead in this piecemeal fashion because it needed to produce candidates who were qualified for government service. In the past, the system that produced those candidates was the imperial examination system; by the early twentieth century, it increasingly was the modern university.

The early modern schools' founders often had firsthand experience dealing with foreign countries or found foreign weapons and technology useful. As their contact with Western learning deepened, they also felt the need to go beyond Western technology to study the more abstract principles behind the applied sciences. This marked a transition on the part of Chinese reformers from a literal adherence to Confucian principles to a broader range of truths. Initially, the more abstract principles, usually from the natural sciences, continued to be viewed in terms of Confucian principles, such as in the case of Prince Gong and his School of Languages (*Tongwenguan*), established in 1861. As Western learning gained greater importance and had an impact of daily life in China in the 1890s, it became subject to the neo-Confucian question: is this knowledge equivalent to moral knowledge? In Zhu Xi's *gewu zhizhi* (investigation of things to achieve understanding of Confucian rules through study), a true understanding of the principles of the world would lead one to a total and sincere acceptance of the Confucian principles and a complete identification of one's sentiments with the Confucian rules—that is, the knowledge of Confucian learning that defined the reality was also the moral knowledge that guided one's behavior. The question was, would Western knowledge be able to define China's moral world? Zhang Zhidong, the chief drafter of the curriculum for Imperial Peking University, tried to address the question in his curriculum.

Prince Gong (1833–1898) was one of the first in the Qing imperial bureaucracy to confront the introduction of Western learning into China, and among all the Qing officials he pursued the policy of learning from the West for the longest period of time. In 1853, when he was twenty, he became the grand councillor (*junji dachen*) for his brother, the Xianfeng emperor. Prince Gong was charged with dealing with the domestic enemies of the Taiping army and the Small Sword Society (Xiaodaohui) rebel forces against the Qing government in the nineteenth century and with negotiations with the United States, Britain, France, and other European countries regarding their demand to revise the treaties they had signed with China after its defeat at British hands in the First Opium War (1839–42). In 1860, British and French troops pressed on to Beijing. The emperor fled the capital, leaving Prince Gong in charge. Eventually, the British and French occupied Beijing and succeeded in having the treaty revised on terms more favorable to them, including an increase of six million taels of silver in Chinese reparations in addition to the twenty-one million taels in the first treaty.[7]

The peace treaty to settle those conflicts, which Prince Gong was negotiating with Lord Elgin, the chief of staff of the English and French allied troops, was delayed because no one on the Chinese side knew English. In the wake of a second treaty with Britain in 1860, Prince Gong proposed opening a language school in Beijing to train interpreters of future treaties with foreign countries, because the English and the French required all treaties to be written in their languages beginning in 1863. However, Prince Gong's decision to build the new school did not envision the permanent incorporation of Western learning into China. His earliest plan was to enroll twenty-four students in his School of Languages so that interpreters would be available when the need arose. Because the Qing dynasty was governed by the Manchus, who were a minority that had conquered the Han Chinese in 1644, for fear of Han disloyalty to the Qing, he also requested that the enrollees be of Manchu origin. In 1862, only ten students enrolled.

From the start, although the school was officially under the supervision of the *zongli yamen* (ministry of general affairs), it was managed by Sir Thomas Wade. The school's main source of income was the proceeds of the maritime customs governed by the Briton Sir Robert Hart. W.A.P. Martin, an American Presbyterian missionary, served as chief supervisor (*zongjiaoxi*) of the School of Languages for twenty-six years.[8]

After the school was established, Prince Gong concluded that a much wider curriculum needed to be offered; in his 1866 memorial to the throne on adding new science courses to the curriculum, he linked scientific knowledge and national power. He suggested a change of student recruitment from teenage Manchus to mature young men over twenty years old of both Manchu and Han origin because they were older, who had good command of the Chinese (Han) written language, so that they could spend their time acquiring a thorough knowledge of the theories of astronomy and mathematics.[9] After that decision was made, Martin added to the curriculum such subjects as algebra, geometry, trigonometry, calculus, physics, chemistry, and calculations in astronomy, geography, and minerals.[10]

Prince Gong was not alone in pointing out a connection between abstract knowledge and practical outcome. So did many of his literary contemporaries, both in and out of government, such as Li Hongzhang, viceroy of Tianjin and founder of several modern military and machinery plants in China.[11] Feng Guifen, Wang Zhichun, Xue Fucheng, and Zheng Guanying, and many other reform-minded scholars linked Western material prosperity and strength with their educational systems and science curriculum.[12] While they aimed to use Western technology and science to transform the Chinese social and economic reality, they were also inadvertently raising the question of whether Western knowledge was also moral knowledge, as the neo-Confucians treated Confucian learning. In his introduction of social Darwinism into China, Yan Fu interpreted nature's survival of the fittest as a willful act, guided by fathomable moral laws.[13]

This treatment of Western learning certainly brought up the question of how Western learning related to the Confucian principles. As in Japan, the Chinese introduced a distinction between Chinese and Western learning as essence versus application, best articulated by Zhang Zhidong in his slogan *zhongxue wei ti, xixue wei yong* (Chinese learning as principle, and Western learning as application). Recent scholarship, however, contends that for many Chinese reformers, including Zhang Zhidong, the distinction indicates not antagonism between Chinese and Western learning but priority.[14] The discussion below uses the example of Zhang Zhidong's 1903 curriculum for Imperial Peking University to explore how he vacillated between Chinese and Western learning.

## Zhang Zhidong and Imperial Peking University

Zhang Zhidong (1837–1909) synthesized the Chinese and the Western in his school curriculum for Peking University in 1903. Although he was by no means the first one to use these approaches in China, his curriculum for Peking

University was the first to impact Chinese studies with these approaches. And his curriculum had a long-lasting impact on the university, even well after the republican revolution. Thus it is important to examine Zhang's curriculum closely. First, it is useful to look at his life experience, which heavily influenced his attitude toward Western learning and the idea of change.

Zhang Zhidong, whose official responsibilities ranged from provincial director of education, Hanlin academician, to governor, also had firsthand experience dealing with instability caused by domestic rebels and foreign powers. He had a turbulent early youth: his father, the prefect of Xingyi in Guizhou province, fought the Taiping army and other rebels, including dissident Miao tribes of Guizhou. In 1855, when he was eighteen, Zhang Zhidong fought alongside his father. He traveled frequently between his native Zhili province, which is adjacent to Tianjin, and his father in Guizhou. Four years later, Zhang Zhidong took charge of a militia force that guarded twenty villages in Zhili. The British and French occupation of Beijing led Zhang to the Zhili militia experience In 1863, his palace examination—the highest of the imperial examinations, presided over and graded by the emperor was a critique of current policies and an attack on the imperial examination system. The examiners were divided in their opinion, but Cixi, the empress dowager, perhaps out of her own personal experience of having fled Beijing with the emperor in 1859, approved of his essay and awarded him the title of *jinshi* (highest level of success in the imperial examination).[15] He served as provincial director of education in Sichuan and Hubei, and later as governor of Zhili, Guangdong, and Hubei.

During his tenure as governor of Hubei and Guangdong, Zhang Zhidong made his name as a modern educational reformer by opening up many new-style schools patterned after the Chinese *shuyuan* (private Chinese institute) system, emphasizing understanding of Confucian learning and current affairs, not preparation for the imperial examinations. After China's defeat in the Sino-Japanese War in 1895, he turned all such *shuyuan* schools to modern, Western-style schools. He also sent students from Hubei to study abroad. Hubei thus became a forerunner in modern Chinese educational reform. Zhang's instrumental role in the 1903 school programs led to the development of Chinese schools at all levels, from primary to tertiary and research institutes, and from normal schools to higher vocational schools.[16]

Zhang's curriculum for Imperial Peking University reflected his awareness of competing classifications of knowledge: the Confucian integration of knowledge, and the Western specialization of learning. Zhang tried to integrate an expanded definition of Chinese learning from the past—history, literature, philosophy, and philology—with Western learning and practical knowledge. Chinese learning was compartmentalized into different disciplines. Even Confucian learning was able to occupy no more than one of the eight academic divisions:

(Confucian) classics, politics and law, arts, medicine, science, agriculture, engineering, and commerce. This classification was closely modeled after that in the Japanese state universities: the Imperial Tokyo University and Imperial Kyoto University, except that, in the Japanese universities, Confucian classics were a subfield in Chinese studies, and commerce was a part of the law and politics division.[17]

In these branches of Chinese learning, scattered in different academic disciplines, Zhang Zhidong tried to create a new integration between the concrete universe and the moral universe, but his approach differed drastically from previous Chinese approaches to education. The official development of Confucian orthodoxy emphasized a literal reading of the Confucian moral exhortations and equation of them to reality. At the Imperial College, instead of a specialized curriculum, students learned through gradual immersion in the classics. The readings over the years varied very little to guide the student gradually into a greater identification with the principles stipulated in the classics. The first level was initiation, including achieving the correct interpretation (*zheng yi*), elevating ambitions (*cong zhi*), and broadening the course of study (*guang ye*). It was offered to those who had a good grounding in the four great books (The Analects, the Mencius, Doctrine of the Mean, and the Great Learning) but were not very familiar with the five classics (Book of Poetry, Book of Documents, Spring and Autumn Annals According to Zuo, Book of Zhou Rites, and Book of Changes). After a year and a half, those who could write fluently would ascend to the level of cultivating the Way (*xiu dao*) and making the heart sincere (*cheng xin*) to give them a deeper immersion in history and the classics. After a year and a half at this level, students would go to the highest level, free exercise of one's temperament (*shuai xing tang*), which would take a year. The third level was based on the assumption that the student had already cultivated the Confucian Way and could now practice administration of government. After passing several examinations, the students would be awarded an office. By emphasizing sincerity of acceptance and the actual practice of the sages' teachings, the Imperial College tried to achieve a combination of one's feelings, motivation, and action, to cultivate a world outlook based on an ethical view of reality imparted by the classics,[18] a neo-Confucian ideal championed by the Cheng-Zhu school.

An implicit assumption in this educational system was the harmony between the individual and society, which was not unlike the assumption behind Enlightenment historical writings, although the reasons for this assumption were quite different in pre-twentieth-century China and eighteenth-century France. The Enlightenment belief in the harmony between the individual and society proceeded from the natural-law philosophies, influenced by science. In neo-Confucian learning, this harmony was also based on a law binding the individuals and society, although such law (*dao*) was based in morality. The results of this belief, however, were somewhat similar: both the Enlightenment philosophes and Chinese Confucians believed that history carried some unchanging essence and historical change only involved contingent elements, so that lessons from history were timeless.[19]

Zhang Zhidong was torn between recognizing the new reality he wanted to achieve as originating from principles that were fundamentally different from Confucian learning and seeing it as simply a manifestation of specific connections between society and the Confucian moral principles. That he continued to uphold the Confucian principles is evident from the division he created for Confucian learning, although this was already different from the past, when Confucian learning occupied the whole curriculum. Despite the special status accorded to Confucian learning, the content was drastically reduced. Specialization, a characteristic of the modern university, was also applied to Confucian learning. Students could specialize in one or two of the eleven subfields/classics in the division: *Book of Changes* (Zhouyi), *Book of History* (Shangshu), *Book of Poetry* (annotated by Mao) (Mao shi), *Spring and Autumn Annals* (annotated by Zuo) (Chunqiu zuozuan), the Zuo, Gongyang, and Guliang annotations of the *Spring and Autumn Annals* (Chunqiu sanzhuan), *Book of Zhou Rites* (Zhouli), *Book of Rituals* (Yili), *Book of Rites* (Liji), *Analects* (Lunyu), *Mencius* (Mengzi), and *Song Dynasty Confucian Learning* (Li-xue). Like the neo-Confucians, Zhang asked for an inferential rather than literal reading of the classics. It meant a greater emphasis on interpretation and the extraction of the most important messages from the classics. He believed that each classic had dozens or even hundreds of common messages, and it was the responsibility of the students to extract them from the classic in which they specialized.[20] The inferences, of course, had to be based on a correct understanding of the classics, including a correct understanding of the words. What Zhang suggested was a combination of the Qing textual exegesis that focused on the understanding of the literal meaning of ancient words and the Song neo-Confucian learning that stressed interpretation for practical use.

The study of these Confucian principles alone was obviously not enough for Zhang to work toward a new social reality for China. Thus he included as supplementary courses comparative studies in ancient and modern Chinese legal systems, history of Chinese and foreign education, Chinese and foreign geography, and world history, which helped relate the classics to Chinese and foreign law, politics, and education. He also assigned elective courses (*xuanxiuke*) for this division, including Chinese literature, Western history, Western legal history, psychology, logic, and sociology.[21] Zhang tried to link the study of Confucian classics with that of Western politics, such as the parliamentary system that Zhang decided China eventually would introduce. He believed that the essence of the Western political system included modern schools, the study of geography, the modernization of methods of finance and taxation, weapons, the legal system, public works, commerce, and trade, all of which were preconditions for parliamentary government.[22] If Confucian learning provided the principles, it had to work alongside these other Chinese and Western subjects in order to bring about the new social reality.

Zhang did not stop at the integration of Confucian learning with other subjects of learning. He tried also to include in the curriculum specific rules governing various aspects of Chinese life and combine them with Western subjects of science and social sciences. Chinese subjects of history, philosophy, literature, and philology, historically subordinate to Confucian learning but closely linked to the classics and perceived as conduits to a better acceptance of the classics, were now studied extensively to focus on the manifestations of Confucian principles on a more concrete level as reflected in these branches of learning. Chinese history and literature—together with foreign history, Chinese and foreign geography, English literature, French literature, Russian literature, German literature, and Japanese literature—formed the Division of the Arts. In the fields of Chinese history, literature, and geography, Zhang emphasized causal analysis and an evolutionary approach to surmise patterns of change that he said had contemporary reference. Unlike the Confucian Learning division, which emphasized interpretation over content, Zhang sought a detailed study of the vicissitudes of Chinese history that went beyond treating history as a moral reflection of the success or failure of meeting Confucian standards. And its focus was on a practical assessment of Chinese policies and society by the standards of wealth, strength, and wisdom. Zhang wanted to search for patterns of establishment and change in political practices, comparative studies between state strength and state policies, changes in people's nature, including wisdom and stupidity, strength and weaknesses, reasons for wealth and poverty of different dynasties, the rise and fall of education, relevance of the literati and scholarship to national strength and social customs, changes in military systems, the ups and downs in agriculture, the difference between useful and non-useful craftsmanship, the relationship between land and water routes and national prosperity, changes in prices, the pros and cons of taxation, different dynasties' financial planning, the pros and cons of criminal law, changes in the strategic importance of the coastal region, reasons for foreign penetration of China, each dynasty's success or failure at foreign policies, reasons for political problems, changes in rituals, music, etiquette, prose, and mourning uniforms, changes in calendars, different institutional emphases in each dynasty, differences between the reforms in each dynasty, and evaluation of historical writing styles of different dynasties. Chinese history, in other words, became a way of expanding the study of Chinese political systems and practices. For that reason, histories that did not follow orthodox Confucian traditions were also accepted for study. Historical genres thus went beyond official dynastic histories—which had usually been considered orthodox histories—to various unofficial histories and general histories. As in the Classics Division, to further link Chinese history with the present and Western culture and politics, Zhang stipulated elective courses including logic, legal history of various foreign countries, Chinese literature, anthropology, sociology, education, archaeology, writings on metal ornaments and stone tablets, finance, and foreign relations.[23]

Like Chinese history, Chinese literature in Zhang's curriculum was coopted to further the study of politics. The Confucian exhortation that literary genres were to transmit the moral messages of the sages and that there should be a special correlation between prose style and moral messages led to the dismissal of many forms of prose, including the novel, from respectable writings in Chinese history. Although the traditional emphasis on writing style persisted—reflected in Zhang's exhortation that students should be selective about literary genres, differentiating between those with and without virtue, with or without scholarship, singling out those that were empty and useless in improving the quality of the people—Zhang introduced to the curriculum a wide range of prose styles, from parallel prose to novels and bibliography, and especially literary genres that were of present practical use. Zhang tried to link literary studies with more direct practical relevance, such as their connection with the nation, geography, world archaeology, diplomacy, and the study of new knowledge and new machinery manufacturing. The elective courses Chinese literature majors were to take included psychology, logic, diplomatic history, Western legal history, sociology, education, Latin and Greek, which were fundamentally similar to the elective courses for Chinese history and Confucian classics, showing that the ultimate goals of the three areas were similar, if not identical. In the field of geography, similar linkages were also built between Chinese and foreign geography and climate, finance, sea and land communications, history, zoology and botany, culture, military administration, customs, and industry.[24]

Therefore in Zhang's curriculum for Chinese learning, one finds a recreated universe *qua* moral universe: the universe now included historical Chinese practices in many areas of life and many Western subjects of learning. On the surface, Zhang tried to show that the principles remained Confucian, hence his famous "essence/application" formula. However, unlike the historical curriculum for the imperial college, where Confucian learning comprised the whole universe, Zhang's curriculum expanded upon the previous Confucian classics and created a new integration between Chinese learning and the myriad reality as represented by the many supplementary and elective foreign and Chinese learning courses associated with the Chinese subjects. With regard to this integrated body of Chinese and Western learning, I agree with the basic premise of

Min Tu-ki. Namely, in his exhortation of Chinese learning as inner (governing body and mind) and Western learning as outer (governing worldly affairs), Zhang Zhidong was concerned not with the logical relationship between "principle" and "utility," but with their functional difference: Western learning was needed so that Chinese learning might be preserved.[25] Although Confucian learning remained a separate division, its status as "principles" or "essence" was primarily in form and its functions in the curriculum did not fundamentally differ from an integrated curriculum in which Confucian learning was offered as subdivisions of different academic disciplines.

The interesting thing about Zhang Zhidong's curriculum was the contrast between the newly constituted universe of Chinese and Western learning, complementing each other to form a new sociopolitical reality, and divisions that comprised only specialized Western learning. As a modern university, Peking University introduced the structure of the Western university, including many specialized areas of learning in the arts and sciences, some of which, such as law, politics, science, and medicine, had very little Chinese learning content. Unlike many nineteenth-century Chinese scholars who traced Western science to early Chinese developments in mathematics and astronomy to show the fundamentally Chinese origins of all knowledge, Zhang made no attempt to integrate Chinese and Western learning in the related areas. If anything, he tried to separate the discussion of certain Western disciplines from Chinese ones, especially those in science, technology, and medicine, traditionally beyond the pale of Confucian learning and the imperial examinations. He did not hesitate to omit these subjects of Chinese learning from his curriculum and replace them almost completely with their counterparts from the West. Chinese law and politics were mostly studied not on their own merits but as supplementary courses to Chinese history and literature for a greater understanding of the Chinese political past. Both criminal and civil laws existed in China and were fully developed in the Qing dynasty, although they largely followed the moral criteria of Confucian learning. In Zhang Zhidong's curriculum for the Division of Law and Politics, he relied almost completely on Japanese curricula and Japanese textbooks. The few courses in the field of politics dealing with China included the *Qing Legal Compendium* (Da Qing huidian), and a history of Chinese legal systems. In the field of law, aside from a few courses on the history of Chinese laws, the focus was on foreign constitutional, civil, criminal, and commercial laws, including Roman, British, French, and German laws, and the lectures were to be based on appropriate books from abroad.[26] The inclusion of Chinese law and politics as supplementary courses in the study of Chinese history and the lack of their coverage as proper academic disciplines reflected a disconnect Zhang created between the modern emphasis on scientific and technological and legal/political developments and traditional Chinese science, technology, law, and politics. On the one hand, there was a greater emphasis on practical learning, as shown in the exhaustive study of the Chinese past for a better understanding of the workings of Chinese politics; on the other hand, the Confucian value system that favored politics and moral studies over the practical arts seemed to persist. Western science and technology were introduced because they would be instrumental for leading China to national prosperity. Chinese science and technology, since they were not immediately associated with a Western-style economic or political outcome, were irrelevant to his curriculum. Yet, although law and politics were deemed superior to science and technology, Chinese law and politics would not be the primary focus of study because the social outcome Zhang was concerned with was associated with Western legal and political practices. Moreover, historically, political practices never gained an independent right on their own apart from Confucian practices. Although law had been practiced in China, it never became a respectful field of study compared with the Confucian ethics and was not tested in the imperial examinations. The result of his treatment of Chinese science, technology, law, and politics was that, despite the new goal of focusing more on the practical and integrating Chinese and Western learning, the continued Chinese hierarchy of knowledge that prioritized political/moral knowledge over any other kind hindered the integration of practical learning into the Chinese value system. And within the body of political/moral knowledge, the emphasis was on integration despite specialization. Chinese law and political studies were studied along with history and literature, but not as specialized fields. Although the core of the reconstituted Chinese political/moral knowledge was more tilted toward what was traditionally considered moral knowledge, namely, history and literature, the encyclopedic listing of courses in these areas of study suggested that Zhang's ultimate goal was an integrated body of both Chinese and Western knowledge that contrasted with the specialized subjects of learning in Western law, politics, commerce, medicine, and the sciences.

What is ironic about Zhang Zhidong's dichotomy of the more integrated curriculum of Chinese learning and the specializations of Western learning is that it was the latter with their detailed rules that would achieve the social prosperity he desired. The former was only a construct that linked the various aspects of the Chinese world, including the Chinese past, to the Western subjects of learning that would ultimately achieve for him the desired social outcome. It could not by itself directly bring about that social outcome but, rather, represented Zhang's moral ideal. Zhang was trying to achieve two things in this curriculum: to reconstruct the Chinese universe *qua* moral universe, and to introduce the specialized fields of learning that would help build China into an industrialized society made up of professionals. Zhang's dilemma over how to balance the two reflected the clash between preindustrialized China—where the moral world loomed larger than anything else—and the industrialized West—which China, however remote from it, wanted to imitate. As such, Zhang was dominated by the pragmatic consideration that specialized Western learning would help him engineer a Western-style social outcome. Guided by such a mindset, Zhang failed to introduce an appreciation of these specialized "practical" trades. The Western "practical" subjects were introduced not for their intrinsic value but for the social outcome they would bring about. Zhang simply refrained from an evaluation of Western learning in his 1903 curriculum. The dichotomy between "essence" and "application" as assigned separately to Chinese and Western learning conveniently allowed him to bypass this evaluation process by resorting to a most pragmatic explanation, although he did include Western learning in the body of moral knowledge to redefine Chinese learning.

Written in 1903, two years before the establishment of the Ministry of Education, Zhang Zhidong's school program provided the basis for not only Peking University but also all modern schools in China from the primary to the tertiary level. The Imperial Peking University not only would be the highest state university at the national level but also would serve as a model for all provincial state universities. This arrangement was based on the Japanese educational model, a hybrid of Japanese, French, and German traditions—whose goal was a hierarchical educational system under state control. According to Zhang's regulations, universities could be established only at the provincial level, and prefectures could only establish primary schools. The national university would be the model for the provincial universities. This was actually part of the original plan for Imperial Peking University. Thus Sun Jianai (1827–1909), who was to become the first imperial minister in charge of education, therefore directly supervising the university, had proposed to the crown in the summer of 1898 that a translation bureau be established and attached to the university so that it could compile and translate standard textbooks for the schools and universities of China.

## Reform of the Educational System: Zhang Zhidong in Perspective

Three drafts of the university curriculum were written between 1898 and 1902, before Zhang Zhidong's the following year. Compared with these, Zhang's was more successful in recreating a Chinese culture geared to current reality. Unlike the other drafts, which often tended to be impatient with the slow pace of practical results from Confucian learning in twentieth-century China, Zhang's was aimed at re-engineering Confucian learning toward a new social reality.

To many early twentieth-century Chinese reformers, from a pragmatic point of view, Confucian learning appeared inadequate. It therefore is no surprise that criticism began to mount against the imperial examination system, which was focused on Confucian learning. Nor is it surprising that the main criticism was the vacuity of the examinations—that they were divorced from life, especially in view of contacts with the West. Although similar criticisms of the imperial examinations had been raised in both the Ming and Qing dynasties, they lacked any real momentum, nor did they bring about change in the examination system. The Ming and Qing governments both tried to reform the examination format, but stopped short because of the enormity of the task .[27] The technical inconvenience of the examination system to accommodate specialized Western learning, and the reluctance of many Chinese scholars to pursue Western learning so long as the imperial examinations on the classics continued, led the Chinese government to end the examination system altogether. The force of the Western entry into China forced the Chinese state to change its educational format, and the reality of Western society fed Chinese reformers' desire for change.

In 1895, many Chinese scholars, led by Liang Qichao, a leading reform scholar, had denounced the examination system in a memorial presented to the emperor, after China's defeat in the war with Japan. Zhang Zhidong also called for reform of the imperial examination system.[28] Later, Zhang and Yuan Shikai (1859–1916), viceroy of Shili Province and later grand councillor, petitioned the throne to cut back on the examination system and eventually abolish it.[29] Even the emperor had issued an edict in 1898 calling on all state officials to study assiduously and, based on classical Chinese teachings, to introduce those aspects of Western learning that were appropriate for dealing with current affairs, so as to save themselves from the problem of vacuity, backwardness, and error.[30] European missionaries also championed learning to bring about social change. One of them, Gilbert Reid, proposed that a university curriculum include Chinese and European languages, writing, grammar, history, politics, law, policies, geography, topology, mathematics, physics, chemistry, astronomy, machinery, minerals, engineering, agriculture, physiology, medicine, and so forth. But, as Chen Pingyuan, a biographer of Peking University, commented, these subjects did not include literature and the arts. Another missionary, Calvin Mateer, who established Dengzhou wenhuiguan (Dengzhou Culture School), the first missionary university in China, also proposed a similar curriculum for an imperial university. Mateer organized a "literature committee" that consisted of various European missionaries in China. The literature they wanted to promote was not classical literature but, rather, popular literature. This was reflected in the works of these missionaries, including Ernst Faber's *German Schools* and Timothy Richard's *Reference on New Education in Seven*

*Countries*. These books had a tremendous influence on late Qing Chinese society, and reformers such as Liang Qichao learned a great deal about the details of Western education through them.[31]

Against the background of this nationwide call for change among the elite, the question was how to change. Before Zhang Zhidong submitted his curriculum, there were three versions of the university curriculum, each with a different approach to Chinese and Western learning. Liang Qichao's tried to compartmentalize the two while privileging Western learning, Sun Jianai's compartmentalized the two and did not differentiate between the practical and the theoretical in Western learning, and Zhang Baixi's aimed at a liberal arts curriculum.

Liang Qichao (1873–1929), one of the most ardent early champions of Western learning and reform, did the first draft for Peking University's curriculum in 1898. His draft put Chinese and Western learning on an equal footing but assigned them to two separate spheres, ethics and science. Sun Jianai appointed Kang Youwei (1858–1927), famous Confucian scholar, together with his student Liang Qichao to draft the first university regulations, which, according to Kang, showed the influence of the educational systems of Britain, the United States, and Japan. The regulations drafted in the spring of 1898 by Liang Qichao, despite the Western influence and emphasis on a standard procedure in educational structure and content, dichotomized Chinese and Western learning into ethics and science, and ultimately privileged the latter over the former. Liang's university plan was divided into comprehensive and specialized studies. The comprehensive studies included Chinese humanities subjects and mostly science subjects from the West: Confucian classics before Zhu Xi (*jingxue*), Confucian classics as interpreted by Zhu Xi and his followers (*lixue*), Chinese and foreign histories, various schools of thought, elementary mathematics, elementary physics, elementary political science, elementary geography, literature, and gymnastics, which the students would study for three years. Students would also choose from among five foreign languages: English, French, Japanese, Russian, and German. The Translation Bureau in Shanghai would compile textbooks. After that, students would specialize in one field of science, such as advanced mathematics, advanced geography, agriculture, mineralogy, engineering, or commerce.[32] Confucian learning, in this curriculum, served as a part of the comprehensive curriculum to pave the way for more specialized fields of study that would be more directly connected to the building of a new social order.

Compared with Zhang's draft, Liang's curriculum had a much narrower conception of knowledge. Dividing Chinese and Western learning into ethical and scientific, Liang compartmentalized Chinese and Western learning into different areas of life in this curriculum. As Liang said to Chinese students while visiting the United States in 1903, they should not specialize in philosophy, literature, and politics but only in the practical fields.[33] Although Liang did not label Chinese learning as "essential" and privilege it over Western learning and seemed to privilege Western science over Confucian learning, Liang's limitation of Western learning to science severely compromised his coverage of Western learning in his curriculum. Like Zhang, however, Liang failed to assign any value to Western science but treated it as an instrument for achieving a particular social outcome.

A similar approach to Western learning was shown in a curriculum proposed by Sun Jianai in 1896. Sun, the first Qing official in charge of the establishment of an imperial university, proposed ten disciplines: astronomy, classics, politics, literature, military science, engineering, commerce, and medicine. As in Liang's draft, Sun's curriculum placed Chinese and Western learning parallel to each other. Furthermore, Sun mixed the practical and theoretical in his taxonomy of knowledge. For instance, he subordinated the sciences to the practical learning of engineering and medicine. The subject of mathematics was put under astronomy; the study of minerals under geology; the study of ships, railways, and telegraphs under commerce.[34] It showed that Sun's attention was not on the intrinsic rules of learning but, rather, on the practical ramifications of specialized learning.

The last curriculum drafted before Zhang Zhidong's was by Zhang Baixi in 1902, after closing down in 1900 and 1901, as a result of the Boxer Uprising. In 1900, Beijing was occupied by troops from eight foreign governments that held the imperial government responsible for the havoc wreaked by peasant rebels who belonged to an organization called the Yihetuan (Boxers). Sun Jianai, the first minister in charge of education, resigned in 1900 because of Empress Cixi's attempt to force the Guangxu emperor to abdicate the throne.[35] Sun was the emperor's former tutor and sided with the emperor on reforms that disagreed with the Empress Dowager. In 1901, after making peace with the foreign governments that had troops occupying Beijing, the Qing government revived educational reform and appointed Zhang Baixi as minister in charge of the imperial university. Before this appointment, Zhang had been minister of education in Chinese provinces including Shandong and Guangdong and secretary (*shangshu*) of several imperial ministries. He was often outspoken in his petitions to the throne on the corruption of the government, including Empress Dowager Cixi's intention to mount a lavish celebration of her sixtieth birthday investing money in a summer palace instead of the Chinese navy as the charge usually went, and on the need for China to modernize. He was responsible for recommending Kang Youwei to the emperor. After the failure of the 1898 reform movement, he was temporarily demoted because of his recommendation of Kang. In 1900, however, he again petitioned the throne for reform of China's financial and educational systems. His appointment in 1901 as minister in charge of Imperial Peking University was controversial and apparently came about through patronage from the emperor, who ratified Zhang's memorial to improve the university through increase of budget, books, housing, and the establishment of a translation bureau on the same day it was submitted. To balance ethnic ranks of the government, the emperor had to put a second minister, Rong Qing, of Manchu descent, in charge of Imperial Peking University, and named Zhang Hengjia general supervisor of the university, thus dividing the power initially entrusted to Zhang Baixi.[36] Zhang, however, still shouldered great responsibility because, in the absence of a Ministry of Education (created only later, in 1905), he was minister in charge of both the imperial university and the education of the whole country.

Compared to Sun Jianai and Liang Qichao, Zhang Baixi paid greater attention to the educational structures of European countries and the United States. In 1902, Zhang Baixi drafted a new set of regulations for the Imperial Peking University. That year and afterward, he sent relevant government personnel to study the Japanese educational system and solicited university curricula and regulations from many foreign countries, including curricula from Harvard, Yale, Columbia, and the University of Pennsylvania as well as primary and secondary schools in Washington, DC.[37] Thus his draft was closer to Zhang Zhidong's curriculum, drafted a year later, which adhered more closely to Western educational structures than did earlier drafts.

The Japanese and American influence certainly left an impact on Zhang Baixi's 1902 university regulations. More than the curriculum of his predecessors, however, his school regulations, including comprehensive and specialized studies, placed great emphasis on research that would build a hierarchy of learning to facilitate specialized research at the very top. Because of the lack of primary and secondary schools in China, Zhang's school program included a three-year preparatory school with an elaborate curriculum. Students entering it would specialize in either politics (*zheng*) or the practical arts (*yi*). Those specializing in the former would advance to the fields of politics, literature, business, and commerce at the university level, whereas those specializing in the latter would go into agriculture, physics, engineering, and medicine. Unlike the drafts of Liang Qichao and Sun Jianai, Zhang Baixi's curriculum integrated Chinese and Western learning. Zhang Baixi adopted Western subjects of learning in the humanities and the social sciences as well as the sciences. In addition to Confucian learning and ethics, Zhang Baixi's curriculum for those majoring in political science in the preparatory school also included Chinese prose and poetry, mathematics, comparative history of China and foreign countries, Chinese and foreign geography, geology, foreign languages, physics, logic, law, finance, gymnastics, and military training. His curriculum for practical arts majors was similar to that for political science majors, except that their natural sciences course load was heavier, including botany, zoology, chemistry, advanced geology. Moreover, the practical arts majors, although they had to take a course in ethics, were not required to take a course on Confucian or non-Confucian schools of thought.[38]

Like Zhang Zhidong's draft, in Zhang Baixi's curriculum the content of Chinese learning included non-Confucian schools of thought, although it still focused on ethical education. Aside from Confucian learning, which included a series of classics and their annotations since the Han dynasty, Zhang Baixi introduced ethics (*lunli*), which covered famous sayings from the Zhou dynasty to the Han and Tang dynasties, important subjects studied in the imperial courts of the Song, Yuan, and Ming dynasties, and the sayings and activities of famous foreigners. The purpose of the study of ethics, according to Zhang Baixi, was its influence on practice. There was a third field of study dealing with the various schools of thought in Chinese history, including Legalism, Militarism, Sophism, and Daoism. Here, Confucian and non-Confucian learning were treated as contributing equally to Chinese culture. Zhang Baixi went even further than Zhang Zhidong in integrating Chinese and Western learning, especially in the curriculum for the college proper, where Confucian learning became a subdivision of study in the Division of Literature together with other subjects of both Chinese and foreign studies, which included Confucian classics, history, neo-Confucian schools of thought, history of institutional changes (*zhanggu xue*), Chinese prose and poetry, and foreign languages and philology.[39] Zhang Baixi's curriculum presented a specialized Chinese studies curriculum without giving Chinese subjects more universal moral relevance. It resembled a liberal arts curriculum at a Western college.

The great ambiguity toward Confucian learning in Zhang Baixi's school program was perhaps one of the causes for the dissatisfaction of Rong Qing and other conservative members of the Qing government. Regarding the imperial school program drafted by Zhang Zhidong in 1903, many have pointed out Rong Qing's acrimony with Zhang Baixi as the reason for the need of yet a new draft of curriculum. Zhang Baixi himself, however, made a petition to the throne soliciting Zhang Zhidong's participation in a new and more detailed school program in 1903, which the emperor approved on the same day.[40]

In the face of the Western presence in China and motivated by pragmatic concerns, all four drafters of the university curriculum searched for new knowledge content to achieve the desired social outcome. Of the four, Zhang Baixi and Zhang Zhidong's were most successful in integrating a broad range of Western and Chinese subjects of learning. Zhang Baixi's, however, failed to uphold the superiority or priority of Chinese learning; hence it was soon dismissed, although the preparatory school and other affiliated schools proposed by Zhang

Baixi were established and allowed to continue operation. By contrast, Zhang Zhidong's draft balanced the pragmatic engineering for a new social outcome with the preservation of Confucian and more generally moral principles. Yet Zhang Zhidong's curriculum, continuing the Confucian cosmological identification of the physical with the moral universes, also failed to rationalize the massive introduction of specialized Western learning and justify it using Confucian principles.

Zhang Zhidong's attitude toward Confucian learning was characteristic of early twentieth-century national views. As shown in an official announcement on the new school system proposed by Yuan Shikai in 1905, Yuan not only classified Confucian learning as a specialized field at the university level but also referred to it as national essence (*guocui*).[41] National essence, a term borrowed from Japan by Chinese scholars at the turn of the twentieth century, essentialized a culture as a transcendental spirit. Confucian learning was increasingly treated as transcendental principles that were reified in various subjects of learning. As such, Confucian institutions were ignored, and Confucian studies receded into the realm of individual moral cultivation. The emphasis on Confucian learning as individual cultivation was also shown in Yuan's request that it be extensively taught in primary and secondary schools but constitute only one field of learning at the college leve1.[42] Momentum across the country to bring about a new, Western-style society in China and a corresponding set of principles to describe that new society gradually pushed Confucian learning to the periphery. Zhang's major contribution to the decline of Confucian learning was his instrumental approach to Chinese learning, eliminating Chinese science and technology, while de-emphasizing Chinese medicine, law, and politics—topics he did not consider relevant for his building of a new Western-style reality. This instrumental approach to knowledge was reflected in later generations' attitude toward Confucian learning, including the slogan of "Down with Confucius and Sons," during the May fourth (1919) student demonstrations and after because students of a younger generation saw no logical connection between Confucian learning and a Western-style political outcome.

Zhang Zhidong's curriculum left important legacies for later generations. The first legacy was the elimination of morality from the study of history and literature. For Zhang, history and literature continued to impart moral lessons and theoretically were manifestations of Confucian principles on a more concrete level, but the study of them was integrated with that of other subjects of non-Confucian Chinese learning and of Western learning, which could easily make their linkage to Confucian learning tenuous. For later generations, this development eased the acceptance of a scientific approach to these disciplines, which treated history and literature as not moral treatises, but historical documents. The second legacy was the divorce Zhang created between the Chinese present and much of the Chinese past, due to his elimination or reduction of state patronage practices that would not contribute directly to a desired social outcome. But if one is tempted to blame Zhang Zhidong for single-handedly departing from tradition, one need only look at the curricula for Peking University proposed by Sun Jianai, Liang Qichao, or Zhang Baixi to realize that Zhang Zhidong was by no means the most pragmatic in his treatment of Chinese learning, and that his pragmatism was probably characteristic of many of his contemporaries. Zhang's approach, however, contains one irony. Because most of the subjects of Chinese learning Zhang Zhidong dispensed with concerned applied learning, their disappearance contrasted with Zhang's continued support of Confucian principles, accentuating a Chinese dichotomy between the moral and political and the practical realms, which Zhang seemed to mitigate through his focus on "practical learning."

# 2

# From Imperial to Civil Service Examinations

## Changes in the Relationship Between the State and the Imperial Peking University (1898–1911)

The specialized curriculum of Peking University and corresponding changes in the state bureaucratic structure, including a greater emphasis on professional expertise along Western lines, helped shape the modern university and alter the relationship between the state and the imperial university. This chapter seeks to examine how the relationship between the state and the imperial university changed from the university's founding in 1898 to 1911, the eve of the republican revolution, through exploring the objectives of the university, its personnel, its connections to the state over the first decade of its existence, its institutional structure, and its early curriculum.

The imperial university was founded in the name of the service it could render to politics, as the connection between politics and education continued, as it had during the imperial era, to be a given in early twentieth-century China. This subordination of education to the political perpetuation of the elite and of the government meant that a formal educational system would not be necessary if the political purpose could be otherwise achieved. During the Ming and Qing dynasties, there were few formal schools by Western standards. Although, by 1500, millions of Chinese men were involved in the biennial local examinations and triennial provincial and metropolitan examinations, there were only 1,471 instructors and 3,415 assistant instructors in the entire empire, supervised by education commissioners in the thirteen provinces and the two capital regions surrounding Nanjing and Beijing. Another reason for this absence of formal primary and secondary education was the imperial governments' lack of financial resources for starting a comprehensive educational system. Historically, the Chinese state preferred alternative educational practices such as the imperial examination system to achieve its desired political goals. The content of education was bent to the state's political needs and therefore reflected not so much pure scholarly pursuit as changing political, social, or cultural concerns. For instance, in the early Ming, the emperor Zhu Yuanzhang forbade in the examinations the inclusion of certain Mencian passages on the value of the people in a kingdom, for fear that participants would compare his high-handed control with Mencius's ideals.[1]

The modern Chinese schools being established in the late Qing continued the tradition of having politics as the predominant consideration. Just as the School of Languages was the product of the Second Opium War, so the Imperial Peking University was the product of the Sino-Japanese War, although it was not formally approved until 1898.[2] In both cases, government officials in charge of these new schools realized that the examination system would not suffice to produce government personnel capable of dealing with China's new environment. The modern educational system created by the Chinese state was more than ever charged with carrying out the state's goals, only now the goal was reform of Chinese politics and society.

The Imperial Peking University had a precarious beginning, suggesting an ambivalent relationship between the state and a modern, Western-style educational system. On the one hand, the state deemed it necessary to bring about greater prosperity; on the other hand, when it was actually founded, it was given a more conservative bent than its reform-minded planners had envisioned so that it would be more pliant to the dictates of the state. Just before its founding, the radical reformers Liang Qichao and Kang Youwei fled to Japan to avoid persecution because the more comprehensive reform program that they espoused—including the introduction of telecommunications, newspapers, and factories to China—was shortcircuited by Empress Dowager Cixi. The Guangxu emperor endorsed the so-called Hundred Days Reform in 1898, but the empress dowager's last-minute intervention prevented it from being fully carried out. Still, in contrast to what many have argued, the imperial university was not the only item on the reform agenda that was implemented. The empress dowager allowed other reform projects to proceed, such as the opening of provincial business bureaus and the headquarters in charge of minerals and railways in Beijing.[3] She needed to allow some kind of political reform, and hence the university ultimately opened on December 30, 1898 (November 18 of the twenty-fourth year of the Guangxu emperor Guangxu according to the Chinese lunar calendar). The fact that many foreign instructors had already been hired before Cixi's persecution of the reformers may explain in part why the university survived.[4] But entrance examinations were based again on eight-legged essays on Confucian learning and current affairs. Instruction at the Imperial Peking University was almost completely in the Confucian classics.[5] And Sun Jianai, the first imperial minister charged to supervise education (*guanxue dachen*), and Imperial Peking University, was under great pressure to lean toward the conservative, hence his contradictory behavior before and after the Hundred Days Reform. Although in 1896 Sun had had an ambitious plan consisting of ten academic disciplines for the university, in 1898, shortly after the Hundred Days Reform failed, he immediately suggested that the primary purpose of the university was to teach the classics, so as to cultivate the students' filial piety and etiquette. Only after achieving proficiency in these arenas were the students permitted to pursue the practical disciplines.[6] In a proposal to establish a translation bureau to translate foreign books in 1898 after the aborted reform, Sun deleted from its curriculum his colleague Kang Youwei's innovative argument that Confucius reinterpreted history to make himself the legitimate king, on the grounds that it would teach children that it was good to change the existing system.[7] Perhaps in doing so, Sun was only doing what he had to do under the pressure of a conservative backlash. In 1901 after the university was reopened in the wake of its closing due to the Boxer Uprising, he resigned as minister of education in charge of Peking University.

Once in operation the university was much reduced in scale from Liang Qichao's original plan. Of the five hundred university students envisioned, only a small percentage in fact enrolled. Even so, there was insufficient housing, so not all the enrolled students could attend. The first group of students totaled 160: 30 university-level students who all came to attend the School for Officials (*Shixueguan*), 60 students in secondary school, and 70 students in primary school. Separate primary and secondary schools were not established, however, and there is little record as to what happened to the latter two groups of students which may well be an example of bad planning and the lack of an established educational structure to accommodate the modern university in Chinese society. In addition to the School for Officials and the normal (or teacher training) school, the university also had several other affiliated institutions, such as the Translation Bureau, which was designed to translate textbooks for university teaching from Western languages and Japanese. Although the emperor approved the Translation Bureau in 1898, it was formally established, together with rules and regulations, only in 1902.[8] The university in 1903 opened a School of Translation (*Yixueguan*) to train translators and interpreters to work in China's diplomatic circles and to introduce Western learning into China.[9] The former School of Languages was merged with this new school in 1903.

### Binding Education to the Service of the State: The Japanese Connection

Since university education was to be immediately related to the content of statecraft, the first country China relied on as an educational model was Japan. By 1903, the Japanese model of education had become influential in China. Japan not only shared a geographic, linguistic, and cultural proximity with China, but also had successfully introduced Western learning thirty years earlier. Japan's military success over China (1895) and later over Russia (1905) further convinced the Chinese that copying the Japanese model was the path to national strength. Furthermore, the Japanese model emphasized state control over education and absorbed elements of European education that furthered this goal. Japanese influence permeated the content of almost all courses, as almost all the textbooks were translated from the Japanese, and under the slogan of "same culture, same language" (*tong hua tong wen*), Japanese instructors staffed almost all modern Chinese schools in the first decade of the twentieth century. For Japan, it was a way to bind the Chinese to itself and use this alliance to offset the hostile Western countries in competition with Japan for expansion in China. For China, all this would guarantee conservative educational reform.[10] The school regulations promulgated in 1904 laid out a national educational system similar to that in Japan.[11] It specified a national university in the Chinese capital and other educational institutions paralleling the levels of regional administration. Thus universities could be established only at the provincial level, and primary schools only at the prefectural level. The national university, by contrast, would be the model upon which the provincial universities were to fashion themselves. The national and provincial universities would also supervise lower levels of education. Therefore the state subjected all levels of education to the leadership of the national university, which was under direct state control. The primary purpose of this regulation was to thwart local initiatives to build institutions of higher learning and alternative intellectual centers. Zhang Zhidong inhibited local attempts to create universities by stipulating that provincial universities had to include at least three of the eight divisions in his proposal before they could be considered universities.[12]

After 1915 Japanese influence started to wane for a variety of reasons. First was heightened hostility between China and Japan: Japan was becoming more aggressive in China after World War I began and in 1919 demanded that Germany hand control over its former territory in Shandong province directly to Japan—an event that sparked what became known as the May Fourth movement (named for the massive demonstrations that broke out in protest on May 4, 1919). The increasing number of Chinese students studying in Europe led to a corresponding rise in European educational influence in China.

## Institutional Connection to State Bureaucracy

After Sun Jianai's resignation as director of education in 1901, Sun's position was conferred on Zhang Baixi, who laid the groundwork for an institutional connection between the university and government bureaucracy, so that the university's primary task was retraining government officials and updating them on some modern knowledge. In the 1902 university curriculum by Zhang Baixi, in addition to college proper, there were two other parallel schools: one for officials who needed retraining in practical knowledge, and the other to prepare instructors capable of teaching Western subjects. The students of the former school were largely officials of ranks five to eight with a *juren* or *jinshi* degree (second highest and highest degrees in the imperial examinations). The latter school enrolled officials as well, although they were usually of lower rank, and their students' academic credentials ranged from degreed *juren* down to students preparing for the imperial examinations. Both schools had a three-year accelerated curriculum, covering topics from Chinese history to law and the natural sciences. Whereas the students at the teacher training school took courses in ethics and Confucian classics, those in the officials' school presumably because the officials were already proficient, were not required to take these subjects.[13] After graduation, the officials would either return to their previous post or be promoted or demoted depending on their examination results. These two schools started enrolling students immediately while the university proper was not started until 1910.

Students who enrolled at the School for Officials in 1898 did not graduate because of the Boxer Uprising and its aftermath.[14] The first class of Zhang's normal school students were enrolled in 1902, scheduled to graduate in 1906, but did not graduate actually until 1907. The ninety-eight graduates from the normal school were divided into three groups according to their grades. There were seventeen in the first category, sixty in the second category, and twenty-one in the third category; all were conferred with the title of *juren* if they did not already have that title and were either returned to their original positions or given priority consideration for the position of compilers of the Ministry of the Interior (*Neige zhongshu*) for the first category, compiler in the Department of Compilers (*Zhongshuke zhongshu*) for the second category, and secretaries of the various imperial ministries for the third category.[15] The School for Officials also graduated its first class, thirty-four students, in 1907.

A new school to provide modern instruction for *jinshi* was established in 1903. This school unofficially merged with the School for Officials in 1906. Their classes were identical although conducted separately. The *jinshi* school might have been opened to provide rapid training of more senior officials. Many students there were formerly compilers at the Hanlin Academy—the highest academy of the imperial state. Seventy-three former Hanlin compilers graduated in 1907, and mostly returned to positions at the academy. Those who did not originally come from the academy could either consider jobs in the imperial ministries or be given priority consideration in provincial government positions.[16]

In contrast to the alacrity in establishing the School for Officials and the normal school, the university proper did not open until 1910. Because an established educational system did not exist in China and no ready candidates for the university proper were available, a preparatory school as first proposed in Zhang Baixi's school program was finally started in 1905, the same year the imperial examination system was abolished and a modern educational system after the Japanese model was started. In 1909, the first class, totaling 132, graduated, and in 1910 the university itself, with eight divisions as proposed by Zhang Zhidong, was finally opened to the graduates of the preparatory school and others. Only seven divisions were in operation, however (the Medical Division was not opened), and the specialized fields were much reduced from Zhang Zhidong's 1903 school program.[17]

Despite the educational reform of 1905, the direct connection between the state and higher education seemed to be a given right up until 1910. When Chen Hanzhang, a famous scholar and *juren* degree holder who was hired as instructor at Peking University, learned that a university graduate would be awarded a *jinshi* degree and a title of Hanlin scholar, he changed his status to that of a student and worked on his degree for six years. His dream of getting the highest imperial degree was aborted by the 1911 revolution, but he was still awarded an instructorship at the university after 1912.[18]

## The Attenuated Linkage Between the University and State Bureaucracy

In the summer of 1911, four months before the revolution broke out, the Ministry of Education announced that it would stop conferring government positions on university graduates. Graduates would still be given the title of *jinshi*, but that was all.[19] This flew in the face of Qing school regulations, which decreed that graduates from middle schools to graduate schools would be awarded imperial titles and government positions.[20] A rumor began to spread from the respected *Educational Journal* (Jiaoyu zazhi) that, after the university divisions started operation, imperial titles and government positions would no longer be awarded and would be replaced with Western degrees such as the Ph.D., master's, or bachelor's degree.[21] Although the rumor had some basis in fact, the imperial titles such as *jinshi* and *juren* were kept for school graduates; nonetheless, the abolition of the awards of government positions could indeed be due to influence from Western educational systems. One explanation for the end of this practice was that the Qing government ultimately intended to replace the direct hiring of university graduates with a modern civil service examination system as early as 1903.[22] This explanation is plausible because many modern schools were being established in China in the early twentieth century, and the number of school graduates could not be adequately absorbed by the various state bureaucracies or even the local governments. The previous linkage between the state and education via the imperial examination system was disconnected with the abolition of the examination system in 1905. Between 1905 and 1910, the students at Peking University who actually were awarded government positions all graduated from the accelerated schools for *jinshi*, for officials, and the normal school and were already imperial degree holders or government officials before they came. In 1907, after the students from the schools for *jinshi* and officials graduated, the two schools hitherto merged but run separately were again merged into the Imperial Peking School of Law and Politics (*Jinshi zhengfa xuetang*) that continued to enroll government officials or officials-in-waiting, separate from Imperial Peking University.[23] After the graduation of its second class in 1909, the normal school also separated from the university and became a higher normal school (*youji shifan xuetang*), which later became the Peking Normal University.[24] Obviously, the government did not intend to award positions to the university graduates as it did to the former officials from the accelerated schools. The separation of the former accelerated schools from the university was an indication that, instead of the training and retraining of officials, the goal of the university, as stated by the Ministry of Education in 1908, was to train specialized personnel who would pursue deep scholarship.[25]

After the establishment of the republic in 1912, the republican government adopted the civil service examination system practiced in Japan and the Western countries. University graduates who passed the examination were eligible to join the state bureaucracy. But the content of the civil service examinations, as in Japan, focused on law, politics, and economics. Consequently, a majority of students at the university entered the division of law and politics. Other disciplines had only a tenuous connection with the civil service examinations. The specialization of learning, in other words, eventually contributed to a separation between education and government service.

## University Administration and the State Bureaucracy

The initial connection between education and state bureaucracy was also reflected in university administration. From 1898 to 1911, a rigid adherence to seniority in scholarship and official ranking was followed in university administrative appointments. With few exceptions, all university administrators up to 1904, and all presidents up to 1912, held a *jinshi* degree and had previously served in the Qing bureaucracy in various capacities. Most of them were distinguished officials. Sun Jianai had served in various offices in the Hanlin Academy, including as tutor to the Guangxu emperor, examiner in the imperial examinations, and heads of various imperial ministries, before his appointment as minister of educational affairs in charge of the establishment of Peking University.[26] Zhang Baixi, who succeeded him in 1901, had been in charge of education in several provinces and served as imperial minister in several capacities before his appointment.

Before 1904, the imperial minister in charge of education directly supervised the university, making the university appointments and other major decisions. The university had a chief supervisor who had very limited powers. In 1903, Zhang Zhidong changed that and established a director position just for the university. Zhang Hengjia, the chief supervisor of the university in 1904, was the first university supervisor with the authority to appoint other university faculty and staff. In that sense, he was the first president of the university.

The university's early appointments below the level of chief supervisor/director were also almost without exception imperial officials. Sun Jianai hired exclusively senior members in the Qing government. His initial appointments of the university's supervisors included Huang Shaoqi as supervisor of the university and Xu Jincheng as chief supervisor of Chinese learning. Huang, a compiler in the Hanlin Academy, was a scholar with a solid grounding in both Song philosophy and Han learning. He also participated in the reform of the imperial examination system between 1885 and 1897 and supported the 1898 reform measures. Xu was a former Chinese minister to many European countries, including Germany, France, Austria, Italy, the Netherlands, and Belgium, and was in charge of inspecting the vessels that China ordered from Germany before they were delivered. He had been instrumental in the negotiations about Chinese and Russian borders in the Pamir region and had supervised customs in Manchuria.[27]

The exception Sun made was in his appointment of W.A.P. Martin as supervisor of Western learning. Martin was formerly head of the School of Languages (1869–94). The appointment of a foreigner to such a high position was quite unusual, and, as Chen Pingyuan, a biographer of Peking University, speculated that the appointment signified a power struggle between Sun and prominent reformers like Kang Youwei. Kang, appointed by Sun to draft the university regulations, had revealed his intentions to be its chief supervisor at an early stage. The school program that Kang's protégé Liang Qichao drafted gave almost exclusive power to the university supervisor and left the imperial minister in charge of the university little room for maneuver. Political differences between Kang and Sun as well as power considerations made Sun avoid nominating Kang as chief supervisor. The appointment of Martin, an American familiar with modern Chinese education and Western learning, was both for practical purposes and to balance the power of the Chinese appointees at the university so that Sun, minister in charge of the university's establishment but not its direct supervisor, could retain his hold over the university. Martin's appointment, which lasted until 1902, did not fit the assumed qualifications for leaders of the university since he was not a *jinshi*, nor had he worked directly in the Qing bureaucracy. Sun had to petition the crown to give Martin a nominal bureaucratic position, "hat of a second-ranking official" (*erpingdingdai*, a position analogous to a second-ranking official), in order to make his appointment possible.[28]

Curiously, a candidate who seemed well qualified to be chief supervisor of both Chinese and Western learning, Yan Fu, despite his interest in the post was never seriously considered, partly because he did not hold a *jinshi* degree—which had also prevented his ascension to a prominent position in the Qing bureaucracy. Yan was well known in late nineteenth-century China because of his translations of numerous Western works, including those of Spencer, Huxley, and J.S. Mill. *National News* (Guowenbao), the newspaper he edited, kept close track of the selection of candidates for that position and hinted that Yan was well qualified for it before the Qing government squelched the 1898 reforms. After he returned to China after studying at the British Naval Academy, he was appointed chief supervisor and then president of the Tianjin Naval Academy by Li Hongzhang. Later he also headed the Beiyang Naval Academy, but Li did not intend to promote Yan any further. Li considered Yan's position in the naval academy merely window dressing. To improve his chances at promotion, Yan took the *jinshi*-level examinations several times but failed every time. It was not until 1909 that Yan was awarded an honorary *jinshi* degree by the emperor. Yan's tenure at Peking University before 1912 was only as the chief supervisor of the Translation Bureau affiliated to the university from 1902 to 1904. Only in 1912, after the downfall of the empire, was Yan appointed president of the university.[29]

Zhang Baixi followed closely the Qing procedure of appointment of *jinshi* bureaucrats at the university, although he also appointed a few non-*jinshi*, non-bureaucrats to university supervisory positions. His first chief supervisor was Wu Rulun, a scholar of the Tongcheng school of writing, developed in the Qing dynasty and known for its emphasis on the elaboration of the meaning of the classics in the form of beautiful prose that emulated the writings of the Tang and Song dynasties. Despite having a *jinshi* degree and having worked for Zeng Guofan, one of the most famous imperial ministers of the late Qing, Wu did not seem sufficiently qualified for the position because he was not a senior enough bureaucrat, and Zhang Baixi petitioned the crown to give Wu a bureaucratic ranking. In 1902, the emperor granted Wu the rank of fifth-degree official (on a scale from eight to one) so that he would be sufficiently qualified to serve as chief supervisor of the university. Wu, however, died before he was able to assume the position.[30] Wu's successor, Zhang Xiaopu (also known as Zhang Heling), was a scholar who belonged to the Yanghu school, a famous school of prose writing, although it is not clear that he was a senior Qing bureaucrat.[31] Yu Shimei, the provost, was a *jinshi* scholar and minister of military affairs who had accompanied Li Hongzhang on visits to half a dozen Western countries. Yu was the only person who held a government position while serving at the university. Later he resigned his post at the university to further his career in the imperial government.[32] Zhang Baixi fired Martin because of a clash of personalities, among other things. However, Zhang Baixi hired two Japanese scholars, Iwaya Magozo, and Hattori Unokichi, as supervisors of the accelerated normal and cadre schools starting in 1902.[33]

After 1904, acting on Zhang Zhidong's suggestion in his 1903 school program, the imperial minister in charge of Peking University was entrusted with the responsibility of national education. The supervisor for the university would now make all university appointments. Zhang Hengjia, the first university supervisor who had relatively autonomous power, was a *jinshi* and an official, having served as compiler in the Hanlin Academy and supervised a reform in Hunan Province to streamline the educated class. He also examined the provincial candidates with Western topics of politics and education when he was educational supervisor in Zhejiang province in 1901.[34] Li Jiaju, Zhu Yifan, and Liu Tingchen, later successors to Zhang, were all *jinshi* who had served in the imperial bureaucracy. Li Jiaju had served in imperial bureaucratic positions in Hubei and Manchuria, and was a general supervisor of the university in 1898 and associate administrator in 1902. Liu Tingchen had worked in the Hanlin Academy and Ministry of Education before assuming the position of president of Peking University.[35]

Despite the close connection between the imperial bureaucracy and university administration throughout the years, the university leadership did not always concur with the state. During the 1900 Boxer Uprising, two university administrators, Xu Jincheng, general supervisor of Chinese studies, and Zhu Zumo, an associate supervisor, opposed the prevailing attitude in the Qing government to use the Boxers to scare off the foreigners. They petitioned the crown to protect foreign embassies and punish the imperial ministers who used the

Boxers to attack the foreigners, for which Xu was executed in 1900. Zhu was also on the list for execution, but foreign troops entered Beijing before the Qing government had a chance to carry out the order. Zhang Hengjia, then an imperial minister, followed Xu and Zhu in opposing the government policy toward the Boxers and persuaded the empress dowager to suppress the Boxers. He escaped persecution only because his heavy Fujianese accent made him incomprehensible to the empress dowager.[36]

Even with a close connection between state bureaucracy and university administration, the latter often displayed great innovations in thinking, as can be seen below. Ideologically, almost all recognized the need for change, and innovations abounded among both administrators and faculty members in the content of learning.

## Evolution, Historicism, and Early Curriculum

The new interpretations of Confucian and Chinese learning embodied in the early drafts of the university curriculum were also reflected in the writings of many university administrators. Zhang Xiaopu, initially associate academic supervisor in chief at Peking University and later named university supervisor in 1902, creatively synthesized Confucian learning with the laws of evolution and competition in his lectures on ethics at Imperial Peking University. Zhang taught many different courses at the university, including ethics, self-cultivation, and education. In his ethics class in 1903, he reversed the Confucian interpretation of social harmony. He viewed the Confucian goal of a harmonious society as compatible with the laws of evolution and competition because, through the elimination of the weaker competitors, the survivors would be more or less equal biologically; hence social equality would be achieved.[37] Zhang did not even try to smooth over the difference between the Confucian emphasis on caring for the weak and sick and the elimination of the weak and sick in the course of competition. His contention that competition brought about social equality not only opposed a literal adherence to tradition, but also represented advocacy of self-interest. His texts on self-cultivation and ethics also reflected early twentieth-century Chinese reformers' more positive attitude toward individual self-interest and their adoption of the Western concept of rights (*quanli*).[38] Zhang Xiaopu regarded self-interest, including taking care of oneself and one's family, as private virtue and therefore the basis for public virtue: public virtue could not be established in the absence of self-interest.[39]

Zhang Xiaopu's arguments were an interesting twist on Confucian teachings about history. Confucius and Mencius had both directly linked individual self-cultivation and the cultivation of the family with the prosperity of the state, but neither identified self-cultivation with self-interested behavior. In Zhang's lecture notes, taking care of oneself was not identified totally with self-cultivation in a moral sense, but with one's livelihood and self-value as an individual. It was connected with his Darwinian interpretation of society and closely resembled the ethical interpretations of rights that Stephen Angle found in Liang Qichao and Kang Youwei.[40] It was about survival in a Darwinian competition with an ethical consequence for society on the whole, as the survivors of the competition would naturally be intelligent and know how to behave under different circumstances. Zhang Xiaopu dismissed preservation of a reified national essence, calling it an attempt to preserve the leftovers and the odds and ends, because principles always manifested in different ways at different times, and specific practices adapted to social changes.[41]

Although reformers who were Zhang Xiaopu's contemporaries tried to justify individual self-interest through finding precedents in the writings of Ming and Qing Confucians such as Huang Zongxi, Dai Zheng, Chen Que, and Gu Yanwu, their views were not accepted by all. The idea of *quanli* was criticized by Zhang Zhidong, who feared conferring political rights on individuals. As the university supervisor who was directly subordinate to the imperial minister of education and in charge of a national university that would oversee all educational institutions in China, Zhang Xiaopu's argument for a pursuit of self-interest that would eventually translate into political rights in a society of survivors of a Darwinian competition contrasted with Zhang Zhidong's school program in 1903, where Zhang criticized free interpretation of Western political concepts by some Chinese, including the concepts of popular rights (*minquan*) and liberty (*ziyou*) and identified them with Western law and politics.[42] In Zhang's mind, political rights carried dangerous consequences.[43]

If Zhang Xiaopu was innovative in his introduction to the university curriculum of the idea of self-interest, his successors displayed an even wider range of innovations. Despite his loyal adherence to the crown, which resulted in his resignation from the university presidency upon the downfall of the Qing dynasty, Ke Shaomin, a *jinshi* scholar and dean of the Confucian Learning Division before assuming the presidency (December 1910–December 1911), was innovative in his scholarship after the end of his university tenure. He specialized in Yuan history, and his scholarship was of the most advanced of his time, covering not only the classics and philology, but also medicine, astronomy, calendars, geography, and writings on metal urns and stone tablets, all of which he applied to his new history of the Yuan dynasty, for which he was given an honorary Ph.D. degree by Imperial Tokyo University in 1924.[44] His successor, Lao Naixuan, president of the university for only one month (November–December

1911), who likewise left his position because of the downfall of the Qing dynasty, also displayed a wide range of learning. A *jinshi* scholar, Lao had acted as secretary of foreign affairs to the superintendent of customs at Tianjin and served as county magistrate in northern provinces, suppressing the Boxer rebels. He had also served as supervisor to several famous modern academies in China. His concerns for Chinese and Western learning transcended the prescriptions by either Zhang Zhidong or Zhang Baixi. He worked at mathematical problems and at the imperial legislature, and invented a phonetic system for the Chinese language inspired by Western languages in the interest of spreading literacy in China. He wrote extensively on Chinese and Western culture.[45]

Similar innovations in thinking also existed among the instructors beginning in the early twentieth century, spurred to a great extent by the new treatments of Confucian and Chinese learning in Zhang Baixi and Zhang Zhidong's curricula. The curricula's treatment of Confucian learning as transcendental principles encouraged Wang Zhouyao, instructor of Confucian classics in 1903, to stress the importance of discerning the essence (*ti*) and its manifestation (*yong*) in history. For instance, in the *Mencius*, the essential message was the goodness of human nature and its manifestation was humaneness. In Mencius's view, with respect to state administration, the people were the essence, and the schools and the well-field system, a feudal land distribution system, were the manifestation.[46] A more innovative course in the 1904 curriculum was literary history, which had no precedent in Chinese history. In introducing this course in his curriculum in 1903, Zhang Zhidong was obviously referring to Western and Japanese curricula. As with other aspects of Chinese literature, its purpose was to help fashion a Chinese core of knowledge that proved of universal relevance. Zhang Zhidong stipulated that the instruction of Chinese literary history should be modeled after how the course was conducted in Japan.[47] Because it had no precedent in Chinese history, it posed great difficulty for Lin Chuanjia, the first Chinese instructor to teach this course, "Literary Trends in the Different Dynasties," at the university in 1904.[48] Lin made an encyclopedic list of topics to be covered that would strictly adhere to Zhang Zhidong's encyclopedic requirements for the course on literary history. In the end, Lin had to abandon the more irrelevant topics because it was too difficult to follow Zhang's requirements literally. Compared with other courses from the early 1900s, however, Lin's adhered to Zhang Zhidong's curriculum the most literally, simply because all the others had some kind of precedent to follow, but Lin's did not.[49]

Evolutionary and comparative history was all the rage in twentieth-century China. One of the first to write a periodized, evolutionary history was Tu Ji, instructor of Chinese history at the Imperial Peking University from 1903 to 1904, who learned it from Hattori Unokichi, professor at the Imperial Tokyo

University who served as an academic supervisor at the accelerated schools at Imperial Peking University and who taught experimental psychology and history. Unokichi's lectures on psychology included both a physiological and a less physiologically based discussion of human emotions. His experimental psychology emphasized a physiological approach, including the way external stimuli on the human nervous system affected human perception and thinking.[50] In addition to psychology, Unokichi also taught the history of foreign countries, focusing on ancient Western civilization, from Mesopotamia to ancient Persia and ancient Greece.[51] His periodization and presentation of history in the form of chapters greatly influenced Tu Ji, who followed suit and became one of the first Chinese historians to write history in the form of chapters. Tu's history started with the legendary beginning of Chinese civilization to the Warring States period as recorded by the *Spring and Autumn Annals*. More than Zhang Xiaopu, Tu applied evolution directly in his history, emphasizing historical development. He also aimed at a comparative history of China and the ancient East.

In the early twentieth century, another intellectual trend in China was the search for the historical origins of Chinese civilization. This was influenced by archaeological work in Europe in which some archaeologists claimed that Eurasia had a common origin in civilizations that stretched from ancient Babylonia to Central Asia bordering on present-day Xinjiang. The implication of that theory was that the present-day civilization of China, among other Asian countries, was the result of the achievements of conquerors from this Eurasian civilization. (For more discussion of Chinese scholars' response on this topic, see Chapter 6.) It stirred up rather heated debates in China. Tu, despite his interest in linking Chinese history to world history, and especially to Western history, as many Chinese scholars did at that time, asserted that the indigenous Chinese were the original Asians and not Eurasians from the Central Asian civilization. Tu argued for a history of Chinese civilization that was independent but parallel to that of ancient Sumer. He made use of a form of periodization of this phase of Chinese history into ten stages that was once considered apocryphal. These ten stages spanned 276 million years. He adopted this method of history because it paralleled the legend of the existence of ten kings before the great flood in ancient Sumerian history as recorded on the ancient Sumerian bricks. Their rule lasted 430 million years, a period that matched that of China's ten stages of ancient history. Through a comparison of ancient Sumerian and Chinese history, Tu hoped to find some common rules governing human evolution from primitive times to the present. He began a reinterpretation of the ten stages theory of ancient Chinese history, tracing Chinese development from fire making and learning to weave, to cave dwelling groups and then hierarchical tribes, from matriarchal societies to patriarchal ones, and finally to the feudal system of the Zhou dynasty, borrowing concepts here and there from Western histories.[52] His evolutionary approach to Chinese history reversed the traditional Chinese reverence for the golden age of ancient Chinese societies before the Zhou dynasty. It also showed Chinese culture as having developed independently from ancient Mesopotamian civilization.

Between 1902 and 1910, one can also see a fairly lively range of intellectual content through the students' examination topics. The normal school's examinations from 1902 to 1909, before the school separated from Peking University and became an independent higher normal school to accommodate the imminent opening of the university divisions in 1910, ranged from Chinese and foreign geography to Chinese and foreign history, physics, chemistry, mathematics, and essays in Japanese and Russian. One year, its examination on education included essay topics on two different subjects: the differences and similarities between Confucius's argument that the superior people were wise and the inferior people were stupid and the Mencian argument that everyone had the potential to be a sage; and why education was based on ethics and psychology. In the examinations on education in 1909, the questions included: who founded the study of education and when, who were the founders of naturalism, what were the connections between ethics and knowledge, physical education, and skills training; and what were the pros and cons of the practical arts.[53]

## Conclusion

The early development of Peking University before 1911 followed certain patterns. First, the state itself implemented policy aimed at building a modern educational system patterned after those in the West. The 1905 decision to abolish the examination system and establish a modern educational system from the primary to the tertiary level and the 1911 decision to stop assigning university graduates to government positions allowed education a certain degree of internal autonomy. A specialized curriculum and the eventual introduction of the civil service examination in 1912 linked only the study of politics and law directly to government service, reducing the immediate connection between much of the curriculum at Peking University and government service.

In comparison to education in earlier periods of Chinese history, the ultimate purpose assigned to education upon the founding of Peking University in 1898 continued to be service to the state, and initial appointments to the university administration until 1911 were almost exclusively state bureaucrats. But a closer examination of the university's early instruction and the writings of university administrators and instructors who served before 1912 show many innovations in Chinese learning. To a great extent, these innovations were structurally supported by new definitions of Confucian and Chinese learning in the 1902 and 1904 curricula, which not only broadened the scope of Chinese learning but allowed a freer interpretation of Confucian learning—a new freedom in scholarship. Both structurally and ideologically, the direct connection between state bureaucracy and education was crumbling. Consequently, by 1911 the conflict between an integrated world of moral knowledge and specialized learning that had preoccupied Zhang Zhidong became less problematic. For many, a more creative production of moral knowledge through a more eclectic synthesis of the Chinese and Western had begun.

# 3

# From a Defense of Confucian Moral Knowledge to New Construction of Chinese Culture

## Academic Developments at Peking University (1912–1937)

The dissociation between the state bureaucracy and Peking University that started in the first ten years of the twentieth century became more prominent at the establishment of the republic in 1912. The republican goals accorded more with Western social and political values. There was now an even stronger reliance on Western learning as the selection criteria of university presidents and other administrators. Political instability after the 1911 revolution and state withholding of funding to the university in the 1910s and 1920s furthered the dissociation of direct state control over the university. By the 1920s and 1930s, under the presidencies of Cai Yuanpei and Jiang Menglin, the university achieved a role as the center for the production of not only scientific but also moral and ethical knowledge.

Structurally, with the abolition of the imperial examination system in 1905 and the fundamental change in the Chinese polity in 1912, university administrators were no longer appointed by virtue of their imperial examination degrees. From 1912 to 1937, Western educational credentials dominated the selection criteria of top university administrators. Although some new university presidents appointed in the early 1910s still held a *jinshi* degree, others were degree holders from Japanese and American universities. And even *jinshi* degree holders, such as Yan Fu—who had been given an honorary *jinshi* degree by the Qing government in 1909—and Cai Yuanpei had won their appointments for reasons other than their degrees: Yan for his numerous translations of Western works, and Cai because of his intellectual renown in both Chinese and Western educational circles. Jiang Menglin, the last president of the university appointed before 1937, had a Ph.D. from Columbia University.

A specialty in Western learning characterized all university presidents from 1912 to 1937. Yan Fu (March–October 1912), whose term of office followed that of Lao Naixuan, was appointed as president of Peking University by the republican government. In order to stimulate Western learning, Yan encouraged the use of English in class instruction to the point that speakers at faculty meetings used English rather than Chinese. Moreover, all courses except those in Chinese studies were conducted in foreign languages, which aroused some protest from faculty members who could not speak a foreign language.[1] Yan's successors, first, Zhang Shizhao and, then, Ma Liang were both respected educators in China and champions of Western knowledge. Zhang Shizhao, a prominent scholar who translated Western philosophy into Chinese and coined the Chinese term *luoji* (logic), was actively involved in anti-Manchu activities in the early twentieth century and founded *Tiger* (Jiaying) magazine in Tokyo in 1914 to discuss contemporary politics. However, Zhang Shizhao declined the position of president because he was aware that the university was in a difficult financial situation (see below).[2] Ma Liang was a famous Catholic educator who founded several universities, including the predecessor to Fudan University in Shanghai and Furen University in Peking. He accepted the presidency at Peking University but left after three months also because of the school's financial problems. After Ma came He Yushi and Hu Renyuan, both students of engineering. He Yushi (December 1912—November 1913) was a graduate of Zhejiang University in China and the Imperial Tokyo University, where he studied mining and metallurgy beginning in 1896. After his graduation in 1905 as the first Chinese to earn a Ph.D. in Japan, he returned to China to assume the position of minister of education and instructor at the Imperial Peking University, later becoming the dean of Engineering Division before assuming the presidency of the university. His tenure was cut short because of disagreement with the Ministry of Education over university administration and monetary issues. Hu Renyuan, dean of the Preparatory School during He Yushi's presidency, had completed studies in shipbuilding in Sendai, Japan.[3]

This growing reliance on Western-schooled experts to govern the university showed the pragmatic decisions of the Chinese governments—whether the short-lived republican government of Sun Yat-sen, the Beijing warlord governments from 1912 to 1928, or the Nationalist government after 1928—to introduce more Western knowledge to China. Yet, precisely because of the authority the Chinese state granted Western learning, the university presidents often could maintain greater independence from the state and exercise some degree of autonomy. Dissociation between the state and the university was accelerated by the woeful financial situation the Beijing government caused the university. Government corruption led to a constant shortage of funding for the university. The situation was not so serious before 1911 because of the relatively small size of the university and the financial contributions from the provinces. At that time, students at the Imperial Peking University did not need to pay tuition, room, and board and often received monthly stipends. According to Hu Xiansu, an Imperial Peking University alumnus, the allowances were cut in 1909, and students had to pay for their own food. Still, there was no tuition until after the republican revolution.[4] After 1911, the now-renamed National Peking University's growth contrasted with the shortage of funding from the state, which often could not collect sufficient taxes from the provinces. From the 1910s to the late 1920s, the university suffered constant financial crises and a revolving door of university presidents, from Zhang Shizhao, Ma Liang, to Yan Fu. Hu Renyuan was perhaps the only president between 1912 and 1917 whose departure was not due to the university's finances. The resignations of Yan Fu and He Yushi were especially dramatic because of their connection to the university's finances. Yan resigned because of a severe cut in faculty and staff salaries and he could no longer raise money for the university.[5] When He Yushi assumed the presidency in December 1912, financial problems and student unrest prompted the Beijing government's minister of education, Wang Daxian, to merge Peking University with Beiyang University in Tianjin, under the pretext that China was then practicing the university district system borrowed from Japan and France (see discussion of Cai Yuanpei below), and there could be only one university in the university district of Beijing and Tianjin. He Yushi protested the merger, and although it never took place, he resigned in 1913. The university never received its budget in full in the late 1910s and early 1920s. In 1921, faculty members of polytechnic high schools and tertiary universities in Beijing, including Peking University, went on strike and petitioned the Ministry of Education for three months' salary owed them. The demonstrators were met with police clubs. Ma Xulun, professor of philology at Peking University, was struck in the head. Jiang Menglin, then deputy president of Peking University, threatened to resign together with seven polytechnic college presidents from Beijing. The problem was not solved until four months later. In 1923, the same financial shortage occurred, but on a larger scale. Salaries and funding for schools were nine months behind. The joint conference of the eight colleges and universities decided that if they could not receive the money owed them, they would have to close. Jiang Menglin was responsible for collecting the outstanding funding from the Ministry of Education and persuaded the presidents of the other seven schools to continue operation.[6] Although part of the university funding came from the Russian portion of the Boxer Indemnity fund—monetary payments the Chinese government was to make to the countries that fought with China in 1900 during the Boxer Uprising—forfeited by the Soviet Union in 1924, only around four percent of the outstanding fund that was to be paid to the Soviet Union was spent on education. The distribution of the fund was conducted by a committee that suffered from serious administrative problems and possible embezzlement. In 1926, faculty members at Peking University received only 40 percent of their salaries.[7] Shortage of funding again made many faculty members reluctant to teach. In a vote on whether to continue the semester in October 1926, of the more than eighty faculty members and thirty staff members present, forty-seven voted for continuing teaching, and eighty-four voted against.[8] Many faculty members—such as Lu Xun and Gu Jiegang from the humanities, Wang Shijie from the social sciences, and Wang Xinggong from the sciences left the university for better-paid southern university positions.

After Jiang Menglin assumed the presidency of the university in 1930, he began to exercise his personal initiatives to get funding for Peking University. An extremely resourceful person, he signed a contract, based on personal connections, to borrow money from Jincheng Bank for the university. In addition, the China Foundation of Culture and Education, founded with Boxer Indemnity funds from the United States, had a five-year contract with Peking University such that beginning in 1931, the foundation and the university would each provide 200,000 yuan to fund chaired professors, library books and facilities, and new construction.[9] Peking University received funding not just because of its prestige but because Jiang Menglin was on the Board of Trustees of the foundation. Even so, in 1931, Peking University was able to pay only 50,000 yuan of its obligation, and in 1932, it borrowed 111,000 yuan from the China Foundation. It was finally able to resume the cooperative relationship with the China Foundation with the establishment in 1932 of the Association to Maintain Educational Expenses in Beiping (Beijing) and Tianjin, which made possible Peking University's 200,000 yuan annual matching fund to the 200,000 yuan grant from the China Foundation, whose matching contribution however was reduced to an annual 100,000 yuan in 1934. The contract expired in 1936 and was not renewed.[10] From 1932 to 1936, the years immediately before the Japanese invasion, the university was financially most sound, thanks not to state patronage but to the ingenuity of the university president.

Greater reliance on Western learning and financial instability also allowed the university greater academic autonomy after the establishment of the republic. This academic autonomy was reflected in a more unequivocal attitude toward Confucian moral knowledge and a greater embrace of academic specialization. Between 1913 and 1917, Confucian scholars were replaced with scholars of philology. Gradually, a new discourse replaced the previous emphasis on an integrated body of knowledge that perpetuated Chinese moral knowledge with an integrated body of both Chinese and Western knowledge that furthered Chinese nationalism. This transformation was completed under the tenure of Cai Yuanpei, first as minister of education and then chancellor of National Peking University.

### The Exit of the Tongcheng School and the Appointments of Classical Scholars

Political corruption and the deterioration of the republican government pushed Peking University further along in asserting its independence. In 1915, when Yuan Shikai, president of the Republic of China, wanted to crown himself emperor, he tried to obtain the consent of Peking University faculty members. The-then president of the univesity, Hu Renyuan, informed Yuan's representative to the campus that the faculty members would not support such a development.[11]

The university also self-consciously fashioned itself as the center of cultural transformation. During the tenure of Presidents He Yushi and Hu Renyuan, there was a significant faculty reshuffling in Chinese studies: the dismissal of a number of faculty members who belonged to the Tongcheng school, and the appointment of classical scholars who had studied under Zhang Taiyan, a famous Chinese scholar, in Japan in the early twentieth century. Compared with the Tongcheng scholars, who specialized in elaborating Confucian messages in ornate prose, the classical scholars' emphasis on the exact meaning of ancient words resembled scientific accuracy, and the prose style they championed, Six Dynasties (*Liuchao*, 420–589) prose, was most free of Confucian influence. The hiring of the latter school of scholars accorded with the university administrators' plan to tailor the fields of Chinese history and literature along Western academic lines.

During his tenure as imperial supervisor of the university, Zhang Baixi hired scholars of the Tongcheng school to teach Chinese literature. The Tongcheng school's prestige led to Zhang Baixi's appointment of Wu Rulun and other Tongcheng scholars, although Wu died before he could take office as general supervisor. Others from that school of prose appointed at Peking University were Yao Yongkai, Lin Shu, Ma Qichang, and Yao Yongpu. Among these faculty members, the most flamboyant was Lin Shu. Strictly speaking, Lin was not a member of the Tongcheng school, but because of his vehement defense of it, he is often mentioned as a member. The Translation Bureau affiliated with Peking University initially employed Lin Shu in 1903. He was appointed in 1906 as an instructor of classical studies at the preparatory and normal schools affiliated with the university and from 1910 to 1913 taught in the Classical Studies Division at the university, where, among other things, he produced a paraphrasing of standard neo-Confucian writings.[12] A native of Fujian province, Lin made his name as a translator of numerous Western classics into Chinese.[13] He was quite popular among the students, capturing their full attention in his 1 P.M. class.

Lin and his colleagues from the Tongcheng school taught literary appreciation through writing. In a tangible and concrete way, they tried to capture certain timeless themes of Confucian teachings in Tang and Song dynasty styles of prose and poetry. Although he taught ancient Chinese prose and a few other courses,[14] his passion lay elsewhere. His colleague Yao Yongkai, dean of the Division of Arts, also diligently taught literary stylistics.[15] To He Yushi and Hu Renyuan, Lin Shu's prose style and values were outdated. He Yushi was said to comment that Lin was no scholar and could do no more than chat about novels in his class.[16] The decision to oust the Tongcheng scholars had already been made, but it was not clinched until their replacements were found. The replacements were classical scholars with a historical approach to Chinese history and literature, who had increasing social influence because many of them were involved in the language reform movement to spread literacy more broadly.

The classical scholars that were hired en masse in 1914 were almost all students of Zhang Binglin (Taiyan), a philologist who fled to Japan in 1907 because of his anti-Qing articles in Chinese newspapers. They had gone to study various subjects in Japan. Shen Jianshi, for instance, had enrolled in a Japanese railway school.[17] While in Japan, many of them were also actively involved in *Tiger* magazine, in which, they launched vehement attacks on the Qing government. They studied Chinese philology under Zhang Binglin: textual exegesis and identification of the meaning of ancient words through pronunciation or word parts. Their scholarly approach drew on a seventeenth-century intellectual movement to stem libertine interpretations of Confucian learning and seek understanding of the ancient past in solid, authentic evidence,[18] a style that many Chinese scholars praised as resembling scientific positivism. Many of them returned to China after the republic was declared in 1912.

The first of this group hired was Shen Yingmo, who had sojourned in Japan while his brother Shen Jianshi was attending school there and being tutored by Zhang. Although Shen Yingmo was not under Zhang's tutelage—a fact that was not clearly known to He and Hu—his affiliation with the classical scholars, especially Zhang, led to his appointment by He Yushi in 1913. Shen Yingmo then became an instructor of Chinese literature in the preparatory school of Peking University.[19] The following year, after he became president of the university, Hu Renyuan appointed several of Zhang's actual students, including Zhu Xizu, Ma Yuzao, Shen Jianshi, Qian Xuantong, and Huang Kan.[20] Because they had a more historical approach to Chinese learning, these classical scholars were also more prepared to offer literary history courses than were the Tongcheng scholars.

Compared with the Tongcheng scholars, who found it increasingly difficult to preserve the moral messages in the classics through classical prose, these younger scholars championed a prose style that celebrated an independent spirit and many of them emulated the Six Dynasties prose, which most deeply explored the human life experience.[21] In addition to having greater intellectual independence from Confucian learning, many of them advocated something that promised to have a tremendous impact on Chinese society, namely, language reform. In 1913, when Shen Yingmo embarked on his journey to Beijing to assume his teaching position at Peking University, Zhu Xizu (hired at Peking University in 1914) accompanied him to a conference organized by the Ministry of Education on language reform and the formulation of a phonetic writing system.[22] To spread literacy, the ministry promoted a project to standardize the vernacular and bridge the gap between classical and spoken Chinese. Such a goal required the standardization of pronunciation in a national language, in contrast to the variety of pronunciations used by the many regional dialects. A Chinese dictionary and codified grammar—hitherto attempted only in the late nineteenth century—would also be needed. Because many classical scholars worked to identify ancient pronunciations of words to understand their historical meaning, they could easily apply their expertise to determine standard pronunciation based on patterns of change over time. By 1918, Qian Xuantong, Shen Jianshi, and Ma Yuzao, were all actively involved in this project. Huang Kan was one of the few classical scholars who, because of his temperament and intellectual outlook, opposed language reform and left Peking University in 1919 over disagreements with colleagues and the university administration.

## Building an Integrated Body of Knowledge for Chinese Nationalism

In the 1910s and 1920s, Cai Yuanpei (1868–1940), who became minister of education and later chancellor of Peking University, more systematically built the university into a center of scientific, cultural, and moral knowledge. His early anti-Manchu activities and clashes with the Yuan Shikai government and later Beijing warlord governments prevented him from identifying with the Chinese state. His zealous nationalism eventually found expression in the German model of education that he applied to Peking University, a model that allowed the academic to develop political and cultural influence beyond academia while maintaining a separate existence from the state. He redirected the discourse about knowledge from Zhang Zhidong's conscious distinction between integrated (Chinese) knowledge versus specialized Western technical knowledge to integrated knowledge for Chinese nationalism, based on the equal treatment of Chinese and Western knowledge.

A look at Cai Yuanpei's early life helps explain much of his later behavior. Cai was a precocious child and studied neo-Confucianism in his youth. He passed the highest imperial examination in 1890, and was put on the waiting list for an editorship at the Hanlin Academy.[23] Despite having a high position in the government, he was a fervent anti-Manchu revolutionary and an active member of the Revolutionary Alliance (*Tongmenghui*), founded by Sun Yat-sen. He experimented with explosives that he hoped to use to kill Manchu officials. In 1911 he participated in the anti-Manchu revolution that ushered in the Chinese republic. In January 1912 Cai Yuanpei was appointed by Sun Yat-sen as the first minister of education of the Republic of China. Sun's cabinet comprised former members of the Revolutionary Alliance and prominent officials and scholars of the Qing era. His initial choice for education minister had been Zhang Taiyan, who both declined the position, and was anyway rejected by several candidates from the various provinces. The nomination of Cai Yuanpei won unanimous approval. If he had any hopes about a worthy and strong government, however, Cai was quickly disappointed. Three months after accepting the position as education minister, he resigned because of disagreements with Yuan Shikai on many issues. His bitter experience with the successive Chinese governments in his adult life deeply affected his views toward politics. Instead of direct participation in the government, he actively sought to fashion nationalism from the realm of education, severing the traditional connection between education and politics.

In 1900, Cai started a School of Eastern and Western Learning (*Zhong xi xuetang*) in his hometown of Shaoxing. The following year, he became the chief instructor for a special class in the South Sea Public School (*Nanyang gongxue*) in Shanghai, started by Sheng Xuanhuai, a prosperous Chinese entrepreneur and politician, to train students in communication with the West. One of Cai's students was Hu Renyuan, who later became president of Peking University. In 1902, around two hundred students, the entire student body of the South Sea Public School, quit school en masse in protest of the school's policy blocking them from reading materials in support of reform, including the *New Citizen* (*xinmincongbao*) journal edited by Liang Qichao. The following week, led by Cai, a new school was formed called the Patriotic School (*Aiguo xueshe*), which regrouped many of the former Nanyang School students for the purpose of cultivating future citizens. In his inaugural speech as president of the new school, Cai outlined his three goals: to teach knowledge, the basis of citizenship; to practice self-government in order to acquire the skills of self-government in society; and to develop ability and spread the ideal of the school all over the country. A subsequent girls' middle school was established within the Patriotic School that began classes a week later.[24]

If Cai hoped to build nationalism through education, European universities provided him with the rationale and procedure to do it. When the Qing government sent members of the Hanlin Academy to study abroad in 1906, Cai was assigned to study in Japan, but, determined to go to Europe, found the means to support himself to study in Germany in 1907. The Chinese minister to Germany was a friend of his and agreed to give him thirty taels of silver a month. Shangwu Press also signed a contract with him, agreeing to pay him 100 yuan a month for editorial work. Thus the first year he was in Berlin, Cai studied German while editing and translating books. In 1908, he attended classes in philosophy, literature, the history of civilization, and anthropology at the University of Leipzig, concentrating on anthropology and aesthetics.[25] For Cai, national salvation lay not in the salvation of Confucian learning but in the independent development of the university as a center of a new culture, which was a synthesis of both Chinese and Western knowledge.

As to why Cai chose to study in Germany rather than Britain or another European country, it may owe to happenstance, for example the fact that the person from whom he was able to gain financial assistance was minister to that country. It is also true that he was influenced by German philosophical writings to which he had been exposed before his trip.

Before he left, he had translated a series of lectures by Oswald Kulpe, a German philosopher and psychologist who taught briefly in a Japanese liberal arts university at the turn of the century.[26] Kuple synthesized Hegel, Kant, and Hartmann with experimental psychology that emphasized the subjectivity of human thoughts with their origins in human feelings and emotions. Such a synthesis was in line with the thesis in his *Outlines of Psychology*, published in Germany in 1893 when he was a *privadozent* at Wilhelm Wundt's laboratory of experimental psychology at the University of Leipzig. Kulpe explained the beginning of religion as a subjective construct based on the perception of fear. Philosophy, with inner contemplation and self-reflection, would lead one to an understanding of feelings.[27] What Cai gained from Kulpe was a theoretical tool for dismissing established morality and other social authorities by exposing their subjective origins. One of the most systematic guides to moral autonomy that Cai encountered was *A System of Ethics*, by Friedrich Paulsen, one of the most influential German philosophers of the nineteenth century. During his first year in Germany Cai started translating Paulsen as part of fulfilling his contract with Shangwu Press. Like Kulpe, Paulsen pointed out the origin of morality in human feelings. By ultimately rooting moral power in man himself, Paulsen tried to achieve moral autonomy from both God and various social forces. Like Kant, Paulsen argued that free will constituted a person's ability to determine his life independently of sensual impulses and inclinations by reason and conscience, according to purpose and laws, and it constituted the essence of man.[28] If Kulpe meant to destroy the existing moral system by exposing its subjective origins, Paulsen meant to establish a constructive moral system by combining a Kantian world outlook with nineteenth-century individualism. Paulsen's emphasis on individual initiative to achieve morality certainly appealed to Cai, thus he chose this work (700 pages in English) as the only foreign work to translate into Chinese while he was in Germany. Cai translated only the second part from both the German edition and the Japanese translation, including conscience, ideals, duty, virtue, and qualities that Paulsen considered as constituting the process of moral realization, in his book of ethics to the secondary school children in China.[29]

If Paulsen pointed the way to the constructive and autonomous development of individual morality, the classes in aesthetics and experimental psychology at the University of Leipzig seemed to help Cai find universal moral principles that transcended history and culture. Cai took both experimental psychology and philosophy courses with Wilhelm Wundt, then one of the most prominent leaders of experimental psychology in the West. Pinning down human thought to predictable physiological movements such as the work of the nervous system, Wundt and his colleagues rendered all mankind subject to similar rules of behavior, establishing universal accountability. The courses in experimental aesthetics offered by Professor Ernst Meumann from the Wundtian School also helped Cai relate individual experiences with universal ones.

The German university provided the connection between autonomous moral knowledge and nationalism. Cai's frustration with Chinese politics over the years led him to search for an alternative route for the exercise of the political energies of Chinese scholars. He found it in the German model of a university envisioned by Wilhelm von Humboldt, the Prussian minister of education in the late eighteenth century. The pre-industrialization German university provided Cai with a model for integrating academic knowledge with nationalism and Chinese with Western knowledge. According to Ruth Hayhoe, in German universities the idea of academic freedom was premised on idealist and theoretical knowledge, based on a duality in epistemology that allowed the university to champion academic freedom on the theoretical level, while abstaining from direct political participation.[30] Von Humboldt integrated in his ideal German university three types of knowledge unified by a transcendental Spirit: scientific, ethical and social, moral and political.[31] In the German model, autonomy (*Lehrfreiheit*) granted the university teachers exclusive authority over intellectual matters. The German rhetoric of intellectual autonomy rested on a tacit, mutually beneficial contract between the German states and academics. German unification, many believed, required the building of a German culture superior to that of France to serve as a center of coalition for the German states. The development of universities in order to build a *Kulturstaat*, a combination of power and learning, would supposedly achieve for Germany the moral and intellectual leadership of Europe. "It was in the untrammeled pursuit of truth and the development of the free man that the university was of political importance, for ultimately these were also the goals of the state."[32] Von Humboldt's university was thus oriented toward the spiritual and moral training of the nation.

The German linkage between university knowledge and nationalism proved a convenient model for Cai, already disillusioned with what the Chinese scholars could do with the ruling regimes from the Qing government to the Yuan Shikai administration. Cai now entrusted the university with the responsibility of developing a core of moral and theoretical knowledge that would ultimately contribute to Chinese national salvation while maintaining its autonomy because the knowledge it produced was linked to a transcendental level of truth not controlled by the state. Presumably Peking University, the only state university in China during his tenure as education minister, would serve as the leader for all other Chinese state universities to come. Cai's goals for Chinese education incorporated five areas: ethics, aesthetics, a world outlook, military training, and practical learning. Among the five, Cai determined that the first three determined the latter two. Although aesthetics and a world outlook belonged to the more transcendental world, they helped complete ethics of this world, which in turn served as the basis for training in both citizenship and practical trades. Thus philosophy would give education an innate rationale.[33] Therefore, although in his program a university would consist of as many as seven divisions ( humanities, sciences, law, commerce, medicine, agriculture, and engineering), the humanities and the sciences have greater weight than other divisions, and a university needed to have more than two of the divisions, including at least one division in the humanities or sciences.[34] Indirectly, Cai hoped this curriculum would create the new knowledge and values necessary for republic building. During Cai's brief tenure as education minister, he abolished the values and orientations associated with the perpetuation of Confucian learning and loyalty to the emperor in schools, arguing that they violated the republican form of government and the freedom of belief. He abolished the practice of awarding modern school graduates with imperial degrees in favor of granting Western degrees, such as bachelor's degrees for university graduates, introduced coeducation in primary schools, and abolished the Confucian learning division at National Peking University. This last act was in sharp contrast to what Yuan Shikai did in subsequent years, when he tried to establish Confucian learning as a religion and reestablish an imperial regime.

By now, Cai had established a rationale for a self-contained educational system that performed important social, cultural, and political functions. He ceaselessly promoted this new alternative to Chinese scholars by advocating it not only at National Peking University but also for all future state universities and other educational institutions. To do so, Cai wanted to adopt the French and Japanese district system under which the country would be divided into certain districts, each equipped with one state university serving as both intellectual centers and administrative agencies that oversaw the lower levels of education in that district. A national university would be established to serve as the national intellectual leader and administrator of all district universities and lower levels of education. This hierarchical educational system, in theory, would maintain relative stability and autonomy from the state. Although the national university president was appointed by the state, the national university's intellectual and administrative responsibilities over national education would maintain relative continuity even at times when the regime changed hands. Cai stipulated that the country be divided into six districts—Beijing, Wuchang, Nanjing, Guangzhou, the northwest, and the northeast—and that National Peking University would be the intellectual and administrative leader of national education. Because he apparently did not think that all these districts were in a position to establish universities, he stated that they would each contain one normal high school. In three of these districts, Nanjing, Hankou, and Guangzhou, a new national university would be established. A fourth national university would be established in Chengdu, which did not exactly fit his district system. The existing high schools, established by the provinces, would gradually be taken over by the Ministry of Education and changed into preparatory schools for universities because of their varying quality and the lack of coordination between them and the needs of university education. This policy inadvertently struck a blow to provincial educational efforts, because by 1916 only two provincial universities existed (Beiyang and Shanxi), and the provincial high schools had served as the principal provincial centers of advanced education. By 1918, Cai's policy had caused all but seven provincial high schools to cease operation.[35] What he intended as an effort to establish educational autonomy turned out to be a high-handed policy that stifled spontaneous efforts to spread education in the provinces.

Soon after launching the plan for Peking University to be the leading educational center and for dividing China into school districts, Cai decided to close down the university because it was too closely tied to the government and most students came to acquire the credentials necessary for serving in the state bureaucracy. Just before his resignation, Cai drafted a plan to dissolve the university on the grounds that it had insufficient funding and the quality of the students was low.[36] In July 1912, the Ministry of Education passed policies for closing the university, stipulating that the students of all divisions would graduate at the end of the year without a degree and that the divisions would not enroll new students in the second semester of the year.[37] Thanks to a petition by Yan Fu and many petitions from the Peking University students, the Ministry of Education changed its plan on July 10, 1912 because of the need for a university in China and because of Peking University's cultural responsibility.[38]

A month earlier, Cai and three other ministers of the republican government resigned in protest of Yuan Shikai's attempts to override the constitutional stipulation that presidential power would be checked by the prime minister and the cabinet; their resignations were ultimately approved by mid-July.[39] Cai's 1912 school program continued to serve as the official policies regarding Chinese education until 1919. He Yushi was a direct victim of Cai's university district system: Wang Daxian, the-then minister of education, to cut expenses, decided to merge Peking University with Beiyang University in September 1912, as Peking and Tianjin belonged to the same university district and only one university was allowed in a district. After strenuous opposition by Peking University, the Ministry of Education tried to merge Beiyang University with Peking University on the latter campus instead, meeting with strong opposition by Beiyang as well. After all this turmoil subsided, He Yushi resigned as president in November 1913.[40] One of the positive outcomes of Cai's school program, however, was the establishment of an evaluation committee as the highest decision-maker on university affairs at Peking University in 1915 during President Hu Renyuan's tenure. This followed Cai's regulations that, after the fashion of German universities, the faculty members of a university, rather than the Ministry of Education or other external government agencies, should have control of the orientation of the university. Each of the seven academic divisions would select two members to serve on the evaluation committee.[41] This policy was perpetuated after Cai's assumption of the university chancellorship in 1917 until around 1930. After 1930, with Jiang Menglin's appointment as president, the prerogatives of the professors to judge university affairs gradually gave way to the university president and other administrators.

Cai spent 1912 to 1917 largely abroad, primarily because of his clashes with the Yuan Shikai regime. He returned to the University of Leipzig in September 1912 as a student sent by the Chinese Ministry of Education, taking courses in modern European history, Baroque art, sculpture, and aesthetics. In the wake of Sun Yat-sen's call for overthrowing Yuan Shikai following Yuan's plot to assassinate Song Jiaoren, the president of the Nationalist Party (*Guomindang*), Cai returned to China in April 1913. Along with other revolutionary leaders, Cai issued several ultimatums to Yuan urging him to step down. Cai also wrote several articles in major newspapers condemning Yuan's unconstitutional usurpation of power. After this "Second Revolution" failed, Cai departed for France and stayed there, working with Li Shizeng to promote the "work-study" movement in which many Chinese students participated and studying aesthetics. Despite Cai's condemnation, Yuan sent him 4,000 francs during his sojourn in France to relieve him of financial difficulties. According to Cai, the money was not used for personal expenses, but covered the expenses of a journal he was publishing.[42]

After Yuan Shikai's death in October 1916, Cai was recalled from France by the-then minister of education, Fan Yuanlian, to assume the position of chancellor (a title Cai preferred to use when communicating in English that was derived from his emulation of German universities) of National Peking University. It was rumored that Hu Renyuan had offended Shen Buzhou, a section chief in charge of Peking University in the Ministry of Education, who had subsequently asked to replace Hu with Cai. Cai's distinction in educational circles in China led the Chinese government in Beijing to approve the nomination.[43] The Beijing government was then under the control of Li Yuanhong, an ineffective leader swayed by various warlords. During Cai's tenure as Peking University chancellor, the government changed hands several times among warlords.

## The University as the Center of Integrated Knowledge

Against this bleak political background, Cai hoped both to shield the university from state intervention and to make it relevant for national salvation. Unlike Zhang Zhidong, whose curriculum displayed a tension between Chinese learning and Western specialized learning, Cai went beyond such a dichotomy and created an integral body of knowledge that incorporated all subjects in the curriculum. In doing so, Cai borrowed the concept of a transcendental realm of knowledge—of which both Chinese and Western learning were manifestations—and the emphasis on theoretical knowledge from preindustrialization-era German universities.

In 1917, he followed the German university practice of making all the applied divisions, such as engineering, medicine, and commerce, into independent polytechnic universities. He would have abolished the Division of Law and Politics had he not met with strong opposition from the faculty. This body of pure knowledge linked to a transcendental realm of truth provided the university with a moral autonomy from the state. Meanwhile, Cai also actively discouraged any connections between the university and the state, such as students pursuing a political or practical career after graduation or faculty assuming positions at both the university and in the government. He restricted to lecturer the title of those faculty who also took government positions. This resolve to cut ties with the state also led to his conflicts with the Beijing government, as reflected in his many absences from the university from 1919 to 1926.

Claiming moral autonomy from the state, Cai tried to create a new blend of knowledge with both Chinese and Western learning. He sought to channel former revolutionary and political energies to knowledge construction that had cultural, social and political relevance. This was reflected, first, in his faculty appointments. About a quarter of the new faculty members—among them Tan Xihong, Xu Baohuang, Xiao Youmei, Ren Hongjun, Zhang Jingsheng, Gu Mengyu, and Liang Shuming—that he hired at the beginning of his tenure as university president were fellow members of the Tongmenghui, the anti-Manchu revolutionary organization extablished in 1905 that later formed the basis of the Nationalist Party established in 1912. As a sixteen-year-old Tan Xihong had been introduced to the Tongmenghui by Cai in 1907. Tan worked for the Tongmenghui in a Tianjin telegraph company and later served as Sun Yat-sen's secretary in charge of Sun's telegraph correspondence. Before Sun Yat-sen stepped down as president of the republic in 1912, he asked that many of the young people who had worked for him, including those mentioned above, be sent abroad to study. Ren Hongjun and Xu Baohuang went to the United States. Ren earned a Ph.D. in chemistry and became good friends with Hu Shi, and Xu, whose uncle was a republican martyr executed by Yuan Shikai, obtained a degree in economics and journalism. Ren Hongjun was named professor of chemistry at Peking University, and Xu Baohuang was appointed by Cai Yuanpei to teach journalism in the Chinese Language and Literature Department. Gu Mengyu studied at the University of Leipzig and was a friend of Cai's who again studied there in 1912 and 1913. Gu later became chair of the German Language and Literature Department before assuming positions in the government after 1926. The others mentioned above went to study in France. Xiao Youmei studied music and, upon his return, was hired to teach the literature of music in the Chinese Language and Literature Department. Xiao went on to become a famous composer. Tan Xihong earned a Ph.D. in biology at the University of Toulouse in 1919 and became professor of biology in 1920 also serving as Cai's secretary. Zhang Jingsheng studied psychology in France and, after coming to Peking University, created quite a stir on campus by teaching the history of sexuality.[44]

Too young a member of the Tongmenghui to come under Sun Yat-sen's patronage, Liang Shuming, a young scholar, attracted Cai's attention with an article in *Eastern Miscellany* (*Dongfang zazhi*) that compared Buddhism with the concept of ether, which many scientists thought permeated the universe before it was discredited. Liang, who had never attended college, was then appointed to teach Buddhism and Confucian learning at Peking University. In the early 1920s, Liang recommended Xiong Shili to teach at Peking University. Xiong had also been an anti-Qing revolutionary and once had to flee arrest. Xiong was self-taught in Buddhism and, upon Liang Shuming's recommendation, later studied in the School of Buddhism in Nanjing with the Buddhist scholar Ouyang Jingwu. He went on to become the founder of twentieth-century neo-Confucianism synthesizing Buddhism, Confucianism, and Western philosophy. (See Chapter 4 for a discussion of Liang Shuming and Xiong Shili.) These former revolutionaries now channeled their nationalistic energies in the cause of the construction of a new Chinese culture.

Aside from the Tongmenghui, another source of Cai's candidates for Peking University faculty was acquaintances from the work-study movement in France who were not members of the Tongmenghui, but often also actively participated in political or revolutionary activities in China or in France. The most prominent of the appointees from this group was Li Shizeng, who in the late 1920s became a strong rival to Cai Yuanpei in university administration in Beijing. An anti-Manchu activist, Li was the son of Li Hongzao, an important imperial minister during the reign of the Guangxu emperor who used his connections to send Li Shizeng to France in 1912 as the assistant to Sun Muhan, the Chinese minister to France. While there, Li and a few others, including Zhang Jingjiang and Wu Zhihui, started the Chinese student work-study movement, in which Cai Yuanpei also participated.

Another group of revolutionaries Cai hired came from Japan in 1917. Liu Shipei (see Chapter 6) and Ma Yuzao were classical scholars who took refuge from the Qing regime in Japan with Zhang Taiyan and his students in the early 1910s. Cai also hired Zhang Shizhao, a veteran scholar and newspaper editor against the Manchu government who had sojourned in Japan and founded the *Jiayin* (*tiger*) magazine while in Japan, to which many of Zhang Taiyan's students contributed articles, to teach logic at Peking University in 1917. Zhang Shizhao was also appointed as the curator of Peking University Library, a position he later found too time-consuming and recommended to Li Dazhao (see below), his friend and contributor to his *Tiger* magazine and *Tiger Daily* (Jiaying rikan, the successor to *Tiger* magazine after Zhang Shizhao came back from Tokyo in Beijing in 1915), which Cai Yuanpei approved. Early in the twentieth century, Li had studied political economy at Waseda University in Japan. Both of them returned to China in 1915 to fight Yuan Shikai. An early champion of communism in China, Li helped establish a Marxist study committee on campus. In 1920, he was also appointed professor of history. The following year, he was one of the founders of the Chinese Communist Party.

Cai's administrative appointments relied heavily on scholars who aimed at transforming Chinese culture. Cai retained the previous dean of the sciences, Xia Yuanli, a returned student from Germany, and appointed as his dean of the humanities Chen Duxiu, editor of the avant-garde journal *New Youth* (*Xin qingnian*). Xia, who introduced Einstein's theory of relativity to China, had been hired by the-then president Hu Renyuan. A chance meeting between Chen Duxiu and Shen Yingmo, a faculty member in the Chinese Language and Literature Department, in Beijing, led Shen to introduce Chen to Cai Yuanpei. Cai urged Chen to move the offices of *New Youth* from Shanghai to Beijing, which Chen finally agreed to do in 1917. All the editors of *New Youth*—including Chen Duxiu, Lu Xun, Zhou Zuoren, Qian Xuantong, Hu Shi, and Shen Yingmo—became Peking University faculty members.[45] Liu Fu, who often wrote for *New Youth* on vernacular literature, was hired at Peking University to teach literature on the recommendation of Chen Duxiu. The choice of his topic of study was related in part to the role he played in the Chinese language reform movement on Peking University campus between 1918 and 1920.

A revolutionary mindframe and Western learning content or approaches were what Cai paid special attention to in his faculty hiring. More than a third of Cai's other appointments in 1917 were of nonrevolutionary returned students from study abroad.[46] While hoping to transform Chinese culture with Western learning, Cai also emphasized the unity of learning, that they would all be united at a transcendental level. In addition to the massive number of Western-educated scholars, Cai also appointed those with credentials in traditional scholarship, such as Cui Shi, a philologist of the New Text school. As recalled by Feng Youlan, Cui was an able scholar but lacked pedagogy. In class, all he could do was to read his book word by word.[47] In his appointments, Cai was careful to balance between people with different approaches to scholarship in order to create an environment where the students had access to multiple interpretations. Cui Shi's lectures on New Text learning, therefore, were balanced by Liu Shipei's exegesis of Old Text learning. The two were courteous and would bow deeply to each other when they met in the street. But in the classroom, they would vigorously attack each other's perspective.[48] Cai's attempt to balance traditional and modern approaches to learning was also demonstrated through the lecturers hired for the course of ethics in the Humanities Division in 1917. The initial lecturer, Kang Xinfu, approached the course from the traditional Chinese emphasis on the cultivation of individual character, which Cai felt was insufficient in introducing Western ideas on ethics. As a counterbalance, in 1918 he hired Yang Changji, who had studied philosophy in Japan and taught subjects in philosophy in normal schools in Hunan province. Unlike Kang, Yang often tried to place Chinese and Western ethical thought into a comparative perspective.[49]

His belief in the transcendental unity of learning led Cai in 1918 to abolish the divisional system and transform all the subdivisions into departments, in order to encourage an integration of learning through cross-disciplinary course selections.

## Lax Intellectual Atmosphere, Liberal Life-style, and Political Autonomy: Peking University in the 1910s and 1920s

Cai Yuanpei's emphasis on lofty ideals and the pursuit of pure learning helped establish a unique identity for Peking University. The result was a combination of the traditional Chinese *shuyuan* style of education that allowed free and independent studies by the students and the modern academic emphasis on scholarship. The emphasis on the untrammeled pursuit of knowledge led to lax enforcement of class attendance. It was not unusual for half the class to spend time in the library rather than in the classroom, to show up only for examinations. It was also very easy to switch from one class to another during the same semester or to switch from one department to another. The free pursuit of learning was overemphasized and applied even to those who were not registered students of Peking University. Anyone could audit a class. Classrooms were often filled with auditors, including Shen Congwen, Ding Ling, and Yang Muo, who later became some of twentieth-century China's best novelists. Although to avoid fees many auditors did not even register their audit status with the school (many could not even afford the audit fees), they could still consult the professors and even have their writings critiqued. Class offerings were extremely diverse. Many courses not offered on other university campuses, such as Sanskrit or Buddhism, were offered at Peking University, irrespective of student attendance; sometimes this meant only one student registered. Thus the faculty welcomed unregistered students. As Zhu Haitao, a Peking University alumnus, commented, such policies helped foster a non-utilitarian pursuit of pure learning. The flourishing of student and faculty academic clubs and journals added to Peking University's distinct identity.

The early specialization in the Peking University curriculum contrasted with that of Qinghua University, which followed the American system in requiring a more rounded education.[50] Between 1917 and 1927, two-thirds of a students' courses were required and one-third were electives. Every department decided its own required and elective courses, and the latter were often interdisciplinary. For example, elective courses for the History Department between 1924 and 1925 included geology, biology, law, history of Indian religions, history of philosophy, and history of education.[51] A course usually lasted a full year, and one class hour per week for the whole year counted as one credit. A student needed eighty credits to graduate, which would translate into twenty per academic year, or between fourteen and forty courses per year (one course ranged from one to three credits)!

One of the products of the free pursuit of learning was Gu Jiegang, an agriculture major at Peking University's preparatory school in 1913. In 1914, he changed his major to art and started to take courses in literature and philology under Ma Yuzao and Shen Jianshi, who had been students of Zhang Taiyan. In 1916, he enrolled at Peking University as a philosophy major. By the time he graduated in 1920, Gu Jiegang had already established himself as one of the most important classical scholars of the twentieth century.[52]

Freedom of thought was one of the most treasured aspects of Peking University. It was also used as a justification of the university's political separation from the state. In 1926, the-then president of the Beijing government, the warlord Zhang Zuolin, decided to merge all the national higher educational institutions into a single university in the capital (*jingshi daxuexiao*) that would be more easily managed by the state. He and his government were becoming increasingly suspicious of any potential dissent as the Northern Expedition army led by the Nationalists and Communists initially headquartered in Canton marched north to unify China and drew closer to his seat of government in the north. Plainclothes police were ordered to perform surveillance at the university. The following year, Peking University faculty members Li Dazhao and Gao Renshan were executed by the regime because of their Communist activities. The situation was very tense.[53] After the fall of the warlords in 1928, peace was temporarily restored, but the university soon found itself in conflict with the newly arrived Nationalist government, which, like Zhang, planned to merge Peking University with eight other higher educational institutions. The idea had originated with Cai Yuanpei, who now as minister of education reintroduced his 1912 concept of educational autonomy based on the French university district model. Viewing the instability of Chinese education, Cai hoped to "replace bureaucracy with scholarship" (*xueshuhua dai guanliaohua*). Under this plan, in August 1928, Beijing and Tianjin together with Rehe and Hebei provinces were classified as one university district, and Peking University was to merge with Hebei University, Peking Law and Politics University, and Tianjin Law and Politics Institute, to form one national university that would serve as the Grand College overseeing the administration of all other educational institutions in China.[54]

Despite Cai Yuanpei's good intentions, this plan met with resistance everywhere it was tried, in both northern and southern China. Many faculty and students viewed the merger of Peking University as an attempt to destroy its unique identity. Eventually, the Nationalist government had to back down and agree to the restoration of the former Peking University. In June 1929, the university district system was finally abolished. Cai Yuanpei, initially the candidate for president of Peking University, ultimately declined the position and assumed the post of president of the newly established Academia Sinica. Chen Daqi, professor of philosophy, was the interim president from 1929 to 1930. In

December 1930, Jiang Menglin, deputy president during Cai's many absences in the 1920s, became the president of the university.[55] Jiang's presidency continued Cai's mission while placing many of Cai's lofty ideals on more solid ground.

## Jiang Menglin, President of Peking University (1930–1937)

In many ways, Jiang Menglin proved a worthy successor to Cai Yuanpei. He shared with Cai the lofty ideals of a humanistic education and the independence of education from political interference. Unlike Cai, who was more a scholar than a bureaucrat and who often valued ideals more than their actual implementation, Jiang was much more pragmatic and resourceful. Jiang sometimes joked that if Cai could be compared to a prize minister because of his contributions to the university's vision and his scholarship, he, Jiang, could be called a prize dog for his dedicated service to the university.[56] During his tenure as university president, Jiang Menglin greatly increased the university's financial resources, making possible funding for student scholarships, appointments of chaired faculty members, equipment, and the construction of a library, a geology building, and a dormitory building. Jiang also introduced a greater emphasis on independent research and study. Despite the uncertainty due to conflict with Japan beginning in 1931, the period of Jiang's tenure turned out to be a golden age for many departments at Peking University.

Jiang Menglin (1886–1964) had a very different upbringing from that of Cai Yuanpei. Like Cai, he was born in a town near Shaoxing, Zhejiang province, which had long experienced Western influence. Unlike Cai, who had pursued a traditional education and won the highest degree in the state examination system at an early age, Jiang had begun private tutelage at the age of six and then attended the School of Eastern and Western Learning (*Zhongxi xuetang*) in Shaoxing, which Cai had founded in the 1890s. Whereas Cai was a visionary who helped bring about changes based on his ideas for China's future, Jiang belonged to a generation that directly experienced the results of such visions and had a more realistic grasp of the interactions between Chinese and Western influences in China. Jiang passed the primary level of the imperial examinations in 1903, but could not decide whether to become a revolutionary or an official. Ultimately Jiang attended the South Sea Public School in Shanghai and in 1908 decided to go to the United States to study . He changed his major from agriculture to education at Columbia University Teachers' College . After earning his Ph.D. in education, in 1918 Jiang was assigned by Cai Yuanpei to Peking University,[57] where he later assumed such important administrative positions as deputy president.

Sharp, industrious, open-minded, and realistic, Jiang Menglin decided that proper university rules and procedures were just as important as ideals for making the university successful. Fundamentally, however, he shared with Cai the ideal of a humanistic education as the ultimate goal of the university. His tenure at the university can be divided into two stages. The first stage, with Jiang as deputy president (1920–26), began with Jiang's vision of an alignment between education, society, and politics: schools and universities were to teach individualism, essential to freedom and equality in a modern democracy. "As these concepts along with 'sovereignty of the people' and 'representative institutions' gained meaning in modern China, the special talents of each person would be liberated and contribute to the overall strength of a democratic society."[58] But after 1922, according to Barry Keenan, Jiang started to place a greater emphasis on a German-style university in accordance with Cai Yuanpei's vision, a university that is more removed from society yet ultimately contributes to social development. This change came about because of his disillusionment with Chinese politics. The educational system that he originally visualized as contributing good citizens to society was premised on a pluralistic democratic society where there is a separate space for professional educators. Jiang was painfully aware that such premise did not exist in China. Thus the German educational model, emphasizing the theoretical, not involving politics, and working for a higher national good, became the university model for him.[59] The Chinese political reality pushed both men, despite their different educational backgrounds, to adopt a scholarship-only approach in their administrations of the university, yet they differed greatly in their methods of administration.

The second stage of Jiang's administration began when Jiang first assumed the presidency in 1930. Peking University was at a low point of its development. Many good faculty members had gone to universities in southern China because of financial difficulties at Peking University. The university curriculum had been greatly disrupted by changes in the university in 1926 and 1928. In 1926, the warlord president Zhang Zuolin merged nine higher educational institutions in Beijing, including Peking University, into one consolidated university (jingshi daxuexiao), establishing state bureaucratic control over the university to better monitor university activities. After the Nationalist Party successfully completed its northern expedition and established a Nationalist government in 1928, this conglomeration of nine higher educational institutions were renamed Zhonghua University. Former Peking University faculty and students vigorously pushed for the restoration of the independent Peking University, and in the second half of 1928, classes stopped, to which the Nationalist givernment responded by suspending university budget, faculty and staff salaries, and coal and other fuels from June to December. The relentless fight on the part of former Peking University faculty and staff finally led the government to back down and agree to the restoration of the independent Peking University in August 1929.[60] In the months when salary ran behind, to maintain their livelihood, many faculty members taught elsewhere in addition to their regular teaching at Peking University. Although Jiang Menglin never eliminated the practice of Peking University professors moonlighting at other schools and universities during the regular school year, he passed new rules and regulations that led to greater accountability of the faculty members. During Cai Yuanpei's presidency, because of the philosophy of untrammeled freedom of learning, Cai entrusted responsibility for faculty appointment and retention to the faculty committee (*pingyihui*), made up of faculty representatives of various departments, which was the de facto highest administrative unit on campus. The committee's other duties included deciding the university's budget, appointing the various campus executive committees, conferring academic degrees, evaluating academic programs, and drawing up the university's rules and regulations. Jiang disbanded the faculty committee and gave the responsibility for faculty appointment and retention to the university president. He ruled that those who taught an excess number of hours on other campuses either would have to leave or would no longer be recognized as regular faculty members at Peking University.[61]

Jiang Menglin emphasized the paramount importance of learning, especially pure learning, as the university's mission. He stipulated that the university should cultivate deep learning, therefore the emphasis on specialization. Much of the university's curriculum was specialized, with a theoretical penchant. In this respect he was in line with Cai Yuanpei's vision for the university. Freedom of thinking continued to flourish during Jiang's tenure as one could see from the many debates among faculty members and between faculty members and students. Qian Mu reminisced that when he taught in class in the 1930s, it was like mounting a debating forum.[62]

To perpetuate the goal of freedom of thought, however, Jiang approached the curriculum and the academic programs from a very different perspective than Cai. Cai Yuanpei had abolished university divisions and established eighteen departments in 1918, so that there would be no divisional barriers to block students from taking other departments' courses. Jiang, by contrast, grouped the academic programs into three colleges: College of Arts, College of Sciences, and College of Law. Common core courses were offered in each college before students would specialize in the required and elective courses in their own departments. These common core courses continued to serve as the philosophical perspective that Cai Yuanpei used to create an integration of knowledge but, unlike in the past, when they could be taken at any time, now they had to be taken in the first year before students could specialize. In the curriculum of the

College of Arts for the 1932–33 academic year, freshmen in the college had to take four common core courses: survey of philosophy, survey of science, Chinese history survey, and Western history survey.[63] Jiang cut a large number of courses that he viewed as overly specialized, arguing that the proliferation of courses was sometimes a waste of time for the students and waste of money for the state, without benefit for the students' specializations.[64] Jiang Menglin's establishment of the three colleges seems a realistic approach to the administration of campus academic affairs, while his course cutting was probably the result of budgetary considerations. Jiang also reformed the university degree requirements. He changed the measurement of credit hours from one hour per week for a one-year course to one hour per week for a semester-long course. A student could graduate after earning 132 credits, or 33 hours per year, in contrast to the 20 credits (40 hours) per year during Cai's presidency. Jiang further stipulated that, in their first two years of college, students could take a minimum of sixteen and a maximum of twenty hours of class per semester and, in the second two years, a minimum of fourteen and a maximum of eighteen hours of class per semester.[65]

On the whole, Jiang's curriculum was a more realistic and structured approach to liberal education than Cai's. Jiang also tried to stop student absenteeism in the classroom, not only stipulating submitting graduation theses in some departments, but also grade deduction for absence in class, including 5 percent deduction for absences during a fifth of the semester, 10 percent for absences of one fourth of the semester, and when students were absent for more than a third of the semester they were not allowed to take the final examination. Those who failed two or more courses among the required courses or half the courses per academic year or who were barred from the final examination because of excessive absences would have to repeat the entire year.[66] While Cai Yuanpei wanted to implement freedom of thought and academic autonomy through lax institutional rules and faculty self-rule, Jiang Menglin tried to achieve academic vigor through a rigorous institutional structure replete with disciplinary measures. Jiang's approach, however, was not fully implemented in reality at Peking University during his tenure because the colleges and departments were not eager to enforce it.

One secret of Jiang Menglin's success was the financial backing he obtained for Peking University. With his great administrative ability, Jiang made possible a cooperative project between Peking University and the China Foundation of Culture and Education. From 1931 to 1936, with financial contributions from the China Foundation,[67] the university was able to expand: almost two thirds of the funding from the China Foundation was spent on the expansion of the infrastructure, while a third was spent on appointing chair professors. Of the twenty-nine people appointed as chaired professors, ten were department chairs, and one was the dean of the College of the Sciences.[68] Such financial resources contributed enormously to the academic development of Peking University.

With pragmatism and insight, Jiang Menglin gave the university more structure and more realistic measures than Cai Yuanpei to reach the lofty academic goals. He continued Cai Yuanpei's goal of research. Because of the financial support from the China Foundation, with better faculty, library, facilities, and student scholarships, research experienced a golden age at Peking University in the 1930s.[69]

In short, from President He Yushi to President Jiang Menglin, one sees a deepening reliance on Western learning as the rationale for the university. Inability to get along with the warlord governments and financial estrangement from the state led them to increase their emphasis on university autonomy. Among them, Cai Yuanpei was most successful in proposing a new, integrated version of Chinese and Western learning. Cai Yuanpei differed from Zhang Zhidong and avoided a dichotomy of (integrated) Chinese learning and specialized Western learning by integrating both under a transcendental realm of truth, linked to Chinese national salvation. Through converting many colleagues and friends from radical revolutionaries to university professors, he attempted to use the university as a forum to produce cultural nationalism at a time when political revolutions, such as the revolutions against Yuan Shikai and successive warlord governments, did not seem to be the solution. His nationalism was corroborated by President Jiang Menglin, whose curriculum gave a more realistic interpretation of the integration of knowledge by strengthening the university administrative structure and making course offerings more systematic, thereby making departmental curriculum more likely to be implemented.

Sun Jianai, the imperial minister in charge of education and the Imperial Peking University (1898–1901). Courtesy of Guo Jianrong.

Zhang Baixi, the imperial minister in charge of education and the Imperial Peking University (1901–1903). Courtesy of Guo Jianrong.

*Honglou* (red building), classroom building immortalized in the history of early Peking University from the old university campus in downtown Beijing before 1952.

Chancellor Cai Yuanpei (1917–1926). Courtesy of Guo Jianrong.

Cai Yuanpei's bust on the current Peking University campus in western suburban Beijing (since 1952).

Peking University science library on the pre-1952 campus. Courtesy of Guo Jianrong.

Committee on Chinese Language Studies (front row: Qian Xuantong: first left; Mao Heng: fourth left). Courtesy of Guo Jianrong.

Liu Fu (Bannong) and Qian Xuantong, two promoters of the vernacular. Courtesy of Guo Jianrong.

Faculty of Chinese studies (front row, from left to right: Dong Zuobin, Chen Yuan, Zhu Xizu, Jiang Menglin, and Huang Wenbi; second row, Gu Jiegang, first left; Ma Heng, second left; Shen Jianshi, third left; third row, Hu Shi, second left). Courtesy of Guo Jianrong.

1932年與章太炎先生等在北大二院合影（前排右起：朱希祖、錢玄同、章太炎、劉半農、馬裕藻；中排右起：2.莊尚嚴，4.作者，6.馬 準，7.郁泰然，後排右起：4.董彥堂，10.周殿福）。

Faculty of Chinese studies with Zhang Taiyan (front row from left to right: Zhu Xizu, Qian Xuantong, Zhang Taiyan, Liu Fu, and Ma Yuzao; second row: Wei Jiangong, second left). Courtesy of Guo Jianrong.

The science compound: where the departments of science and later the College of Science were located. Courtesy of Guo Jianrong.

President Jiang Menglin (1930–1937).
Courtesy of Guo Jianrong.

# 4

# The Transformation of a Discursive Context

## From a Paradigm of Chinese vs. Western Learning to One of Science vs. Metaphysics

By 1917, in the discourse regarding knowledge both at Peking University and nationwide, one sees a marked transition from Zhang Zhidong's dichotomy of integrated Chinese learning and more specialized Western learning to situating Chinese learning in a discourse on materialism versus spirituality and science versus metaphysics. Chinese learning was no longer treated as pertaining only to China but as moral knowledge that converged with the moral and metaphysical knowledge of European countries. In such discourses, Chinese knowledge continued to be classified into history, literature, philosophy, and philology—the four academic disciplines Zhang Zhidong and later Cai Yuanpei used to categorize Chinese learning—but it was incorporated into a more universal discourse on learning.

In Cai Yuanpei's curriculum for Peking University, erasing the dichotomy between Chinese and Western learning was based on a transcendental perception of learning, typified in the curriculum of the Philosophy Subdivision of the Humanities Division (1917–19) and the subsequent Department of Philosophy (1919–26), where many courses on classical Western philosophy from Descartes to Kant were offered, which dealt almost exclusively with the issue of epistemology. According to F.R. Ankersmit, the rise of epistemology was the result of conflicting interpretations of knowledge in the seventeenth century: whether knowledge came from the transcendental ego or was rooted in human experience. René Descartes was the first to use the modern notion of the mind as a *forum internum*, in which truths about the world and about the physical self were mirrored. Conflicting interpretations of the source of knowledge led to the subsequent acknowledgment by many Western philosophers that "[o]nly those beliefs that have come into being in accordance with the rules and under the jurisprudence obtaining in the *forum internum* can count as knowledge."[1] Epistemology especially appealed to Cai Yuanpei, perhaps because it was the product of conflicting interpretations of reality, like the times in which Cai actually lived, and although it admitted the limitations of human understanding of truth, it was optimistic about greater human knowledge and explored avenues of fuller human understanding of truth. Moreover, it assumed the existence of a transcendental order of knowledge that was superior, though accessible, to human beings. The study of epistemology, therefore, offers an understanding of how humans explore this independent and transcendental order of knowledge.

An increasing number of courses in classical European philosophy were offered in the early 1920s, after the appointments of scholars who completed their studies abroad, such as Zhang Yi. Before 1917, only a few Western philosophy courses were available. In 1914, the first year the philosophy subdivision enrolled students since its opening in 1910, courses in ethics, logic, aesthetics, linguistics, and psychology were listed alongside a survey of Western philosophy and Song and Ming Confucianism. But apparently not all were actually offered. In 1916, the Philosophy Department offerings included a course on Indian philosophy, ethics, Gongyang's annotation of the *Spring and Autumn Annals*, Confucianism, anthropology, and ethnology.[2] After 1917 courses increased significantly in number. By 1922, courses in Indian and Western philosophy included history of Western philosophy, aesthetics (taught by Cai himself), behaviorism and Comte's positivism, Descartes and Leibniz, epistemology, history of modern epistemology, history of Christianity, Indian philosophy, history of ancient Indian philosophy, Consciousness Only (*Weishi*) philosophy, philosophy of religion, and history of religion.[3] In the 1925–26 academic year, the only Western philosophy course not dealing with classical continental philosophy was on Auguste Comte. Compared with Qinghua University, which put greater emphasis on mathematical logic, Peking University never had a logic specialist, although Zhang Shenfu and Jin Yuelin, professors of logic at Qinghua University, often came there to guest lecture. Peking University focused more on the history of classical Western philosophy, largely ignoring contemporary Western philosophies such as American pragmatism and philosophers Alfred North Whitehead and Bertrand Russell, a situation that lasted well into the 1930s.[4] Most of the European philosophers that were taught at Peking University—Spinoza, Descartes, Locke, Hume, Berkeley, Kant, and Hegel—dealt with epistemology and tried to explain the relationship between human beings and knowledge, and the human ability to understand truth.

One can say that European epistemology formed the basis of Cai Yuanpei's transcendental approach to knowledge, making it possible for him to be even-handed with respect to both Chinese learning and Western learning. It was also the basis of his famous slogan *jianrong bingbao* (all subjects of learning would be tolerated and included), which he used to justify the coexistence of Western and traditional Chinese learning in his curriculum. Cai's penchant for epistemology was reflected in his deep interest in aesthetics, which he thought bridged the human sensual perceptions and transcendental knowledge. Although not all shared Cai's synthesis of Chinese and Western learning, his colleagues at Peking University also tended to discuss Chinese learning in a more international context. In addition to discussing Cai Yuanpei, this chapter also explores Liang Shuming's and Xiong Shili's approaches to scholarship. Liang and Xiong both distinguished themselves with a synthesis of Confucian, European, and Indian philosophies to create a new conceptual framework of knowledge. A lecturer in philosophy from 1917 to 1924, Liang, created a three-stage transcendental cultural structure based on European, Chinese, and Indian cultures. By treating the three as universal human stages on the evolution ladder, he pointed out the inevitability of Western learning in China but also asserted the superiority of the Chinese culture because it was the second stage of human development that Chinese and Europeans alike would enter into. Xiong, who lectured in philosophy (1917–37), created a universal and transcendental realm of knowledge based on a synthesis of Buddhism, Daoism, Confucian learning, and the theories of Henri Bergson.

They did not have as lasting an impact as Cai Yuanpei's aesthetics since both Liang and Xiong left the university without proper successors to their causes in the 1920s. Nevertheless they had a profound influence on the twentieth-century Chinese classification of knowledge, including the separation of the arts from the sciences and the development of neo-Confucianism in Taiwan and Hong Kong. Together, they redefined Confucian learning and situated Chinese learning in a more universal framework. Their new definition of Chinese learning, however, was premised on a new definition of the human being that many Chinese came to accept in the early twentieth century.

## Biological Evolution, Aesthetics, and the Definition of Humaneness

By the 1910s, a new definition of humaneness started to develop that drew upon Western humanism and a Darwinian depiction of the human being and gave a freer reign to the development of human attributes than in Confucian teachings. The biological depiction of man, as transmitted through social Darwinism, deeply affected Chinese scholars. Their familiarity with the theory came primarily from its use in their attack on the Manchu government. After the downfall of the Qing dynasty, social Darwinism was convenient to use in the biological criticism of the Chinese culture. Most Chinese scholars, even those who later became conservative and pro-monarchical swallowed the

Darwinian biological description of humans in terms of races and their need to adapt to the external environment. Biologizing human nature also enabled many to link Chinese cultural degeneration with biological decay and pit nature against culture, something learned from the fin-de-siècle European criticism of culture.[5] Under these circumstances, many not only gave freer rein to emotional spontaneity but also saw how they could use it to transform culture. Liang Qichao, for instance, championed fiction writing as a means of changing China because it was aesthetically compelling, easily accessible to the majority of the Chinese, and the most effective medium for shaping and regulating their moral complexion precisely because of its affective-impact.

In his new definition of morality, Cai Yuanpei saw spontaneous emotions as essential to its fulfillment. In his "On the Evolution of Aesthetics," for instance, Cai discussed the German aesthetician Alexander Baumgarten's *Aesthetica*, the seminal work in modern Western aesthetics, stressing Baumgarten's citation of the Greek etymology of the word "aesthetic" as denoting feeling and sensation. Yet Cai was also drawn to the aesthetic for its affective values with respect to moral education, seeing in it something that would help the people develop along the path of noble habits and refined tastes, with their desires sublimated to higher ethical principles. Like Cai, many others in China also saw the moral value of an aesthetic education. Wang Guowei, an important scholar and aesthetician of the early twentieth century, saw in aesthetics an ideological function akin to that of religion, something capable of penetrating people's deep psychology and curing the emotionally depressed and morally degenerate society.[6] The emphasis on natural expressions of emotions was not entirely new to the Chinese. The neo-Confucian learning of the Cheng-Zhu school placed emphasis on sincerity of purpose, meaning a sincere, natural expression of Confucian teachings in everyday life. In the twentieth century, however, Zhu Xi came under increasing attack for his dichotomy between heavenly rules (*tianli*) and human desires (*renyu*). Scholars like Hu Shi and his followers championed Confucians like Dai Zhen of the Qing dynasty, who gave greater affirmation to the human being than the Cheng-Zhu school. The introduction of the Darwinian biological depiction of the human being also led to a search among many scholars for "authentic" human sentiments apart from Confucian teachings, which developed into an important intellectual movement at Peking University in the 1920s.[7]

## Aesthetics and *jianrong bingbao*

For Cai Yuanpei, spontaneous human sentiments underlay the introduction of aesthetics as a way of helping connect the individual and universal, transcendental truth, and balance between an overemphasized scientific approach and a Confucian paradigm. Between 1919 and 1920, Cai gave about ten public lectures on campus on Western aesthetic theory, stopped only by his hospitalization for treatment of a fungal infection of his foot.

When science was first introduced to China, many Chinese scholars wanted it to replace Confucian cosmology. Some people employed the scientific paradigm to deal with all problems of nature, society, ethics, aesthetics, and metaphysics. Like the Confucian cosmology, it covered every aspect of life.[8] For believers in science, the confrontation between Eastern and Western cultures was a difference not of kind but of degree, between the new and the old, tradition and modernity, which would eventually disappear with the development of science.[9] Cai had no intention of unconditionally defending Confucian learning, nor did he intend to flood China unconditionally with Western. Although Cai actively promoted science in China, he scorned the material forces that science unleashed, which to him stunted any emotional cultivation that was formerly the province of religion.[10] Cai rejected Confucian learning because for too long it had been associated with Chinese politics. Still, he appreciated the emphasis on humaneness and emotional cultivation in Confucian learning. Those aspects of Confucian learning that he favored were now associated with the characteristics of Western aesthetics, without the this-worldly political orientations of Confucian learning. Although in his first history of Chinese ethics Cai adopted a linear, progressive approach to Chinese thought, judging as ethical anyone who actively promoted social progress, and as unethical anyone who passively blocked it,[11] Cai quickly abandoned this linear, progressive model. After completing *A History of Chinese Ethics* (*Zhingguo Lunli Xueshi*), Cai translated a part of Friederich Paulsen's *Principles of Ethics*, in which Paulsen argued for the existence of an ethical world that transcended the world of concrete phenomena.

The rise of aesthetics in Europe was a response to the growing conflict between transcendental truth and the rise of human values. Alexander Baumgarten, one of the founders of aesthetics, argued that it is the contemplation of beauty. Moses Mendelssohn, another founder, further combined sensation and contemplation in his discussion of beauty: the human mind is too limited to be able to sensuously observe the variety in unity of ontological perfection, which is discernible only by reason. But we can sensuously contemplate the variety in unity of the mind's own acts and passions, sensations, thoughts, and emotions. Perfect perception gives rise to disinterested, aesthetic pleasure in the harmonious play of our faculties.[12] To J.J. Winckelmann, an eighteenth-century German philosopher, aesthetic depiction of beauty depended on human emotions distilled or creatively reworked, such that the depiction gains independence from the external influence initially prompting emotional response, and external impressions were transformed into a purely internal mental activity.

Therefore an emphasis on aimless aesthetic appreciation would not only help retain certain elements of Confucian learning that Cai continued to appreciate, but also perpetuate the practice of human self-cultivation that Cai, who at an early age had been steeped in neo-Confucian learning, must have held dear, through the emphasis on the balance between the emotional and the cognitive. What lay at the heart of aesthetic appreciation was free human mental activities that derived from sensual and visual contact with beauty. Free expressions of sentiments served as the foundation for this freedom of mental activities.

This type of free, or aimless, mental activity helped balance the goal-oriented activities encouraged by both Confucian learning and the introduction of science. Cai found the ideal expression of this idea in Kant. During his stay in France in 1916, while writing *Kant on Aesthetics* (*Kangde meixueshu*), Cai translated Kant's definition of the beautiful, pointing out that the aimlessness of aesthetic appreciation differed from concrete goals of the good and the useful. These two were to serve human will and were not the ultimate goals of life. The aesthetic beautiful, however, was not constrained by any desires and completely free, was never overly serious and originated from interest. It was concerned not with bodily desires but ethics.[13] Intellectual pleasures were derived from the achievement of a certain goal through the use of mental observations and research, but the pleasure derived from the beautiful did not involve any concepts or goals. Pleasure itself was not a goal; otherwise, it would be a desire and not pure appreciation, concerning not its external form but its content.[14] Cai affirmed the importance of emotional cultivation and placed specific ethical rules below the aesthetic cultivation of emotions. As he quoted Kant, morality came from a sense of responsibility and was easily overemphasized.[15]

Aesthetics, as a subject of study, was popularized in the German states to adjust the students to an industrial era. It was an important component of German education in the eighteenth and nineteenth centuries, especially in personal cultivation (*Bildung*), initially to enable moral freedom through personal harmony, achieved through aesthetic appreciation, so as to ease transition into a disciplined, impersonal, and industrializing society. Aesthetically "cultivated people would find an occupational outlet for their creativity without having to internalize collective imperatives," thus ensuring "voluntary commitment to duty."[16] For Cai Yuanpei, however, the ultimate goal of aesthetic cultivation was not to reconcile one to this world, but to transcend human self-interest and ultimately abandon one's hold on the material things in this world,[17] in other words, the absolute transcendence of the sensual world and human sentiments. To some extent, even national salvation was a specific goal secondary to this transcendence of concrete pursuits because, with all its urgency, it was too utilitarian to be the rationale for a new knowledge structure in China, for example, by flooding China with science, which displaced the study of ethics and other metaphysical subjects. Cai carefully distinguished between specific moral conduct and aesthetic self-transcendence, viewing regular ethical and intellectual standards as part of a low echelon of morality. At that level, humans were working to prolong life and self-benefit and avoid death and cost. To serve this goal, morality could not be called a good. Only completely altruistic behavior was the highest form of good. It was free and beautiful because it completely transcended individual interests. At the lower level, humans needed to be guided with general knowledge, but at the higher level, one would need aesthetic education because the motivation for altruism proceeded entirely from emotions.[18]

Perhaps because Cai hoped that the individual faculty members and students could transcend their individual disciplines and fields and come to the realization of this higher, universal realm of knowledge, his discussion of self-transcendence differed from Kant's description of aesthetics. This was revealing of different approaches to knowledge and human understanding. To Kant, the transcendental world was beyond human understanding, although there were a priori concepts connected to that world that provided humans with the means of explaining their experience.[19] Humans could not understand these concepts as they were and could only intuit them through aesthetics using the free play of mental faculties such as imagination and understanding.[20] The pleasure from the free reign of the faculties would enable one to understand such concepts as "absolute totality" or "transcendental freedom." Although Kant's end was realization of morality—that an awareness of the universality of the aesthetic experience would enable one to prescind from a preoccupation with personal gratification or advantage and regard things instead from a universally shareable perspective—his emphasis was on the aesthetic experience, and to Kant, there was never a complete self-transcendence because man could never advance to the order of transcendental knowledge. The aesthetic experience simply bridged man and that order, making the transition from the charm of sensual experience to habitual moral interest possible without too violent a leap.[21] Kant's focus was on the individual.

In comparison, Cai's emphasis was more on transcendence from this world to reach a state of unity of individuals. Cai's argument was closer to another part of Kant's aesthetic theory of the sublime, treated by Kant as an independent theory from his work on the aesthetically beautiful. To Kant, sublime feelings, caused by extraordinary events such as violent storms and volcanic eruptions, did not bring immediate pleasure of the faculties but, rather, evoked immediate resistance. A struggle between oneself and nature ensued, which finally reconciled one to nature and awakened one to the conception of oneself as a self-determining moral agent who could rise above the lures of sensuous impulse and make one's conduct conform to the principles and ends laid down by practical reason. Thus, in experiencing a feeling of the sublime, we are conscious of being more than creatures of sensibility—here conceived as a susceptibility to natural desires and fears—and are raised to a presentiment of the preeminence of our rational state. The actual source of sublimation lies in the superiority of our rational powers to those of sensibility. To achieve this goal, one needs to be able, at the level of practical life, to respond to hostile or menacing circumstances in such a manner as to withstand the pressures of sensuous inclinations.[22]

Most of Cai's examples of aesthetic appreciation were about transcending one's original sensual self to arrive at a higher level of being, with little or no discussion of the individual experience in the process. Unlike in Kant's conception, where transcendental truth was not directly connected with human experience, in Confucian learning, a higher level of mentality was not alienated from human experience and could be achieved through intuition. Therefore, a good neo-Confucian scholar like Cai did not need to distinguish the sensual and intuitive from the rational in his discussion. Similarly, for Cai, to achieve transcendental truth did not require a triumph of the rational self over the sensual self, because the two were connected and formed a continuum. What often led him to challenge the intangibility of truth was his belief that humans could completely grasp truth. He was more interested in discussing what happened after total truth was grasped—when the gap between individuals would be erased—than how that process was achieved through human mechanisms. For that matter, in his discussion of the sublime, he easily ignored Kant's discussion of the inner conflict before one could achieve a greater alignment with rationality. He did not think there was a distinct demarcation between the human stage and the stage of greater rationality. The continuum Cai built between the ideals and human pursuit seemed to be characteristic of many Confucian scholars in twentieth century China, the most notable being Mo Zongsan, reputedly the most vocal leader of twentieth century neo-Confucian learning. Like Cai, Mo was deeply interested in German classical philosophy and reconstructed Confucian philosophy by using the framework of Kant's practical rationality. Unlike Kant, however, Mo idealized innate human nature and saw the possibility of internal transcendence, such as the self-elevation of the ethical heart.[23]

Cai's lack of distinction between the transcendental and the immanent truth made him ignore the difference between various schools of aesthetics that emphasized one or the other.[24] The humanistic order of knowledge that Cai aimed to establish, although taking human emotions and intuition into consideration, focused more on how to channel individuals to completely and seamlessly merge with the universal than the consequence of this process on the individuals. His major concern was the final realization of the unity of knowledge.

The aesthetic approach enabled Cai Yuanpei to bypass the questions of the division between Eastern and Western cultures and between science and metaphysics. It explains his equanimity in carrying out the *jianrong bingbao* policy. It also showed his distinction between the university and the political goal of national salvation.

University learning now served as an integral body of knowledge that was linked to a transcendental realm of knowledge. It would benefit national salvation in providing the nation with a highly developed culture, but its knowledge content went beyond the immediate goals of national prosperity, especially material prosperity. National salvation, if used to define the university identity directly, would be too narrow a goal.

Whereas Cai's aesthetics enabled him to develop an integral body of Chinese and Western learning according to certain universal categories such as human cultivation, metaphysics, and science, Liang Shuming adopted a different, comparable-but-separate approach to integrating Chinese and Western learning. Liang saw Chinese and Western learning as comparable because they represented universal patterns of civilization, but would form exclusive stages in the evolution of human societies. Liang also emphasized the polarity of science and metaphysics, which he used to differentiate between Chinese and Western cultures. Therefore while acknowledging the inevitability of Western educational influence, he also conveniently compartmentalized Chinese and Western learning. Xiong Shili proposed a universal order of knowledge based on a synthesis of Chinese, Western, and Indian philosophies. Both Liang and Xiong opposed a scientific paradigm in their thinking. In doing so, they both drew on anti-rational, anti-materialistic Western thinkers such as Arthur Schopenhauer and Henri Bergson for ammunition.

## Liang Shuming: Ethical Evolution and the Aesthetics of Confucian Learning

In his famous series of lectures on the philosophies of the East and West from 1920 to 1921, in which Western, Chinese, and Indian civilizations constituted three separate stages of universal human development, Liang Shuming, one of the youngest faculty members at Peking University, proposed a very different transcendental and universal system of ethics and knowledge from the one proposed by Cai Yuanpei. He developed an aesthetic approach to Confucian learning such that, in his scheme, the Chinese stage, which followed the Western stage as represented by the scientific paradigm, was typified by ethics, belief, and feelings. Science and metaphysics became two defining paradigms indicating two different stages of human development. They were both necessary but exclusive of each other and were related diachronically. This was Liang's way of solving the problem of the East-West cultural conflict and the universal paradigm of science.

Liang was initially hired in 1917 to teach Buddhist philosophy but became more and more interested in Chinese philosophy. He had been sent by his enlightened father to a Western-style primary and high school and was immersed in Western education. After experiencing reversals in his personal and political life, Liang retreated to Buddhist studies for comfort. Eventually he turned to Confucianism, although Buddhist influence still showed in his writings.[25] He equated Chinese learning with Confucian studies. In his lectures on comparative studies of Chinese, Western, and Indian cultures developed at Peking University in 1920 and again in Shandong in 1921—published in 1921 as *The Cultures and Philosophies of the East and the West* (*Dongxi wenhua jiqi zhexue*)—he approached the three cultures as three exclusive stages on the road of human evolution. As Liang's intermediate stage, Confucianism represented a harmonious mesh between man and nature. The first stage was the Western conquest of nature, and the third stage was Indian retreat from the external world.[26]

Based on the modern world, Liang treated the three different cultures as prototypes that were detached from their geographic loci and represented three different stages of human civilization. Incorporating Chinese history into world history, yet resisting the dominance of Western science, Liang tried to assert the truth of Chinese culture by making it an objective stage in world civilization. Chinese civilization, Liang argued, was precociously mature and skipped a stage of human development: the conquest of material culture as represented by European civilization. Therefore it must experience this stage before it can proceed to the more mature and universal stage represented by Chinese civilization, in order to fit the scheme of world civilizations. He thus simultaneously permitted and resisted the introduction of science to China. The acceptance of science and technology in China would lead to a discontinuity with the Chinese past, but only this way could China be incorporated into the international community and eventually realize the apex of civilization following the end of Western civilization's dominance in the world.[27] Despite Liang's resistance to Western science, he had transcended the East-West division in the characterization of Chinese and Western cultures and reduced the differences into metaphysical qualitative differences about generic cultural types, so he was free to incorporate Western idealist philosophers into his new system of thought.

Liang's exegesis on Confucian learning was strongly influenced by German idealist philosophers, including Arthur Schopenhauer and the French philosopher Henri Bergson, who was influenced by German idealism. Like them, Liang strove to employ ethical and metaphysical means to integrate truth and individual behavior, man and the world. Reacting against industrialization, mechanization, and a mechanistic explanation of the world, Schopenhauer and Bergson tried to reintegrate humans to the world and merge the subjective and objective into which Kant had divided the world. To Kant, the world of truth and human attempts to grasp it in daily life experience constituted the objective and subjective realms; the first was intelligible through the concepts provided by the second. Absolute truth, the "thing-in-itself," as Kant called it, was not linked to human experience. To Kant, it could not be understood by human beings, although humans used concepts that derived from that realm. German idealists from Goethe and Schiller to Schelling and Schopenhauer all tried to do away with this detachment of the human being from natural truth. Schopenhauer and Bergson differed from their predecessors not only in their exposure to industrialized society and positivism in the nineteenth century but also in the influence of Darwinian evolution and Indian philosophy, where many Western philosophers tried to rediscover the lost soul or spirit in a materializing world. Both Schopenhauer and Bergson proceeded from Kant's premise and located human knowledge of truth in the human consciousness or intuition. Following Kant's division of the world into the phenomenal and the noumenal, Schopenhauer nonetheless disagreed with Kant that absolute truth was inaccessible to the human being. Instead, he believed that human will, or consciousness, enabled one to see the immediate reality behind the phenomenal behavior of our own bodies. Human will, which existed in all objects in the world, directly constituted the essence of truth and was fully accessible to the human being.[28] Going beyond Schopenhauer, Bergson tried to avoid the partition of the world into the subjective and the objective. His idea of intuition posited a gradual progression, or "duration," wherein the mind, fixed in introspection, could transit from images of the external world to feelings, memories, and eventually to the incommunicable depths of one's personality—what traditional philosophy called the essence of the soul perceived in itself and by itself, thereby completing the penetration of the essence of things by transporting oneself with them. "Intuition," the name of this process, made a merger of the subjective and objective possible and actually made one coincide with the object known.[29] Despite Schopenhauer's influence over Bergson, the two men's ultimate solutions to the separation of the subjective and objective were different. They both viewed human will as manifested as desire. Desire caused human suffering, and Schopenhauer's solution, in which he followed Buddhism, was to stop desire. The resignation and the asceticism that arose from the cessation of desire were the only alternative to a life of continued suffering. Resignation was the outlook attained by the human being who fully grasped that the same will is the inner reality within all phenomena. One then would no longer want to compete with other phenomena.[30] Bergson's idea of intuition interpreted evolution in the light of Buddhism, giving the latter a material goal. Buddhism enabled Bergson to attempt to transcend set intellectual concepts and to fight the scientific rationalism of his time, as rational ideas, in light of Buddhism, only had nominal value. The human goal was not to build a material reality of science but to enter into spiritual reality: a sort of a universal consciousness in which waves of perception propagated and criss-crossed, where being was regarded as a transitory residuum of becoming and action, and memory conceived as the mind itself subsisting on its acts and as a past that endured.[31] What was used by Buddhists to negate the intellect and human striving in life became, in the hands of Bergson, a way to describe the forever changeable movement of the life impulse and the material forms in which the vital impulse was manifested and to fight a rigid rationalism or scientific positivism. Bergson concluded that the substance of things was an active duration and signified continuity of change, perpetual growth, and incessant creation. Evolution became interpreted as the continuous assertion of human consciousness, an instinctive and spontaneous will, which would affirm itself in contingent acts. The self was a living and continually changing duration. Body and soul formed one continuous whole of duration. Matter was the inversion of the creative impulse, what it became when interrupted. This, to Bergson, was the path of evolution, which, pushed by the creative impulse, led to a multiplicity of life, including two general genres, the animal and the vegetable.[32]

Schopenhauer's idea of human beings' indefatigable will and Bergson's explanation of the evolution of life forms with the idea of a vital impulse or consciousness deeply affected Liang Shuming. They provided the theoretical rationale for an interpretation of civilizations, of how humans are integrated with nature, by not scientific but spiritual means. However, Bergson's creative use of Indian philosophy in his interpretation of evolution and life affirmed material life and its spiritual dimension and avoided a mechanistic understanding of the world. This seemed to corroborate the affirmation of this world and priority of human life in Confucian learning.

Liang also drew on social psychology and employed terms such as "instinct" to describe the workings of Confucian learning. Liang equated an alignment with nature with the spontaneous work of the vital impulse. In his *The Cultures and Philosophies of the East and the West,* Confucian learning was described as approaching life in a lively and spontaneous way and in the process connecting with the truth of life. The Confucian instinctual approach to life contrasted with rational calculations and conscious desires in life. Liang saw the Confucian *Analects* as abounding with the talk of happiness. Understanding the *Analects* in the light of Bergson, Liang realized that human desire was instinctual, an objective existence, and as long as humans followed their instincts instead of erecting arbitrary barriers to living, life would be happy, and if the instinctual flow of living were blocked, life would be miserable.[33] This description of Confucian learning was a reminder of the Confucian and neo-Confucian propensity to build a continuum between natural human sentiments and ethical principles and conduct and comparable to an aesthetic experience because, through their very experience, humans spontaneously and naturally moved toward the higher stage of truth.

This aesthetic description of Confucian learning formed part of a deliberate strategy to distinguish Chinese learning from any rational system of thought represented by Western science. In his reinterpretation of Confucian learning under the influence of Bergson, Liang demarcated between a spontaneous, instinctive Confucian life that revealed transcendental truth and a human life based on rationalization and misleading desires that needed to be avoided. Some, including his friend and colleague, Xiong Shili, were critical of Liang's purely ethical approach to Confucian learning. Xiong chastised him for avoiding facing the real nature of Confucian learning, such as its family-centered social structure perpetuated at the cost of the public and the nation.[34]

Yet aesthetics also helped Liang equate concrete Confucian practices with the realization of transcendental truth without having to evaluate the workings of Confucian learning in a social context. By its very nature, aesthetics was a bridge between the concrete and the transcendental through intuition. It only concerned the mental state. The actual workings of Confucian learning, in this way, could not be evaluated since it was not the concern of aesthetics.

In Bergson's view, aesthetic experience, like instinct, was objective and universal because it was the manifestation of the intelligence of God. Much of the truth in Bergson's philosophy was not so readily available to human knowledge as it was to intuition. Liang subscribed to the outlook of Bergson, who allegedly did not read any Hindu or Buddhist texts directly,[35] and a revision of an Indian Buddhist school called Vijnaptimatra (in Chinese,*Weishi*). Liang's criticism of rational principles and conscious desires resembled the Weishi Buddhist school's criticism of sensual perceptions, which separated men from one another and from nature. But Liang imputed that the solution was not to escape from this world but to adopt the Confucian approach to life.

The Vijnaptimatra school focused on breaking down the illusions of apparent reality—the phenomena in this world—which was also what gave each individual distinct forms and led to artificial barriers between people. Illusive reality was created by the six senses and the sense of self-existence, from which one needed to free oneself.[36] In *Cultures and Philosophies of the East and the West*, Liang did not deny the importance of sensual experience, but emphasized that man must transcend the separation between individuals created by sense perceptions. Life consists of infinite efforts motivated by infinite desires, conscious and unconscious, forming a continuous process that resembled the life process of Bergson.[37] But since desires are informed by one's senses, which are illusory, the only way to transcend sense perception is to avoid desires. Although appearing to conclude on a Schopenhauerian or Buddhist note, Liang pointed to an alternative solution offered by his reinterpretation of Confucian learning. The Confucian way of life, he believed, is devoid of conscious desires, but based on intuition. Intuition (*zhijue*) is spontaneous and unreflective whereas desire (*yiyu*) comprises the conscious use of rational calculation.

> One should act by responding to the external environment and following one's instinct. The conscious pursuit of goals from the outside world will get you nowhere. Man naturally follows the most appropriate route in life . . . thus Confucius says, following one's character [*shuai xin*] is called the Way. . . . It is not that one should not have feelings of worry, enjoyment, and fears, but that they should not become a fixed part of oneself independent of the environment that first evoked them. These feelings should be natural and instantaneous responses to external happenings.[38]

Liang's use of instinct and the spontaneous and unconscious to describe Confucian learning made it possible for him to weave a critique of a prototypical Western material culture with Indian and Bergsonian philosophy. Liang distinguished between conscious desires and intuition. Desires dealt with the material world and intuition the essence of the world. This resembled the Weishi Buddhist or Kongzong (emptiness of the universe) Buddhist schools' division of the world and Bergsonian philosophy. Liang repeatedly emphasized that Confucian learning was the exercise of intuition, and Confucian humaneness (*ren*) was the human instinct of the good. Humanity became something driven by intuition and instinct, a totally spontaneous biological function to restore psychological balance. Humaneness, said Liang, was not an ethical principle, which would be detached from life and lose its spontaneity as well as its real meaning.[39] Liang equated conscious activities with knowledge and calculation that separated man and material nature in the West. Material nature, with its negative connotation in Buddhism, also denoted the negative and illusive nature of knowledge since it resulted from man's pursuit of material things. Thus knowledge and conscious desires were seen as inferior to the Confucian intuitive approach to the essence of life.

In Liang's schema, the ultimate stage of mankind was Indian culture. Despite his attachment to Confucian learning, Liang never completely abandoned his belief in Buddhism. After World War I, the questioning of European civilization by many Europeans, including Bertrand Russell, had an obvious impact on Chinese reformers. Although they did not abandon what they came to characterize as a universal process of modernization patterned after the Western model, they found new ammunition for critiquing the modernization process. For critics of Western civilization like Liang Shuming, an exclusive, prototypical treatment of three local cultures as three stages in a transcendental, universal culture both criticized Western material culture and science and justified China's acceptance of that culture—a necessary stage before the "more mature" (in Liang's words) Chinese culture could be realized worldwide. Liang viewed Chinese culture, with its merger of individuals and nature, as having reached its maturity prematurely, while Western culture, with its material acquisitiveness, represented a younger stage of culture. To become compatible with other countries in the world, Chinese culture had to reexperience its growth process and acquire Western material culture, in order to enter the stage of Chinese culture at the appropriate time. This way, Liang both criticized Western culture and placed Chinese culture in the context of an international cultural system.

But explaining Confucian learning as a spontaneous pursuit that would merge with the universe was problematic, as Liang soon found out. Soon after his book was published, he tried to deny his own connection between transcendental truths and instinctual striving among individuals. He quickly embarked on redressing his concept of the natural and spontaneous human being because it could be easily confused with animal behavior and tried to assert the Confucian model of a rational and ethical being. In subsequent works, he stated that in *Cultures and Philosophies of the East and the West* he discussed human beings not merely as emotional beings but also as rational beings.[40] In *Human Heart and Human Life* (Renxin yu rensheng), completed in 1975, he recounted that in his youth he was influenced by Russell's stress on encouraging the flow of human instincts and William McDougall's emphasis on instinct in *An Introduction to Social Psychology* and therefore changed his emphasis from consciousness to instinct. Although an instinctual explanation of ethics was sanctioned by the Russian anarchist Piotr Kropotkin in his *Mutual Help* and *The Ethical Views of Anarchism*, it seemed to Liang that few in the field of instinctual theory would agree with the equation of instinct with morality, as the use of instinct could easily be confused with instinct of animals.[41] In *Human Heart and Human Life*, Liang admitted his own early confusion of animalistic and human instincts. He defined the latter, quoting from Mencius, as inherent knowledge. Liang wrote that he was more inclined to accept Russell's definition of man as composed of instinct, intellect, and spirituality, considering the last an important component that he had previously neglected.[42] In particular, he used the concept of rational temperament (lixing) to replace instinct, indicating the human heart liberated from animal instincts. Rational temperament referred to unselfish human feelings based on rational understanding (lizhi). Such feelings were experienced only by man and were a product of evolution. Human and animal instincts were parallel in some ways, but human unselfishness was conscious and not a result of instinct.

Here, Liang admitted that rationality was not all negative, and instinct had its limitations, including the instinct of selfishness. His criticism of science and Western material culture led him to the depiction of Confucian culture as a spontaneous, instinctual pursuit of the good that completely differed from a rational, intellectual culture. Yet his criticism of Western culture did not return him to the past, and in his system Western culture only represented a temporary stage Chinese culture needed to pass through in order to proceed to the higher stage of Chinese culture. As Wang Hui points out, despite his antagonism toward Western science, the basic premise of Liang's conceptual framework was European: modernization.

## Xiong Shili: Ethical Evolution and Moral Efforts

Even though Liang Shuming's discussion of Confucian learning bypassed discussing it as social praxis, he never treated learning as separate from life. According to Liang, his own writings were the result of his unresolvable problems.[43] Although the answers to his questions could be theoretical or transcendental, a more prototypical than real description of the world, Liang Shuming held that his beliefs would be implemented in action. That was why in 1924 he left Peking University to start experimenting with modernizing the Chinese countryside, in Zouping, Shandong province. In contrast to Liang, Xiong Shili was less interested in combining theory with practice. Although he joined Liang Shuming in Zouping in 1924, Xiong's stay was very brief, and he had no intention of transforming China through practice. By contrast, he believed that his philosophy offered China an alternative to Confucian learning. Xiong synthesized Buddhism, Daoism, Confucian learning, and extensive borrowings from Bergson's theory on the continuous flow of life to establish a theory of the constant movement of life. Like Liang's, his theory comprised a transcendental and universal system. Unlike Liang's system, where the different stages of culture were distinct from one another, Xiong's system integrated elements of the different cultures he studied into one dynamic whole, in the process emphasizing a spiritual fundamentalist view of the universe while confirming the value of the material world.

Like Liang Shuming, Xiong Shili was a revolutionary turned cultural reformer. Frustrated with Confucian learning, he wanted to develop a philosophy of life that could truly guide the Chinese. Born in 1885 to a poor peasant family in Huanggang, Hubei province, Xiong developed an extremely independent character beginning when he was quite young. After his father died, when Xiong was thirteen, he had to help his brother with the family farm and received only intermittent education. His extensive reading including Yan Fu's translation of T.H. Huxley's *Evolution and Ethics* and other works on reform led him in 1904 to join the New Army of Hubei Province's. Meanwhile he participated in anti-Manchu activities and had to flee, fearing arrest. After the outbreak of the 1911 revolution in Wuchang, Hubei, Xiong joined in efforts to recover Huanggang, Guangdong province from Manchu rule. He continued to work on and off for the republican cause after 1911, including Sun Yatsen's "Second Revolutuion" of 1913, but beginning in 1918 the instability of warlord politics led him to withdraw into scholarship, immersing himself in Confucian learning and Buddhism. He became acquainted with Liang Shuming through their scholarly exchanges on Buddhism. Liang recommended that Xiong study at the Buddhist Institute in Nanjing, under the well-known Buddhist scholar Ouyang Jingwu. In 1922, Liang had already made up his mind to leave Peking University for Shandong to start experimenting with practical education there and asked Xiong, with Cai Yuanpei's consent, to take his place at the university teaching Weishi Buddhism. The years he spent at Peking University enabled Xiong to develop a systematic philosophy that reinterpreted Buddhism in the light of Confucian learning, thereby transforming Confucian learning. His teaching greatly affected his students, including Tang Junyi, Mo Zongsan, and Xu Fuguan, who went on to become the most vocal leaders of the neo-Confucian school.[44]

Based on his extensive knowledge of Buddhism, Bergsonian philosophy, and Confucian learning, Xiong created a universe in constant flux where the ultimate truth was spirituality. Rejecting the Buddhist abandonment of this world as antihuman and destructive to the universe (*fan rensheng, hui yuzhou*),[45] Xiong nonetheless absorbed much of the Buddhist descriptive style of the universe: amorphous and constantly in flux. At the same time, using the philosophy of Henri Bergson and Confucian writings by the Ming dynasty neo-Confucian scholar Wang Yangming, Xiong affirmed material life while still keeping it subordinate to the spiritual realm. Unlike Liang Shuming, who split the spiritual and material, Xiong put the two in a dialectical relationship, which adhered more faithfully to Bergson's philosophy. Bergson posited two concepts, the vital impulse and matter. On the one hand, they were different. The constant movement of the vital impulse, the impulse of life and the manifestation of God, contrasted with matter, which was its inversion, a lack of impulse, and which emerged when the movement of the vital impulse was interrupted. On the other hand, they were intertwined and inseparable. Within the vital impulse was tremendous tension; the vital impulse was interrupted, and space was thus created, which was none other than the ideal limit of the falling movement of matter, formed when the vital impulse slowed down.[46] The vital impulse, therefore, was perceptible to humans only when it slowed down and formed into matter.

Thus Bergson built a continuum between spirituality and material forms by subjecting the latter to the superiority of the former, with the latter being the default of the former. However, the significance of the material world was not denied. Even when the vital impulse was interrupted, relaxed, and appeared in material form, something of the original impulse remained. Although matter tended to solidify and fall downward, the life force that lingered in it tended to move upward seeking to retard the fall of matter, utilizing the energy of matter in order to create new material forms and release contingency. Matter formed the reality and as such was a positive thing: it was the way in which the vital impulse manifested itself. Life was, first, a tendency to act on inert matter and to obtain from this act the affirmation of the liberty of the creative will.[47] This argument not only affirmed the material world but also resembled the Daoist discussion of the two extremes of the Supreme Ultimate (*taiji*), which appeared in early neo-Confucian writings in the Song dynasty, such as those by Zhou Dunyi. The two extremes, movement and stillness, and their different combinations led to the creation of the myriad things in the world. In particular, according to Tu Wei-ming, Xiong was influenced by two neo-Confucians Zhang Zai and Wang Yangming. Xiong's cosmological duality, contraction and expansion, is reminiscent of Zhang Zai's fusion and intermingling of material force (*qi*) wherein lies the "subtle, incipient activation of reality and unreality, of motion and rest, and the beginning of yin and yang, as well as the elements of strength and weakness." The influence of Wang Yangming, however, could be seen in his emphasis on the mind as not only cognitive knowing but also affective acting, and on the integration of the external and the internal, of knowledge and action.[48]

Borrowing from Bergson, Xiong Shili's discussion of the material no longer referred just to the West, as material also comprised the human heart, traditionally a locus of ethical knowledge in Confucian learning. Contrary to Confucian teachings, Xiong denied the human heart the inherent ability to generate ethical truth. From a *Weishi* Buddhist causal point of view, Xiong decided that there were many causes that decided how the human heart would perceive, but these causes were related to infinite other causes. Therefore, Xiong argued, there were no true causes to decide how the heart perceived that was inherent in the heart, and the heart, as a material thing, did not have an entity in itself.[49] This definition of the human heart and its capacity for perception differed from Bergson's definition of true human intellect, which could ultimately be sought within oneself. This statement of the heart was his criticism of

Confucian learning, which to him had been corrupted for two thousand years. Xiong believed that, although early Confucian learning was brilliant philosophy, it had been declining since the Qin dynasty (221–206 B.C.) because of government abuse of it. In response to Liang Shuming's argument that Chinese culture had reached its apex prematurely, Xiong contended that, par contre, the previous two thousand years of Chinese civilization had produced regression and transformation into a country of foreign customs, robbers, and slaves.[50] Unlike Liang Shuming, Xiong Shili did not tie his nationalistic identity to an idealized Confucian culture. Xiong did, however, affirm early Confucian learning and borrowed from it the concept of moral cultivation or self-improvement. But to Xiong, cultivation no longer emphasized practice, as in Liang Shuming's case, but a pursuit of true knowledge.

What underlay Xiong's argument was an epistemology based on Bergson and Buddhism. Xiong delineated an essence of life, approachable through cultivated intuition, and life's manifestations, which were the material world. Bergson's "vital impulse" was based on a synthesis of Buddhist reality and a spiritualistic interpretation of evolution, and as such did not refer to a definite, easily definable quality. Xiong's essence resembled the Chinese naturalistic and Buddhist concepts of "nothingness," the amorphous and invisible basic constituent of the universe. As Bergson's definition of knowledge was situated against the background of his definition of the essence of life, so was Xiong's. Because of his antagonism toward scientific positivism, Bergson denied the veracity of intellect as such. To Bergson, knowledge or intelligence, like matter, was a deficiency of the creative impulse, as the function to bind like to like, and knowledge of facts that repeated themselves. But the more we detach ourselves from the external, the less we need this kind of reasoning, as we increasingly bring ourselves to coincide with ourselves.

Instead of denying the importance of intellect, Bergson distinguished two kinds: one primary, related to consciousness, and the other secondary, related to matter. It was the second type of intellect that Bergson criticized. In the first kind, the intellect, in perceiving a thing, attained the thing (idea) in its actual existence and singularity. Not only would the first kind of intellect grasp the essence of the thing through the root and in a way that was entirely manifest, but also exhaust its intelligibility. This was the case of an intuitive understanding like that of the Angels in Christian theology. The second kind of intellect did not receive its ideas from God, but drew them from things by means of the senses and by abstraction. It therefore apprehended natures only as their operation or their properties reveal them, but could not grasp all the predicates that could be attributed to an essence.[51] To a great extent, Xiong borrowed the two definitions of intellect and wove a dynamic relationship between the two. He viewed knowledge as human reflections of material matter—not reality, but its specific manifestation. Despite some resemblance to truth, knowledge or intellect contained many illusory elements. That it was often taken as the truth added to its illusory nature.[52] To arrive at truth, one did not rely on knowledge, but on one's intuition.[53]

To Xiong, the ultimate human goal was to become one with consciousness, which lay in constant human moral effort to purify oneself of the secondary kind of intellect in order to arrive at the pure intellect. Although he emphasized the transcendence of truth, Xiong rejected the complete denunciation of the material world in Buddhism, thus affirming the value of human life. But he subordinated individual human life to transcendental spiritual truth. This subordination was achieved through a critical adoption of the Indian Mahayana schools (*Weishi*) Buddhism as transmitted through the *weishi* and *kongzong* denominations in China. *Weishi* divided human knowledge into eight consciousnesses, with the eighth, *alayavijnana*, being the storage-house consciousness, which contained the seeds of the other seven consciousnesses and was influenced by the goings on outside. Thus the seeds and their fruitions the consciousnesses mutually influenced each other. "Each of the eight consciousnesses was supposed to be a separate reality, demanding a type of analysis suitable to its own nature. . . . Intent on 'penetrating behind the veil of impermanence to attain to the level of absolute knowledge that transcends all conditions and relativity,' the school focuses its attention on the purification of *alaya*, seeds of consciousness. This task involves, among other things, raising the level of consciousness."[54] *Kongzong* denounced all phenomena in the world as an illusion and argued for an ultimate reality.

In Xiong's use of the two schools, he drew upon their understanding of a transcendent level of ultimate reality but rejected any attempt either to separate the transcendent from the temporal or to deny the true existence of the ultimate reality. Xiong rejected the division between seeds and their outgrowth in *Weishi* Buddhism to indicate cause and effect, arguing that this would create a world of truth separate from its manifestations. To Xiong, the essence of the world, although invisible and amorphous, was in constant movement and manifested itself in infinite material things. Although he drew on the teachings of Kongzong that dismissed the material world, Xiong's purpose was to destroy human hold on the latter. Xiong believed that *Kongzong* was so vehement in its attack on the material world that it destroyed the concept of the essence of the world out of fear that people would not easily detach themselves from it. That was why the world of Kongzong was quiet, devoid of life and movement: the ultimate reality could not be sought from the outside world, only from within one's heart, through intuition.

Yet Xiong viewed the value of the human being, who lacked an independent entity, as subordinate to the transcendental spiritual realm. Neither Zhang Zai nor Wang Yangming was so transcendental as to deny the human entity. Zhang's argument about *qi* (breath, life force) affirmed the material existence of the earth as reality, and Wang Yangming's boast that his mind contained all the knowledge of the world proved his mind as a true entity. Given the human limitations, Xiong gave an outline of cultivation by positing several dichotomies: essence (*benti*) versus pure habits (*jingxi*) and tainted habits (*ranxi*), function (*gongneng*) versus habit (*xixing*), essential knowledge (*xingzhi*) versus mere knowledge (*liangzhi*), contraction (*yi*) versus opening (*pi*). They were all dichotomies contrasting the essence of the world and the (often misleading) human perceptions (habits) of it.[55] Xiong interpreted the Confucian concept of humaneness as one way to transcend the illusory world and unite man and nature through constant purification of one's habits to recover the original pure habits not exposed to the outside world.[56] This view cohered with his belief in the virtue of early Confucian learning and the latter's later corruption. But, in this formulation self-cultivation was no longer about the restoration of true Confucian learning, but about reaching a higher spiritual realm: the essence of the world that was universal.

The glorification of consciousness as the essence of the universe, to Bergson, was an outcry against the mechanistic modern thought and its determinism of nature that enslaved man.[57] To Xiong, it was a way to affirm human moral integrity in the face of scientific and material determinism. Morality was no longer confined to the specific Confucian tenets, but became a general call to spirituality and moral exertion that had universal implications.

The morality Xiong advocated, captured well by his biographer, emphasized:

> individual sense of responsibility, mission, sense of self, and infinite freedom. Just like in a battle, even though the leader could be captured, the individual soldier's spirit belonged to himself and could not be taken away. This exercise of morality was a show of free individuality, because individuals under specific circumstances were often not free and without spiritual guidance. . . . Self-sacrifice motivated by an inner spirit was a form of freedom, the freedom to abandon the random and changeable individual self.[58]

In other words, Xiong established a universal and transcendental system that, on the one hand, affirmed the importance of life and moral cultivation and, on the other hand, subordinated individual cultivation, and individual selves, to the higher, transcendental, and unchangeable cause of truth. That Xiong's world was ultimately moral could also be seen from his difference from

Bergson. For the latter, life was a blind snowballing style of self-expansion, but to Xiong, individual lives were purposeful. Unlike Liang Shuming, who developed prototypical cultures based on particular local cultures, Xiong Shili's discussion of the spiritual and the material was based not on a demarcation of the West and China but the subordination of both the material West and humanistic China to a transcendental and spiritualistic system. Humaneness, the hallmark of Confucianism, no longer indicated interpersonal relationships in mundane life, but complete spirituality. His favoring of the spiritual over the material was his criticism of Western science and material determinism. Nevertheless, he also affirmed the importance of the material, treating it as a necessary and vital part of life and demonstrating the inevitability of introducing Western material culture to China. His ultimate goal, however, was a universal culture of spirituality.

Xiong's discussion of knowledge and human nature was not fundamentally different from an earlier effort in a similar direction by Zhang Binglin (also known as Zhang Taiyan), one of the greatest philologists at the turn of the century. Beginning in 1906, Zhang started to combine German idealist philosophy, especially Kantian philosophy, with *Weishi* Buddhist preaching. He compared Kant's "thing-in-itself" to the truth in *Weishi*. All phenomena, he concluded, owed their true nature to that transcendental truth and were transient, illusive, and changing.[60] This argument was in line with an overall attempt by a group of philologists in early twentieth-century China to redefine human nature through a transformation of the Song neo-Confucian definition of human nature. Song dynasty neo-Confucians had treated human nature as true nature of the universe contaminated by human life, hence human nature should be subject to the universal truth (*li*) and suppressed where a conflict arose between the two. Twentieth-century philologists fought back by arguing that human nature itself was neutral and could not be classified as good or bad. Zhang Binglin's denunciation of the illusiveness of the material world, through the negation of a true and autonomous human nature, dismissed its depiction as in conflict with heavenly nature and the need for its suppression. These philologists often went on to sanctify human desires and called for greater development of humaneness.[61] Although holding a similar view that subordinated human nature to transcendental truth, Xiong differed from them in continuing to uphold the goal of human self-transcendence. His two-pronged attack is clear: Confucian learning and Western material culture. A dichotomy between Chinese and Western cultures existed in his mind, although his ultimate goal for both the Chinese and the Western world was to transcend their respective worlds into the unifying realm of spirituality.

Cai Yuanpei, Liang Shuming, and Xiong Shili were examples of how Chinese scholars transcended the Chinese-Western learning dichotomy and situated Chinese learning in a more universal framework. All three drew on different parts of Chinese learning—including human cultivation, a continuum between natural human sentiments and rational principles, and the moral heroism of Mencius—incorporating them into a discourse based on Western aesthetic and other metaphysical schools of thought.

# 5

# The Uses of the Evolutionary Historical Framework

## The History and Chinese Language and Literature Departments (1917–1927)

In early twentieth-century China, a historical approach resembling a post-Enlightenment European definition of historicism was applied to the new fields of archaeology, ancient Oriental linguistics, history, geology, intellectual history, and popular ethnology,[1] in addition to the existing fields of study, such as Chinese philology, philosophy, and literature, although many of them were not yet classified as independent disciplines. According to F.R. Ankersmit, European historicism was a reaction to Enlightenment historical writings that presupposed a reality made up of entities that remained essentially the same over time: any change was peripheral. Historicism that developed in the wake of Enlightenment histories, by contrast, admitted substantial changes did occur. "For the historicists historical change could not be restricted to what is merely peripheral; indeed, 'substantial' change was seen as the true domain of historical research."[2] The development of Chinese historicism broke away from the largely cyclical history that regarded the world as largely unchanging, with only transient alterations. The use of history to deal with multiple areas of academic studies and the adoption of historicism were related to the modern Chinese need to break from the past and fashion a new identity. Moreover, out of all subjects of learning in China, history most closely resembled a Western academic discipline. Therefore using a historical approach arguably would facilitate the academic development of Chinese learning along Western taxonomies of knowledge.

Such a historicist method was often combined with an evolutionary approach. Evolutionary history conveyed double meanings to Chinese scholars.

Continuous human development embodied in historical evolution usually enabled a meaningful connection between the past and the present. In the Chinese case, historical continuity could be achieved through not just constant self-renewal but a disavowing of the past and reestablishing a new relationship between the past and the present. Historical evolutionism would render irrelevant Confucian moral criteria that would have heaped moral condemnation on events in modern Chinese history—for instance, the repeated defeats in wars against foreign countries. The past's verdict on the present would be too difficult to bear, as Jerome Grieder commented,

> Evolutionary theories helped the Chinese to wrest some meaning, however grim, from their recent experience, as discredited Confucian historiography no longer could. We may speculate further that it was perhaps psychologically less burdensome to share with the human race at large the prospect of an almost unbearably slow progress than it was to accept the verdict of moral delinquency that was the characteristic Confucian response to political and cultural disaster. Spencerian determinism held out at least the hope of a future, albeit a future toward which mankind inched its way as insensibly and ponderously as a glacier approaches the sea.[3]

After the Chinese scholars broke away from the Confucian discourse of the past, an evolutionary historical approach would render the past relevant to the future to satisfy the purpose of nationalism. History enabled Chinese scholars to "tell the final story" about what they would surrender precisely because they could tell this story. According to Hegel, in the words of Ankersmit, "[T]he past must first be historicized, transformed by association into narrative understanding, before, with a subsequent gesture, it can be repudiated, and thereby ensure entry into a new world."[4] Many Chinese scholars covertly hoped to relate to the present by rearranging their relationship to the past. Historians and other scholars organized history more around their contemporaneous concerns. As Tao Menghe, professor of sociology at Peking University, summarized it in 1918: the past could no longer serve as the standard, only as a reference for the present.[5] In this process, historicism, by recognizing change over time, provided a convenient way to dissociate the present from the Confucian past. For many, history had lost its intrinsic meaning, but regained it through reflection of its social, economic, and cultural background. Its context-specific nature resembled the definition of historicism by the German historian Maurice Mandelbaum:

> Historicism is the belief that an adequate understanding of the nature of any phenomenon and an adequate assessment of its value are to be gained through considering it in terms of the place it occupied and the role which it played within a process of development.[6]

As reflected in the curriculum for the History and Chinese Language and Literature Departments (CLLD) during Cai Yuanpei's tenure between 1917 and 1926, a historical approach was applied across the board to these two disciplines with the highest concentration of Chinese subjects of learning on campus. Historicism, combined with progress, situated Chinese history and literature in an evolutionary process, often complemented by an emphasis on scientific methods. The application of scientific methods to the study of society in nineteenth-century Europe, often the result of "the recognition that all human ideas and values are historically conditioned and subject to change." For Max Weber, scientific inquiry was no longer unshakable, as perceived by the Enlightenment philosophes a century earlier. It was not scientific findings, but methods, that possessed universal validity. To Weber, although one coherent meaning in the world does not exist, rational and objective knowledge is possible, and although the very character of science and scientific research excludes any finality, it guarantees progress. In other words, the application of scientific methods to social studies was based on the recognition of the absence of universal truth and the continued hope for a rational and objective underpinning of truth, as well as for universal progress. This to some extent resembled the rise of historicism in nineteenth-century Europe, where it also represented the disillusionment with omnipotent truth or reality and the result of clashing views of the reality. The emphasis on scientific methods in German historiography placed history on a rational, progressive basis and transformed history into disciplined research of the past instead of general studies of culture.[7]

In China, the collapse of the Confucian paradigm and recognition of the relativism of history also led many Chinese historians to seek scientific methods to pursue more universal meaning and truth in Chinese history beyond the fragmented realities of the past devoid of the Confucian moral framework. Therefore, historicism, scientific methods, and progress went hand in hand as important components of the curricula of the CLLD. A historical approach was applied to an increasing number of courses, such as "History of the Evolution of Chinese Geography," taught by Zhang Weixi, author of a six-volume work on the history of communications between China and the West.[8] An evolutionary approach, in the form of periodized histories, was often used to enhance a sense of historical continuity in order to bolster nationalism.

Periodized histories were initially written as a project by the state Bureau of National History, which was merged with National Peking University and gave birth to the History Department in 1917.[9] This evolutionary approach was distinct from a Confucian discourse of history and removed the intrinsic moral meaning associated with Confucian histories. The first periodized histories were compiled in 1917 by the Japanese historian Kuwabara Jitsuzo in his *Brief History of East Asia*, which divided Chinese history as follows: prehistoric to Qin (ancient, end 206 B.C.), Qin to Tang (medieval, 206 B.C.–618 A.D.), Tang to Ming (late medieval, 618–1644), and modern, including the Qing (1644–1900s) dynasty. Whereas the period of medieval Chinese history signified the epitome of Chinese civilization, late medieval history was one of the decline of the Han and the vigor of the Mongols; modern Chinese history saw the dominance of the Manchus and Westerners.[10] Many at Peking University, such as Fu Sinian (a disciple of Hu Shi), later derided this historical periodization as indicating a decline of the Han nationality in China.[11] The History Department in 1920, in the interest of presenting history as continuous and coherent, proposed offering periodized histories that would reflect on society as a whole and on historical evolution.[12] By 1925, the Peking University History Department curriculum was using the following periodization: ancient, from prehistoric to Zhou (end 256 B.C.); medieval, from the Qin and the Han dynasties to the Five Dynasties (221 B.C.–960 A.D.); late medieval, from the Song to the mid-Ming (960–c. 1550); and modern, from the mid-Ming to the republic (c. 1550–1900s).[13] This reperiodization emphasized Han integration against foreign invasion because although medieval history did show the country in turmoil (Five Dynasties), the country became reunified (Song) and despite later foreign invasions (Manchus) a unified republican government led by the Han nationality was ultimately established. Starting in 1921, the nationalist *qua* racist narrative of Chinese history implied in the periodization was supplemented by a course on anthropology and ethnicity, an elective course in the History Department that included discussion of a social and natural evolution of the races as well as their consequent prosperity or decline in the world.[14]

In this new historical discourse, historical events gained meaning from their sociopolitical contexts or meaning assigned to them by the historians in relation to the values they wanted to champion in the present. Chinese scholars' approach to history was frequently to view it as a reflection of a particular social context; such an approach was employed by a majority of the historians at Peking University. Lao Gan, one of the most illustrious Chinese history faculty and an expert in textual exegesis at Peking University in the 1930s, brought to light ancient Chinese social practices with a blend of textual exegesis and history as a reflection of society. In an article on stone relief sculptures depicting Han dynasty banquets on the occasions of burial and military examinations in three places in Shandong province, Lao depicted the sculptures as a reflection of their time. The banquets and the items entombed revealed the elaborate burial rituals of burials of the Han dynasty. The soldiers in some relief sculptures revealed a spirit of militant knighthood (*you xia jingshen*) in the Eastern Han dynasty, in contrast to its relative absence in the Western Han. The greater laxity of law in the Eastern Han allowed for revenge to be sought, although the avengers were still depicted as outlaws. The relief sculptures of carts, including those that were ox-drawn, Lao explained, indicated a reduction in the number of horses during the war-torn years of the Western Han.[15] Here, the specific characteristics of the Han society became the ultimate goal of Lao Gan's study.

The same was true of literature, historically an appendix to the study of the Confucian classics that was often treated as data devoid of intrinsic meaning, but now seen as a reflection of the society that produced it. Literary histories were also arranged in an evolutionary framework to affirm the trend of their progress over time. In 1918, literary history was divided into ancient (Yellow Emperor (c. 26th century B.C.) to the Warring States period (c. 321 B.C.)), medieval (Qin, Han, to mid-Tang (c. 221 B.C.–C. 800 A.D.), and modern (mid-Tang to the end of the Qing (c. 800 A.D.–1911)).[16] The literary periodization in the CLLD emphasized literary revival after periods of chaos and division, for instance, the Spring and Autumn period, the post-Han and pre-Sui period, and Mongol, Manchu, and other foreign invasions of China from the post-Song to the Qing dynasties. This periodization also stressed the triumph of Chinese culture over geographical divisions (Warring States period) or foreign rule (Tang, Qing). Periodized offerings in Chinese literary history changed the focus from the transmission of literary schools to a more detached overview of a spectrum of literature over time. In the revised curriculum of 1917 for the Subdivision of Chinese Language and Literature in the Humanities Division, following a survey of literature were courses on periodized literary history.[17] The content of Chinese literary topics was expanded, including novels, drama, and poetry. The definition of prose given in 1918 classified it as anything written except poetry and song lyrics, in contrast to traditional literary classifications, which excluded writing that did not conform to certain literary styles or content. Inclusion of such materials in the department in the 1920 curriculum was justified with the argument that novels and drama were derived from ancient genres. It was said that novels derived from nine writing methods of the Zhou dynasty, while drama descended from *yuefu* (ancient poems set to music practiced in praise of virtue) during the Han.[18] Literature thus changed from a vessel of the sages' teachings to a mirror of society and historical changes.

Many faculty and students were also engaged in the study of the evolution of literature. An evolutionary approach to literature treated different editions of literature as a reflection of the changes in society, a method first used by Hu Shi. A student of John Dewey's at Columbia University in the 1910s and arguably the most influential propagator of Western learning in China in the 1920s, Hu started to teach at Peking University in 1917. For Hu, literary appreciation became an examination of the historical development of literature. This objectified history of literature contrasted with traditional arguments that literature was the vessel of the eternal *dao*, or Way.[19] One of the common practices of these scholars was comparing different versions of folksongs. Peking University took the lead in the collection and organization of popular folksongs and folklore. Various organizations such as the Folklore Society (*Fengsu diaochahui*), and later the Society for the Study of Folksongs (*Geyao yanjiuhui*), led to the publication of folksongs and folklore in journals such as *Folksongs Weekly* (*Geyao zhoukan*), *Weekly of the National Studies Institute, Beijing University* (*Beijing daxue yanjiusuo guoxuemen zhoukan*), and *Monthly of the National Studies Institute, Beijing University* (*Beijing daxue yanjiusuo guoxuemen yuekan*). Gu Jiegang, Liu Fu, Zhou Zuoren, and Rong Zhaozu, among others, took the lead in this enterprise, through which they hoped to gain a picture of China's true past uncontaminated by Confucian values.[20]

Applying an objective approach to literature and history and seeing them as a product of their time, Hu Shi historicized the development of the vernacular in Chinese history and thereby became the first to contrast the vernacular with the "elitist" classical-language literature. He argued that the vernacular embodied the dynamic of Chinese literature, which classical literature often appropriated but never successfully perpetuated.[21] Hu examined literature against particular historical backgrounds, researching historical novels by tracing their different editions and evolution in these editions over time, studying the transformations of legends and novels through examining the expansions and alterations in their motifs.[22]

Although Hu Shi was the most avid champion of this evolutionary historicism, many others followed suit in their attempts to avoid the moral influence of the Confucian classics on Chinese history. The status of Confucian classics declined to the point that, to reestablish its status, Chinese learning (*zhongxue*) had to be renamed "national essence" (*guocui*) or "national learning" (*guoxue*). In the words of Zhang Taiyan, such names were needed to "drag Chinese learning from the periphery back to the center by linking it with nationalism and racial survival (*yi guocui jidong zhongxin*).[23] From Wang Guowei to Chen Yuan and Chen Yinque, leading philologists and historians of the late Qing dynasty and the early republic, the focus was less on China's golden ages (c. 26th century B.C.–17th century B.C.) Shang (17th–11th centuries B.C.), and Zhou dynasties and the two Han dynasties, and more on the Liao, Jin, and Yuan dynasties and beyond, periods that had witnessed a cultural mixing between Chinese and foreign populations and practices. Chen Yuan, a historian who taught at Peking and Furen universities, avoided discussions on the classics in teaching Gu Tinglin's Records of Understanding (*Rizhilu*), saying Chen himself was not familiar with the classics. Chen Yinque, also a historian known for his erudition, refrained from studying the classics as well. Most scholars who leaned toward new types of learning focused on history after the Han dynasty, as pre-Han history consisted primarily of what were later called the Confucian classics.[24]

Many historians even avoided the study of dynastic histories influenced by Confucian teachings, as both the messages they conveyed and the historical materials they included became suspect. To avoid Confucian-guided histories, radical and moderate reformers alike engaged in a massive search for new historical primary sources, fueled by the archaeological excavations of the ancient Shang dynasty, the discovery of the Dunhuang grottoes in Gansu province that housed numerous historical documents from the Tang dynasty, the discovery of Han dynasty bamboo-slip writings, and the numerous documents of the Ming and Qing that were sold to the public in the 1920s.[25] This trend became so prevalent that, for Fu Sinian, the study of history meant the study of (mostly unstudied) primary sources.[26] The proportion of archaeology and ancient philology courses as part of required courses steadily increased in the CLLD in the 1920s.[27] The courses on antiquity included both written texts, often on metallurgy and stones, and non-written materials such as tombs, ancient river routes, paintings, sculptures, and utensils. By 1925, archaeology had become an independent major in that department, along with philology and literature.[28] This meant that almost two-thirds of the department's emphasis was on the study of ancient texts and understanding of ancient word formation through archaeology and philology.[29] Archaeology often supplemented philological studies on ancient word formation because of the unearthing of ancient texts. From 1931 to 1935, students would engage in specialized fields of study, such as philology, literature, and archaeology. Although archaeology was removed from the department in 1934, courses on ancient characters on tortoiseshells and on bronze bells and containers were still offered because of the importance of these studies on archaeological findings. In part because of the archaeological findings in the late 1920s the listing of philology courses became much more extensive.[30]

The study of archaeology was aided by the numerous archaeological discoveries of twentieth-century China. To many Chinese scholars—for example, Fu Sinian, whose Institute of History and Philology in the newly established Academia Sinica participated in these discoveries in the 1930s—these discoveries would provide a more authentic picture of past history than written documents, whose authenticity was sometimes difficult to establish. The historical discoveries from the archaeological findings also tempered the general agnostic attitude toward history and encouraged greater historicism. Fu Sinian himself changed from being an agnostic on antiquity to someone arguing for a reconstruction of history with new historical materials.[31] As Wang Fan-sen comments on the contribution of archaeology to Fu Sinian's historicism:

> Especially important was his hypothesis on the plural origins of Chinese antiquity. Several other working hypotheses also shed significant light on the field

> of ancient Chinese history. The major characteristic of these projects was the dissolution of systems into multievolutionary processes. Many traditional Chinese descriptions were dissolved into unrelated clusters that no longer supported Confucian moral teachings. For example, the morally constituted Three Dynasties were dissolved into a history of struggles between eastern and western ethnic groups.[32]

Traditional Chinese scholarship had paved the way for understanding ancient history. Beginning in the Song dynasty, collections of ancient urns and stone tablets with written inscriptions by both government and private sources contributed to a better understanding of ancient writings, which paved the way for an understanding of inscriptions on tortoiseshells found in the twentieth century. These tortoiseshells had been carved with divination inscriptions during the Shang dynasty, had been buried in the ground, and had fallen into oblivion after the fall of Shang. As tortoiseshells, they were often sold as medicine and were rediscovered in the late Qing by Duan Fang, then an imperial minister who, as a collector of antiques, eagerly bought many pieces of shells with ancient inscriptions. In 1899, after Wang Yirong, a student of ancient metal and stone craftsmanship, stumbled upon them accidentally after encountering an antiques dealer, they became widely known in the scholarly community. Subsequently the value of tortoiseshell inscriptions was recognized. The tens of thousands of pieces of tortoiseshells discovered, followed by the unearthing in 1928 of the ancient ruins of the capital of the Shang dynasty and the discovery of ancient inscriptions elsewhere, led to greater understanding of the ancient past. Thereafter followed a surge of interest in Chinese antiquity in Western countries in the late nineteenth century.

A Western interest in Chinese archaeology developed in the context of worldwide archaeological excavations in the nineteenth and early twentieth centuries. Napoleon's invasion of Egypt in the late eighteenth century and his discovery of the Rosetta stone increased interest worldwide in archaeological excavations. The improvement of paleontology techniques during that time led to better understanding of prehistoric civilizations in Europe and the Aegean, as well as arousing interest in prehistoric India, China, and the Americas. In 1899, an international organization was established to explore Central and East Asia thanks to the activities of numerous archaeologists from Russia, Britain, Germany, France, Sweden, and the United States in China, convening the International Oriental Society in Rome. The same group, meeting in Hamburg in 1902, formed many international committees on the history, archaeology, linguistics, and ethnology of Central and East Asia, to coordinate the archaeological excavations of the various European countries in China, especially in Xinjiang, and Gansu, on the ancient Silk Road. From then on, waves of British,

French, Russian, German, and Japanese expeditions traveled to Xinjiang, Gansu, and Mongolia. They discovered writings on bamboo-slip writings in Xinjiang and Mongolia and Buddhist sutras in the Dunhuang temple, written from the fifth to the eleventh century. The Dunhuang excavations are considered the largest archaeological excavation to have taken place in twentieth-century China. The monk who discovered the documents in Dunhuang in 1900 was followed quickly by European and Japanese antiques dealers and sinologists, who smuggled large numbers of documents into Britain and France. The first Western explorer to reach the Dunhuang collection was a Hungarian Marc Aurelstein, and the most assiduous collector and organizer of the Dunhuang documents was Paul Pelliot, a French sinologist in the early twentieth century. The Chinese scholarly community did not become aware of the Dunhuang documents until 1909, when Pelliot came to Beijing to purchase some Chinese books for the French National Library and brought along with him some Dunhuang documents. It was not until the late 1970s that the microfilming of all the Dunhuang documents was completed in Beijing, London, and Paris, and the microfilms started to circulate.[33] In the 1920s and 1930s, many Chinese scholars either had access to the partial microfilms of the Dunhuang documents from Paris or gained direct access to some documents while in Paris. Qing scholars such as Luo Zhenyu rescued countless Qing dynasty documents from destruction by the republican Beijing government who found them useless. This newly available wealth of historical documents in the twentieth century allowed many scholars to re-examine China's history from a wider range of sources.[34]

Many faculty members in Chinese studies at Peking University became involved in the study of these ancient relics, including Huang Wenbi, Rong Geng, Rong Zhaozu, Ma Heng, Dong Zuobin, and Tang Lan. The ancient documents provided more substantial evidence of history than the existing writings and enabled them to arrive at a more historical analysis of ancient practices, including those discussed in the classics, and to put ancient events in historical perspective. The absence of direct historical documentation of the dynasty and earlier history of China had led Hu Shi to start his lectures on the history of ancient Chinese thought from the late Zhou dynasty in the late 1910s and early 1920s. The tortoise-shells unearthed in Anyang, Henan province, were from the Shang dynasty and preceded classics such as the *Book of Changes*; they offered historical background to many practices, including religious worship and social structure, during what Confucius called the golden age of Chinese history. They were the first documents from the legendary Shang dynasty and thereby confirmed its existence. Before the excavations, the Shang was known only through historical documents from later dynasties. The discovery of these engravings enabled a comprehensive picture of the

Shang, including its political system, the forces shaping the structure of the state, social structure, family system, religious worship, calendar, and geography. The significance of this knowledge could not be overestimated. The Shang, one of the legendary dynasties emulated by Confucius, could now be comprehended through historical documents. Moreover, those aspects of its practices that strongly influenced Zhou religious worship, such as divination, now had a historical context.

Archaeological discoveries led to a more historical understanding of the past and reinforced the use of history as data to explore the society from which it originated. The ancient history revealed by the tortoiseshells, for instance, led faculty members like Rong Zhaozu, a philosophy student at Peking University from 1922 to 1926, to decide that the *Book of Changes* was nothing more than a book on divination.[35] Another example of a historical discussion of the past was an exchange between Fu Sinian and Dong Zuobin (a graduate student in the Classics Institute at Peking University from 1923 to 1924 and then secretary of the Vernacular Committee there beginning in 1927) on the original meaning of the Chinese noble ranking system. Dong was one of the chief members on the team that formally excavated Xiaotun Village in Anyang in 1928, unearthing the tortoiseshell inscriptions buried there in the Shang. In 1930, Fu Sinian wrote an article on the system of noble ranking in the Zhou dynasty, comparing it to the historical rise of the nobility in medieval Europe. Since the Zhou dynasty was the epitome of the golden age glorified by Confucius largely because of the social courtesy displayed by each social rank to the higher one, the question of whether social rankings actually existed in the Zhou was critical. Drawing on the *Spring and Autumn Annals*, the *Book of History*, *Mencius*, and the *Book of Songs* (*Shijing*, supposedly compiled by Confucius), Fu argued that the nobles claimed their ranks only after the disintegration of the Zhou dynasty during the Warring States period, when the ministers broke away and established their own separate states.[36]

Archaeological excavations of tortoiseshell writings allowed Dong to support Fu's argument to a great extent while giving a much more historical interpretation of the ranking system. In response to Fu, Dong tried to discern the original meaning of the five aristocratic ranks in the Shang dynasty (*gong*, *ho*, *bo*, *zi*, and *nan* roughly corresponding to marquis, duke, count, viscount, and baron), showing that they often evolved from place names.[37] Influenced by these archaeological discoveries, Hu Shi wrote one of his best syntheses of historical evolution and textual exegesis on the historical origins of Confucian thought. Hu argued that Confucian learning was actually Confucius's synthesis of Zhou dynasty practices with the literary and religious beliefs and practices of the Shang because Confucius had Shang ancestors. Hu compared the rise of

Confucian thinking with the rise of Judaism after the fall of Jerusalem in 526 B.C.E., as both developed upon the demise of the political and administrative entities of a people. But the specific comparisons between Confucian thinking and Shang society and thought were made possible by the archaeological confirmation of the existence of the Shang dynasty. Confucian teachings became historical reflections of Confucius's time.[38]

This objectification of history differed from a more traditional approach in that it represented a more conscious effort to situate history in a particular framework, either against the sociopolitical background of the time or in an evolutionary-historical framework driven by Western values such as progress. As such it had a distinct narrative structure, which earlier historiography consciously avoided, and required a clear statement of methodology.[39] Scientific methods were relevant because their rational, objective methods, according to Weber, presented an optimistic approach to truth even with the disappearance of uniform and universal truth. A clear statement of the (scientific) methodology helped justify the new historical discourse. To approach history with more scientific methods, Zhu Xizu (professor of history at Peking University from 1914 to 1935 and chairman of the History Department from 1918 to 1930), was inspired by German historian Karl Lamprecht's view that history as a subject of study should be situated in the perspective of various social sciences subjects and thereby changed sociology, political science, and economics from elective to required courses in the 1924–25 academic year. These courses continued to be required for history majors until 1930.[40] In the explanations of the History Department curriculum, which remained more or less unchanged from 1923 to 1927, Zhu argued that history was a part of science, and, out of all the sciences, the most important for history were sociology and social psychology, which had to be studied in the first two years before one could specialize in history. A student would then study the histories of social sciences, such as political history, economic history, legal, and social history, while also taking classes in art, literary, philosophical, and cultural history, including historiography.[41] To improve upon methods, Zhu Xizu appointed Li Dazhao and He Bingsong to teach historiography. Li, a Marxist, taught intellectual historiography and historical materialism, while He, who had studied history at Princeton University, taught historiography by using H.R. Robinson's *New History*. Zhu also taught historiography.

This emphasis on scientific methodology to give credence to the new histories contrasted with a traditional approach to Chinese history, textual exegesis: the study to elucidate the work of ancient sages by clarifying the meanings of texts that had become obscure through the passage of time and changes in usage. Textual exegesis

> expose[d] factual errors and textual distortions through command of an enormous amount of detailed information and through careful comparison of textual variations within a given collation . . . Proper scholastic training not only resulted in an educated command of source materials; it also instilled a profound respect for faithful adherence to textual authenticity down to the last detail.[42]

A textual exegetical approach focused on "textual fragments and factual details," consequently it was "antipathetic to the development of large-scale conceptual generalizations." This approach was often used in the study of history because history served as elucidation of the classics, rather than as a narrative on its own. Historical commentaries, such as the *Zuo Commentaries* (*Zuo zhuan*), became classics on their own because of their relationship to the classics. The *Zuo Commentaries* constituted one of the three primary commentaries of the *Spring and Autumn Annals*. It filled in the historical background of the events to which the classic itself only enigmatically alluded.[43] Although the refrain from a more thematic approach to Chinese history had complex causes, it was a practice that could be traced to Confucius's famous saying *shu er bu zuo* (I transmit but do not create), in order to transmit traditions intact.

Despite the dissemination of scientific methods, the majority of the historical narratives or semi-narratives in the republican era were written with a textual-exegetical style embellished with semi-literary Chinese, a writing style that was being replaced by the vernacular in official media in early twentieth-century China. At first glance, these narratives resembled traditional Chinese history in several respects, including a tendency to efface the author's authoritative voice, the avoidance of generalizations, the use of classical language, and a focus on nuanced details. A closer examination showed that these histories differed markedly from traditional historiography in their very historical treatment of the past and greater narrative structure. The textual exegesis easily meshed with a historical approach because of the evidentiary details it supplied. But a textual exegetical focus on the search for the original meaning of words through tracing their historical origins often put an end to the linear, progressive evolutionary approach. Even Hu Shi's own linear, progressive framework was punctuated with textual exegesis. Hu Shi's methodological masterpiece on the history of ancient Chinese philosophy was praised by open-minded thinkers Cai Yuanpei and Liang Qichao not for the Huxleyian agnosticism and Deweyan pragmatism that Hu claimed guided the writing of that book, but for Hu's exegesis of ancient texts. In time, even Hu himself engaged increasingly in textual exegesis, which he called an inevitable result of living in the intellectual milieu of Beijing, which was permeated by textual analysis.[44] Hu Shi not only engaged in textual exegesis but called it the most important Chinese contribution to modernizing Chinese historiography.[45] Hu championed the scientific reorganization of the national past (*zhengli guogu*), elevating the status of Qing textual exegesis to that of science in the process.[46]

A textual exegetical approach, in a strict sense, did not need to rely on a comparative framework or Western values, since its emphasis was a literal comparison between two specific texts. And the Zhang Taiyan–influenced scholars hired after 1913 were members of the school of textual exegesis. Most of these scholars accepted an evolutionary periodization of Chinese history and adopted an eclectic approach to Western values and scientific methods. But their textual exegetical approach enabled them to remain largely at the level of specific details without weighing historical facts in the context of more universal, or Western, concepts and meanings. This was true of the majority of courses in the 1931–32 curriculum. Almost all of the following prominent faculty members applied a textual exegetical approach to their studies instead of conscious scientific methodology. Ma Heng's course on the study of writings on bronze and stones relied on a systematic study of historical relics. Meng Sen, a specialist on Ming and Qing histories, based his courses on the beginning of the Qing dynasty and topics in the histories of the Ming and Qing with extensive readings of dynastic histories. Qian Mu's course on ancient Chinese history required the reading of reference works from the *Book of History* and *Zuo Commentaries*, to the writings of Cui Shu, a Qing philologist, and Gu Jiegang, his colleague at Yanjing and Peking universities. His course on Han and Wei histories also had as optional readings various histories including *Records of the Grand Historian* (*Shiji*), *History of the Han Dynasty* (*Han shu*), and the *Comprehensive Mirror for Aid in Government* (*Zizhi tongjian*). Zhao Wanli's bibliography courses on Chinese historical bibliography and Qing historical bibliography both included a study of bibliographical methods and a survey of extensive documents. Fu Sinian offered a course on literary styles in ancient Chinese writings, which also included bibliographical studies of the codification of writings. Gu Jiegang offered a course on the *Book of History* with a textual analytical approach. Ke Changsi's "History of the Song Dynasty" also focused on extensive study of Song documents in order to study the various aspects of the dynasty's history.[47] After Chen Shouyi became chairman of the History Department in 1932, he expanded the department reading room's offerings, adding reference works to complement the historical documents there.[48]

The textual exegetical approach also predominated in the CLLD. The juxtaposition of literature, philology, and archaeology in the CLLD stemmed from the close connection between philology and archaeology in textual exegesis because of the need to study the meaning of ancient words. The philological and archaeological emphases deepened the textual exegetical orientation of the research. Often their combination with historicism helped steer Chinese history away from a linear, progressive path and give an internal logic to Chinese historical development.

It was precisely the textual exegetical approach's refrain from generalization that made it work well with both greater and lesser narrative histories of the republican era. Many histories demonstrated a juxtaposition of an evolutionary narrative style and textual exegesis, for example, the novelist Lu Xun, one of the greatest novelists of twentieth-century China. Lu Xun's literary career debuted with his radical socially critical tale "Diary of a Madman" (*Kuang ren riji*) in 1918. Two years later, he was invited by Cai Yuanpei to teach at Peking University upon the recommendation of his brother Zhou Zuoren, who had already started teaching Chinese and Japanese there. Because he was already holding a part-time job at the Ministry of Education, Lu Xun worked only as a lecturer at the university, and the course he offered most often was a history of Chinese novels, based on his study on Chinese novels over the previous decade. Evolutionary historical analyses were subsumed under a textual exegetical style. The analyses showed through a study of the connection between historical backgrounds and novels in each dynasty. However, Lu Xun did not try to build a consistently progressive description of Chinese novels. This resistance to a rational and progressive narrative was also evident in his use of language. His explanation that he wrote his lectures in the classical language to save the copiers' trouble does not seem very persuasive.[49] Even his novels meant to promote a new culture in China were written in semi-classical language.

An evolutionary historical outlook enabled Lu Xun to introduce to his narrative modern Western values, such as popular education, individual expression, and humanism. In his discussion of Song dynasty novels, for instance, he consciously explored the vernacular tradition (*baihua xiaoshuo*) since the vernacular was promoted in early twentieth-century China as a way to promote literacy. The growing emphasis on individual expression at the turn of the century also led Lu Xun to see a growing conscious appropriation of fiction for self-expression in Chinese history, beginning with the Tang dynasty. From simple fantasies (*chuanqi*) during the Jin dynasty (256–420), which were mostly about ghosts, spirits, and preordained fate, fiction gradually developed into an effective mode of self-expression in the legends of the Tang dynasty, reaching an epitome of conscious expression of human sentiments in the Qing.

Textual exegesis characterized the major approach to Lu Xun's history of Chinese novels. Like Hu Shi, Lu Xun used textual exegesis to study different editions of novels, as many significant novels underwent a series of alterations. Lu Xun carefully examined the novels of different dynasties and their influences on one another. *Water Margin* (*Shuihuzhuan*), for instance, had its origin in the true story of a gangster, Song Jiang, in the Song dynasty. Although its earliest version as a novel could not be found, Lu Xun found six later versions, which he carefully compared to show the influence of earlier versions on a later one by Luo Guanzhong.[50] The textual exegetical style, by focusing on the particular origins of a historical fact, be it a novel, a word, or an event, could both present an evolutionary history of the development of a historical event and steer the historical narrative away from some universal patterns of development, hence preventing a linear, progressive narrative. Lu Xun's textual exegetical approach presented a multi-layered history. He traced the origin of the rise of vernacular novels to the influence on Song dynasty writers of Buddhist-related stories, which had often been written in vernacular Chinese in the late Tang and Five Dynasties (*Wudai* 907–960). The Song vernacular novels thus often popularized the Buddhist teachings of performing good deeds while providing entertainment. Similarly, Lu Xun did not depict the linear development of self-expressive novels over time. While covering achievements in self-expression in the novels from the Tang to Qing dynasties, Lu Xun's textual exegetical eye did not omit novels written during the same period that continued the fantasy tradition and focused on interactions between humans and ghosts. Supernatural novels (*zhiguai xiaoshuo*) during the Song, and stories of demons and ghosts during the Ming, similarly reflected their time. A combination of traditional witchcraft and the spread of Buddhism, Lu Xun argued, also influenced novels during the Six Dynasties (*Liuchao*, 420–589) period. Many alchemists at this time wrote about impermanence (*wuchang*), a concept loaned from Buddhism, to trap people who wanted to escape the impermanence of the world.[51]

Lu Xun's historical evolutionary framework accommodated an injection of modern Western values and a progressive interpretation of Chinese novels. Yet his textual exegetical approach, by focusing on the origins of certain novels, prevented a consistent comparison with Western literary developments. The result was that, at times, his narrative did not present a linear or even progressive history. It, however, consistently treated historical novels as a reflection of their time, and in that sense, it followed the scientific approach and was historical.

Textual exegesis, therefore, could assist a scientific approach to history while deterring a linear, progressive narrative. But it could also help develop a progressive outlook while omitting a detailed comparison with modern Western developments in its historical discourse. One example of the latter use of textual exegesis could be seen in the writing of Yu Jiaxi. Yu was a leading Chinese philologist who taught at Furen University from 1927 to the 1950s and was a guest lecturer at Peking University in the 1920s and 1930s. He had received a classical Chinese education in his childhood in the late nineteenth century, although not a strictly conventional one. Along with studying the Confucian classics, he learned history that was not covered in the imperial examinations, thanks to a reading list that broadened the traditional categories of learning, published by Zhang Zhidong. Yu passed the provincial imperial examination at the age of eighteen. At Furen and Peking universities he taught courses on bibliography, studies in *A New Account of Tales of the World* (*Shishuo xinyu*), ancient text editing and analysis, and prose of the Han, Wei, and the Six Dynasties—courses that did not fall strictly into the category of traditional Chinese philology.[52] At the same time, Yu forbade the teaching or use of the vernacular language and did not advocate reform in any way. Whatever innovations he did make were passed off as traditional exegesis under the guise of classical language without an explicit articulation of the methodology used. His writings had less narrative structure than Lu Xun's and read as a series of textual exegetical findings strung together. Some of his works were obviously inspired by contemporaneous interests in Western ideas of science and democracy but did not bear either name and passed as research on a traditional Chinese subject. One of the studies Yu made was of *hanshisan*, a mineral mixture used as medicine to restore physical strength by scholars and officials during the Wei, Jin, and Northern and Southern Dynasties. *Hanshisan* was one variation of what was called *dansha* (red sand), a red dye used for medicinal purposes for longevity starting in the Eastern Han dynasty.[53] The study of *hanshisan* was an exploration of this ancient medicine that was historically perceived to have magical power. Through an exegesis of the medicine and the varying effects it had on different people, Yu concluded that it was unrealistic to use the medicine as a cureall. A strongly implied theme in the article was that the medicine was unscientific.[54] The idea of science inspired Yu's interest in the study of a traditional Chinese panacea, yet his proof of the medicine's ineffectiveness was accomplished not through touting a scientific method but through a textual exegetical analysis of cases over time. The conclusion did not bear any mention of science either, although it was obviously inspired by scientific positivism. Science provided inspiration, but Yu conducted his research using a case-by-case study without reference to the Western criteria of science.

Similarly, in another article on the origin of novels, Yu was influenced by the post–May Fourth value of the novel. He had a dual purpose: to elevate the status of the novel, and to negate the denunciation of Confucian orthodoxy by Hu Shi through a separation of orthodox and unorthodox writings in Chinese history. Unlike previous historians, who decided that the novelist began as a petty official who recorded petty matters and whose job could not be classified as that of a regular official, Yu argued that the novelist had a much nobler origin. He had been the mediator between the emperor and the masses, conveying the latter's views to the former. And because the emperor would not always want to hear serious criticism, the mediator had to insert jokes and stories to leaven his reports.[55] Yu's conclusion that the novelist had originated as a court official was considered one of the best pieces of textual exegesis on this subject in centuries. He attacked the conclusion that Hu Shi had reached in "The Various Schools of Thought Other Than Confucian Were Not Affiliated with Official Positions in History" (*Zhuzi buchu wangguan*). Obviously, Hu wanted to demonstrate that the various schools of non-Confucian thought that he wanted to promote were outside the official orthodoxy and not promoted by the dynastic governments. Yu demonstrated here that the line between orthodox and unorthodox thinking was not so clearly drawn.[56] In a way this was an attack on Hu's ideology, but it was more an attack on methods, to show that specificity would reveal what generalizations would not. Textual exegesis promoted a greater historicism regarding historical details than a simple linear progressive model.

Indeed, for many Chinese scholars, this was one of the most important attractions of textual exegesis: it allowed an evolutionary outlook to Chinese history but, by focusing on particular origins, often prevented a comparison with general Western patterns of development. Textual exegesis focused attention on a closer identification between historical events and the particular Chinese circumstances that spawned them. Yu's aim was to call for a greater attention to historical details in their particular, not universal, context.[57] Later archaeological excavations would prove Yu correct in that the Shang dynasty, the antiquity Hu and Gu doubted, had existed. Yu's textual exegetical method thus also served as a signpost of his philosophy: solid research for a good understanding of particular historical contexts instead of bold and farfetched revolutionary hypotheses.

As can be seen from Yu Jiaxi's example, textual exegesis allowed flexible innovations in Chinese history writing without pinning the historian down to detailed predetermined criteria or explicitly stated frameworks. This same flexibility was also shown in the writings of Meng Sen, professor of Chinese history at Peking University in the 1920s and 1930s who was most famous for his rewriting of early Qing history using a textual exegetical approach. Throughout his historical narratives, however, Meng did not mention anything about the revolutionary changes in his philosophy of history. Unlike many of his colleagues who shunned dynastic histories because of their taint with Confucian values, Meng took on dynastic histories, especially of the Ming and Qing dynasties, with ease, because of the critical methods he applied to their studies and their cross-examination by many newly found primary sources. Possessing an agnostic spirit, Meng paid close attention to the form of the presentations of dynastic histories and the intentions behind them. With their intrinsic value gone, dynastic histories, to Meng, were not just value-free historical data, but human constructs that embodied particular intentions suited to a particular historical context, a position that to some extent resembled the postmodernist deconstruction approach of the late twentieth century. From this belief Meng was able to reconstruct the history of the Manchus through a comparison of different editions of early Qing history to reveal inconsistencies in them. He also asserted his own conclusion that Nurhachi, the founder of the Qing dynasty, revised history to hide the early identity of the Manchus as subordinates of the Ming empire, which they later overthrew. Historically, each dynasty compiled the official history of the previous dynasty, and sometimes when a dynasty was long enough, later emperors would compile histories for earlier emperors of the same dynasty. These histories were usually considered the epitome of truth, and beginning in the Tang dynasty, royal historians completed them. Meng benefited from an agnostic spirit and broad cross-reading of different historical documents. The inconsistencies between documents, for example, between the *True History of Korea* (*Chaoxian shilu*) and different editions of the *Truthful Record of the Qing Dynasty* (*Qingshilu*), a history that had been updated several times during the Qing Dynasty, enabled Meng to pinpoint which past the Qing regime had deliberately repressed. Later editions of the *Truthful Record* located the origin of the Manchus in a place called Jianzhou (in present-day Shandong province). Meng's research showed, however, that Jianzhou had really referred to present-day Manchuria in northeastern China, which was incorporated into the Ming dynasty as a frontier state that the Ming regime had asked the Manchus, who were natives of the region, to govern. Nurhache, then a military supervisor of that frontier state, wanted to develop his own forces and made several attempts to establish an independent state but failed. When he began his rebellion, he wrote a proclamation of the resentments the Manchurians bore the Ming government and their reasons for secession. In earlier versions of the Ming Dynasty history this proclamation was still available. The consequences of this rebellion, with Nurhache begging the Ming troops to leave and promising obedience to Ming once the Manchu demand for a large amount of money and goods was satisfied, were recorded in the *True History of Korea*. A copy of the proclamation was even available at the Archives of Peking University, perhaps as a result of Peking University's collection of many old Ming and Qing Dynasty archival documents. But in later versions of the Ming Dynasty history compiled by the Qing Dynasty and in *Qingshilu*, this proclamation was altered because it would reveal Nurhachi's history of service and subservience to the Ming emperor.[58] Meng's narrative of his discovery of the Manchu rulers' real identity was free of any scientific jargon. The very absence of such terminology might also be a statement of his philosophy: that these values and ideas were to inspire him to new areas of research, and not to confine his research to certain predetermined values. His attention, like Yu Jiaxi's, was to remain focused on the specific historical details and their contexts.

The scholars of textual exegesis overlapped with those championing scientific methodology in their adherence to historicism and a macroscopically evolutionary framework. The same person would often employ scientific methods more consciously in some writings and greater textual exegesis in some others. But the two approaches did not always coexist peacefully in the Chinese studies disciplines, as shown by the students' expulsion of Zhu Xizu in 1930. Although Zhu introduced historical methods into the History Department, his own research employed a textual exegetical approach preoccupied with the details of history instead of macroscopic trends that put Chinese history in the mainstream Western history of progress. The students, asking for more scientific methodology, after the style of Hu Shi, wrote Zhu to ask for his resignation from the department.[59] After the mediation of President Jiang Menglin, Zhu Xizu maintained his position as professor in the History Department but was no longer the chairman. Fu Sinian, and then Jiang Menglin, served as the interim chairman before Chen Shouyi, who had a Ph.D. from the University of Chicago, was appointed to Peking University and started to chair the department in 1932.

In the 1930s, Hu pushed for literary histories in the CLLD, his rendition of a scientific and experimental approach to literature. Before 1934, philologists like Ma Yuzao, chairman of the CLLD, dominated the department and emphasized a textual exegetical approach with no explicit theoretical emphasis.[60] Even He Bingsong, who had studied at Princeton University and come under the influence of the New History School of James Harvey Robinson of the University of Wisconsin, gradually abandoned a positivist approach to history and embraced textual exegesis.[61] Under the pressure of the textual exegetics, Hu himself was also increasingly immersed in textual exegetical studies. But Hu was never a philologist who buried his methodology under weighty research, and in 1934, Hu Shi insisted on more courses on methodologies using a causal and historical approach, and Ma, a philologist, decided that, in the absence of extensive documentation, an emphasis on methodology could not constitute real scholarship. Their disagreement led Hu, dean of the College of Arts, to pressure Ma to resign from his position as chairman of the CLLD in 1934, although Ma still taught in the department as a professor.[62] Hu's triumph over Ma came at a time when an ideological approach to history was in the ascendant, in view of the imminence of war with Japan. A mushrooming of new history courses followed that consciously manipulated historical methods and approaches to glorify the Chinese historical past, explain China's position in world history, or alert students to crises periods in history. Qian Mu's course "Modern Chinese Intellectual History in the Past Three Hundred Years" depicted continuous Chinese intellectual development from the Song to the late Qing dynasty. Jiang

Tingfu's "Modern Chinese Diplomatic History" explained the process of how China joined the international community and its treatment in that community. Wang Tongling's "East Asian History" dealt with China's position in Asia and in the world historically and with the relationship between China and neighboring peoples. With the deepening of the national crisis, new courses were added to highlight periods of foreign invasions in Chinese history as historical background to the crisis of the 1930s. One course added in 1931 was the history of the Liao, Jin, and Yuan dynasties from the twelfth to the fourteenth centuries, when the Jurgens and then the Mongols invaded China and established control first of northern China and then of the entire country. By 1935, new courses on the tumultuous period of the Wei, Jin, Northern and Southern Dynasties and on Sui, Tang, and the Five Dynasties were offered. There were also new courses on the Chinese frontier regions, such as the history and geography of northeastern and northwestern China.[63] Occasionally, ideology overrode pedagogy, such as in Fu Sinian's history of northeastern China: though he was an excellent philologist, Fu presented a history of Manchuria that was full of mistakes, some perhaps deliberate to contradict Japan's justification for occupation of Manchuria.[64]

This more ideological use of history seemed to favor history along linear, progressive lines over textual exegesis as contributing to national consciousness because linear, evolutionary history seemed more capable to present a holistic continuous past than textual exegesis. This also leads to an interesting question on when scholars were willing to adopt a more scientific and linear, progressive approach to Chinese studies. From the above discussion of history inspired by nationalism and the following discussion of philology inspired by language reform, it seems that the amount of relevance to national salvation greatly influenced the style of historical narratives.

## Nationalism, Western Phonetic Systems, and Chinese Language Reform

If philologists like Yu Jiaxi, Lao Gan, and Meng Sen refused to apply Western values directly to their studies, their colleagues who worked on the reform of the Chinese language felt a more urgent need to find rules within the Chinese language that followed a Western pattern of development. In the late nineteenth and early twentieth centuries, champions of Chinese learning, recognizing the role modern vernacular languages played in the development of Western countries, put language reform on the educational agenda.[65] Their primary task was to find rules governing the Chinese language that paralleled the rules of European languages in order to make learning Chinese easier and spread literacy. These philologists had often to battle their own historical tendencies that particularized Chinese philology while trying to make Chinese a phonetic language by finding grammatical rules in Chinese that paralleled those in the Western languages. By historicizing language changes, they used textual exegesis to reveal particular linguistic characteristics and guide their search for rules governing the Chinese language and its changes. The guiding principle of their writings, focusing on change, contrasted with the façade of timelessness that Yu Jiaxi and Meng Sen tried to impart. Unlike the more radical reformers, who advocated replacing Chinese characters with a phonetic writing system based on the Latin alphabet, these philologists believed that using textual exegesis, they could grasp the intrinsic development of the Chinese language and come up with a better version of the Chinese language system than either the phonetic or more traditional ones.

Like their counterparts in modern European countries, Chinese philologists wanted to establish a standard pronunciation system based on a vernacular. To do that, they needed to find out which vernacular(s) they wanted to use as the standard, but they lacked historical rules or definitions guiding pronunciation. Historically, unlike the Romance or Germanic languages, the phonetic and written parts of the Chinese language were not related and there were no clearly established rules to guide an understanding of word pronunciation. Phonetics was studied not for pronunciation but to achieve a better understanding of the ancient classics by clarifying the original meaning of words in these texts. Since the spoken language contained more words than were represented in ancient writings, many written characters were used to signify multiple meanings with identical pronunciation. The difficulty in understanding ancient texts was further complicated by the changes in meaning and pronunciation over the centuries, most notably in the Qin dynasty (221–206 B.C.E.) when the emperor Qin Shihuangdi ordered the creation and use of a new writing system for his empire, leading to the obliteration of several earlier styles of writing that had been employed in the Confucian classics. All this hindered a proper deciphering of words in ancient texts, hence the field of philology seeks to clarify the meaning of words in these texts. But early Chinese grammar paid little attention to pronunciation. One of the first books to study word formation was Xu Shen's *Explaining Texts and Characters* (*Shuowen jiezi*), written in the Han dynasty (206 B.C.E.–220 C.E.). Xu focused on generalizing rules governing the formation of character components and their meaning, rather than on how the pronunciation of words related to their meaning.

A phonetic study of Chinese did not start until the Tang Dynasty and was prompted by influence from Indo-European languages, first from India and then via the Jesuits. Buddhism was introduced to China around the time of the Eastern Han dynasty (25–220 C.E.). In the early Tang dynasty (618–907 C.E.), Buddhist texts originally written in Sanskrit needed to be transliterated into

Chinese. Borrowing from the Sanskrit, reducing its fourteen vowels to twelve, and increasing its thirty-three consonants to thirty-six, Tang dynasty monks created the first phonetic rendering of the Chinese language, called *fanqie*. It used two Chinese characters to indicate the pronunciation of a third by combining the initial of the first character with the final of the second character.[66] For instance, the pronunciation of "tong" is indicated by the initial of the character "tu" and the last of the character "hong." Then, in the seventeenth century, Jesuits who came to preach in China developed a romanized spelling of Chinese to facilitate pronunciation, which was much more accurate than *fanqie*. After the publication of Matteo Ricci's *Western Alphabets* (*Taixi zimu*), Nicholas Trigault, another Italian missionary, wrote a phonetic grammar of Chinese called *Ear and Eye Aid to the Western Scholars* (*Xiru ermuzi*), which largely corresponded with Ricci's phonetic system. Both of them greatly influenced Qing scholars, including Fang Yizhi and Liu Tingxian. In 1669, another Italian missionary, Prosper Intorcetta, used the Latin alphabet to romanize the Four Classics. This Jesuit venture in romanizing the Chinese language was brought to an end by the expulsion of all Jesuits from China in 1723. But Western missionaries who used romanized spelling of the Chinese Bible in southeastern China and directly influenced the first book of phonetic Chinese by Lu Gangzhang in 1892 continued the enterprise in the nineteenth century.[67]

The Jesuits' phonetic study of the Chinese language apparently contributed to a surge of phonetic studies of ancient Chinese characters by Chinese philologists. By the eighteenth century, phonetics had become an important way to decipher changes in pronunciation through history to discern the true meaning of a word in antiquity. But many Chinese philologists focused on the rhyme rather than the actual pronunciation of words because the study of rhyme itself would lead to the establishment of a sufficient connection between different words, their interchangeable relationship in history, and the original meaning of a word.

In the twentieth century, however, more attention was focused on how to pronounce these ancient words because the goal was not only to determine the original meaning of words but also the evolution of their pronunciation in order to develop a standard pronunciation system based on historical usage. Historically, the difficulty of transportation had led to the formation of many regional dialects in China that are not mutually intelligible. Vernacular writing developed after the Song dynasty (960–1279) and remained more or less the same throughout China because of the uniformity of written classical Chinese as a result of the imperial civil service examinations. There was, however, no codified Chinese grammar until the latter part of the nineteenth century, which came about as a result of Western influence, no standard pronunciation, and no punctuation in Chinese writing.

By the late nineteenth and early twentieth centuries, numerous versions of Chinese phonics developed. Most of them based the phonemes on Chinese word components, after the Japanese *kanji* system, but some were based directly on the Latin alphabet. The most circulated phonics text was compiled by Wang Zhao; it sold around sixty thousand copies in thirteen provinces from 1901 to 1910.[68] A nationwide language reform movement was finally started by the republican government in 1913, when the Ministry of Education organized a Unifying Pronunciation Committee (*Guoyin tongyi hui*), which was divided over what to use for the Chinese phonemes: Chinese word components as in the Japanese *kanji,* other symbols, or the Latin alphabet. Some even suggested a completely phonetic Chinese language, which was rejected because too many Chinese words are homophones. Peking University faculty, including Ma Yuzao, Li Jinxi, Qian Xuantong, Lin Yutang, Shen Jianshi, Zhu Xizu, and Lui Fu took the lead in these efforts. In November 1918, the Ministry of Education published a list of phonemes (*zhuyin zimu*) to indicate pronunciation as well as a standard of pronunciation and in 1919, stipulated that this national language with standard pronunciation be taught in all Chinese primary schools beginning in 1920. In 1920, the first national standard vernacular dictionary was circulated by the Ministry of Education, with a synthesis of northern and southern pronunciations as the standard pronunciation of the Chinese language. Faced with opposition from many scholars, this dictionary was eventually replaced by a new standard pronunciation based exclusively on Beijing dialect.[69]

Besides building a system of phonemes based on ancient Chinese characters, a pronunciation system based on the Latin alphabet was also created. The most commonly accepted version was proposed by Peking University philologists Qian Xuantong and Li Jinxi, and Qinghua University linguist Zhao Yuanren. At Qian Xuantong's suggestion, a Chinese romanization booklet was published in 1923, which could trace its influence to Nicholas Trigault and included the contributions of T.F. Wade, the British envoy to China in the late Qing dynasty. The project to standardize the Chinese language pronunciation was not completed under the warlord governments. The Nationalist government in 1928 invited Li Jinxi and Qian Xuantong to resume work on it. In 1931, the Grand College, the institution in the newly established Nationalist government in charge of all educational matters in China, building on work by previous ministries of education from 1918 to 1928, circulated a phonetic Chinese language based on two separate sets of phonemes whose pronunciations corresponded: ancient Chinese characters and the Latin alphabet. The conjunction of government policies of popular education through linguistic reform and the scholars' transformation of the Chinese language for the same purpose seemed to make the goal more immediate and tangible. This was especially so after 1928, when more Peking University faculty were incorporated into the

Unifying the National Language Committee by the Nationalist government. In addition to the aforementioned Li Jinxi and Qian Xuantong, others involved in the project were physics professor Li Shuhua, who was also deputy president of Peking University at the time, Hu Shi, Liu Fu (also known as Bannong), Wei Jiangong, Shen Jianshi, Lin Yutang, and Ren Hongjun. The last was a professor of chemistry. Liu, Wei, and Shen were faculty members from the CLLD whose task was to implement the phonetic system and to complete the *Dictionary of Standard National Pronunciation* (*Guoyu tongyi zhuyin zhidian*).[70]

To discern historical patterns of pronunciation changes, many authors drew on the works of Jesuits and European sinologists such as Matteo Ricci, Nicolas Trigault, and Bernhard Karlgren. Chinese philologists appreciated the contributions of these Europeans with respect to the romanization of Chinese.[71] The Peking University philologists' contributions to language reform were largely in editing the grammars and dictionaries and direct contributions to the standardization of pronunciation or the codification of grammar. A systematic scholarly discussion of the phonetics of the Chinese language started at Peking University in 1923 with a publication by a Russian faculty member, A. Von Stael-Holstein, who, following Karlgren, pointed out that the study of ancient Chinese pronunciation could be facilitated by comparing Chinese transliterations of Sanskrit and the original Sanskrit terms with the local Beijing and Ningbo—a town south of Shanghai—dialects to incorporate both northern and southern accents. His writing immediately elicited a response from his colleague Wang Rongbao, a faculty member at Peking University, who had written a paper the same year tracing the effect of the "a" sound on ancient Chinese language. Wang's work differed from most philological work in that it focused on actual pronunciation. Wang used a comparative approach, with transliterations of Chinese in Arabic, the writings of Marco Polo, Japanese borrowings of Chinese pronunciation in the Tang dynasty, and Chinese transliterations from Sanskrit. His work invited a very mixed response, ranging from extreme approval to extreme rejection, with many views in between aimed at a modification of his arguments. The debate initiated serious scholarly studies of ancient pronunciation at the university and in the Chinese scholarly community.[72]

One focus of discussion in language reform was whether to approach spoken Chinese as a monosyllabic or a polysyllabic language, an argument that was evidently sparked by the fact that European languages are polysyllabic. Wei Jiangong, A member of the the CLLD after graduation from the university as a student in the 1920s, member of the Unifying the National Language Committee in 1928, and one of the foremost philologists in China, participated in the debate, but his generalizations were balanced by his textual exegetical style, which pointed to the particulars of Chinese language development. Wei first pointed out that polysyllabic spoken Chinese existed because oral and written languages in China developed separately: the monosyllabic written language differed from oral Chinese, which could have been polysyllabic. Historicizing language development, Wei suggested that the earliest written language did not have pronunciation—obviously written words did not always correspond with the oral language; words were created for meaning, not directly taken from oral language. After the Shang and Zhou dynasties words with pronunciation were often loaned to stand in for written words that did not have pronunciations. The merger between characters and their pronunciation was not complete until the appearance in the Han dynasty of Xu Shen's grammar *Explaining Texts and Characters*. Xu's gramar, however, was not for daily use but for reading the classics, and the written characters Xu studied were ancient, which differed from the calligraphy of his time called *lishu*, created at the order of Qin Shihuangdi. The Qin Dynasty created a new system of writing. To gain a comprehensive understanding of changes in the Chinese language, Wei called for restoring language to its original spoken form, by studying not just monosyllabic characters, but also multisyllabic character combinations in written language that could have been used in spoken communication, such as *xiamo* (toad) and *kedou* (tadpole). On this basis, Wei called for a generalization of phonetic changes in relation to word roots.[73] The polysyllabic Western languages inspired Wei's historicization of polysyllables as Chinese word roots and his possible intention to pattern the study of Chinese pronunciation more closely along Western phonetic lines. Textual analysis, however, directed his attention as well to the particulars in Chinese language that defied a facile generalization.[74] Wei cautioned against a comparative study of Chinese and languages with similar grammatical structures such as Tibetan, Burmese, and Thai. Instead he called for a comparative study of Chinese dialects (*fangyan*).

The comparative phonetic study of Chinese with closely related language groups was a frequently discussed topic in early twentieth-century China, started by Western sinologists. Based on a hypothesis by Von Stael Holstein, among others, they claimed that Europeans and Asians were originally undifferentiated and originated in a place called the Turan plain, which included present-day Turkestan and Xinjiang; from there they dispersed to Europe and Asia.[75] This hypothesis aroused great interest among many Chinese, who tried to explore the similarity between ancient Chinese and Indo-European languages to prove that the two shared early roots. It also branched into the comparative studies of Chinese and other similarly structured languages. Wei argued that the changes in language could not be pushed too far, and that, although it was sometimes possible, many changes could not be explained with logic or even through analogies.[76]

Shen Jianshi was another professor of philology at Peking University beginning in 1914, who had worked briefly with Zhang Taiyan on philology in

Japan in the early twentieth century, and a member of the Unifying the National Language Committee. He made more specific linkages between historical studies of the Chinese language and modern language reform. Shen hoped to achieve a systematic study of Chinese historical word formation from writings of the Warring States period (around 700–256 B.C.E.) and other early periods, comparative study of local dialects as well as the study of ancient dialects, remnants of which could still be found in the non-Han ethnic tribes in southwestern China and the pronunciations in Japanese of Chinese loanwords from southern China during the Sui and Tang dynasties.[77] Inspired by Western languages, whose words had monosyllabic or polysyllabic roots, Shen in an article in 1919 tried to generalize that Chinese words also had their own roots that could be reduced to their smallest element that embodied meaning. But, he concluded, it was not always easy to reduce words to their smallest form because the written representations had been handed down from many people, allowing for a great deal of incongruity in the writing of a single character. Word formation discussed in Xu Shen's classic *Explaining Texts and Characters* included ancient script that was no longer used in Xu's time, further complicating the discussion. These difficulties notwithstanding, Shen tried to generalize the different combinations of word formation based on the rules in Xu's work.[78]

By now the Ministry of Education was regularly consulting Shen on pronunciation, so his writings shifted to the topics of word formation and pronunciation. Criticizing historical studies of phonetics as too piecemeal, Shen wanted a systematic study that would list all the variations of characters that began with the same initial and their derivations.[79] He suggested creating phonemes in the Chinese language through character components to prepare for a transition to a phonetic system of language.[80] This was to be achieved through finding words that shared both meaning and the component indicating pronunciation. By the 1930s, Shen felt convinced that a phonetic approach to the Chinese language was entirely possible without the kind of drastic language change he proposed in the 1920s. He concluded that over 80 percent of Chinese characters already followed phonetic rules, with their root parts carrying the pronunciation of the words. Following a philologist Wang Shengmei of the Song Dynasty who argued that the right part of a character usually denoted pronunciation and meaning of the word, Shen argued that it was usually the right part of the character that bore its root meaning and pronunciation. He quoted an example that Wang Shengmei had used to illustrate the point, that the words "jian" 贱, "qian" 钱, "qian" 浅, all shared the part 戋, which meant small, and 戋 (pronounced jian, meaning small) not only lent pronunciation to the above words, but also gave meaning to them. Thus a small shell was called "jian" 贱 (since shells were often used as money in ancient times), a small piece of metal was called "qian" 钱, and small water called "qian" 浅. Because not

浅

much had been written on that subject Shen decided to write a historical chronicle for it by studying individual word formations in all the major dictionaries and grammar books from Xu Xhen's *Shuowen jiezi* (*Explain words and characters*), to *Guangyun* (*General thesis on final syllables*), and *Jiyun* (*Collections of final syllables*). The ultimate goal was preparation for a major dictionary of the Chinese language. This was a daunting task as characters that formerly shared components indicating meaning and pronunciation would either diverge on their own or come to stand for other characters and in the process change meaning. Despite the challenges, Shen was optimistic that general rules could still be formulated regarding how these irregularities occurred. Here, Shen the historian was stopped short by Shen the language reformer.[81]

Shen's proposal invited much criticism from his colleagues including Wei Jiangong. Wei argued that, because of language changes, many characters changed meaning although their written representation remained the same. Thus to discuss pronunciation one must start from a relationship between character components and meaning as well as character components and pronunciation to trace the transformation. Although phonetics aided in clarifying character components and pronunciation, it did not help explain the changes in meaning and the related changes in pronunciation. Since the earliest words were formed based on meaning, and not pronunciation, phonetics could not determine word roots and original meanings.[82]

Another critic of Shen, his colleague Tang Lan—who started teaching ancient philology at Peking University in 1934—concurred with Wei that, contrary to Shen's thesis, writing was associated first with meaning, not pronunciations. Thus to trace the development of words, it was erroneous to focus on components that indicated pronunciation. Because he had extensive knowledge of archaeology, Tang was in a better position to discuss ancient word formation than most of his colleagues. He argued that the then-current tendency in phonetics was to overlook the importance of understanding character components, which ultimately determined the meaning of words. Despite his disagreement with Shen Jianshi over approaches to decipher ancient language, Tang Lan was very involved in language reform and agreed with Shen on the creation of a phonetic language by using the right component in a character (such as 戋 in 浅) to indicate pronunciation. They battled with more radical colleagues who were bent on a creation of a Latin based alphabetical Chinese language or a Romanized pronunciation system. Tang said it was better to keep the Chinese characters and reform them by rendering each word into two parts, the left part indicating meaning and the right pronunciation, indicated by ancient Chinese character symbols. The difficulty of turning Chinese into a completely alphabetical language lay primarily in the high number of homophones: Although regularly used words numbered some nine thousand, there were only 265 different distinct syllables to represent them. English, for example, has a greater stock of different sounds to represent the same amount of vocabulary (author's example: one word in the English language, such as "mean" is just one word although with different meanings. The Chinese words with the same pronunciation, such as "tong" can be 35). Tang decided that a better understanding of ancient words would facilitate the process of word transformation to better link writing with pronunciation. In theory, words created with a greater continuity with the past would be not only viable but superior to words that claimed a more abrupt break from the past.[83] Tang Lan hoped to fathom the historical trends in Chinese word formation through tracing word developments from tortoise-shell words. In practice, however, Tang was only able to claim an understanding of seventy-four tortoise-shell words that he arrived at on his own, despite his acclaimed methods at deciphering tortoiseshell words.[84]

While Luo Changpei, Wei Jiangong, Shen Jianshi, and Tang Lan discussed and debated the rules of language reform, Liu Fu, professor of Chinese philology and literature who had been a writer of "Mandarin ducks and butterflies" (a genre of pop novel) novels in Shanghai in the early 1910s, created a more technical approach to establishing rules governing pronunciation. He researched Chinese regional dialects with the assistance of machines and sound charts. Liu worked as an editor at the publisher Zhonghua shuju from 1913 to 1916. His articles on literary reform in *New Youth* caught the attention of Cai Yuanpei, who hired him as a professor of literature at Peking University in 1917. Chen Duxiu, then dean of the humanities at Peking University and editor of *New Youth*, asked him to teach at the Peking University preparatory school, and, in 1919, Cai made him a member of the Unifying the National Language Committee that had been established by the then Ministry of Education. Following Hu Shi's call for a literary revolution, Liu championed writing in the vernacular, the expression of genuine emotions, and punctuation.[85]

Liu went to the University of Paris from 1921 to 1925 to earn his Ph.D. in experimental linguistics, a decision apparently based on his perception of the need of language reform in China. Liu's interest in language reform seemed to be twofold: to create a standard national language to facilitate literacy, and to give voice to the common people, who lacked an outlet for literary expression.[86] Even while in Paris, he designed equipment to record the different pronunciations of various dialects in the hope of discovering the most prevalent characteristics of spoken Chinese and the general characteristics of different Chinese dialects.[87] His Ph.D. dissertation was a study of the four tones expressed in the dialects of his hometown area in Jiangying, Jiangsu province. In addition to charting the tones of his own dialect, he wanted to draw up a chart of the tonal inflections of all the regional dialects, to compile a dictionary of dialects, and draw up a map of dialects patterned after similar maps in France.[88]

Liu's study of tones, which he continued after his return to China, correlated with his involvement in the vernacular movement and dictionary compilation. After his return to Shanghai in 1925, he was asked to help compile a dictionary there by the publisher *Qunyi shushe*. After that deal failed because the money for it was diverted to a coalmine, another publisher, *Beixin shuju*, asked him to compile a dictionary for primary and secondary school students. He also participated in the compilation of the standard dictionary of commonly used words published by the Unifying the National Language Committee, authorized by the Ministry of Education. That dictionary comprised more than six thousand words and was indexed by radicals, a procedure adopted in dictionary indexes in the twentieth century.[89] Liu's work, however, was cut short by his untimely death in 1934.

The legacy of standardization and codification of Chinese language pronunciations in early twentieth century continues to be felt today. The standard vernacular that the Ministry of Education codified in the 1930s, including a phonetic system indicating pronunciation with standard phonemes and with the alphabet, has remained the basis of the Chinese language in Taiwan and mainland China. The Taiwan government continued with the dual phonetic system with both romanized pronunciation and an emphasis on the set of phonemes based on Chinese characters (*zhuyin fuhao*). However, in mainland China, the Communist government emphasized the use of romanization using the Latin alphabet, starting from 1958, called *pinyin*. Although the twenty-six letters of the alphabet used to represent *pinyin* sometimes carry a different pronunciation from English, the pronunciation is close enough that it allows English speakers to learn Chinese sounds with little difficulty.

## Conclusion

In introducing Western academic disciplines to early twentieth century China, many Chinese scholars wanted to turn Chinese learning into a modern academic discipline. They adopted evolutionary historicism and objectified Chinese history, stripping it of its intrinsic value and treating it as historical data that derived meaning from its social and cultural context. Archaeological excavations, at least up to the 1930s, were also closely associated with creating a more objective historical discourse of Chinese culture. In their striving for change, many Chinese scholars also avoided over-reliance on a linear, progressive framework of Western origin. Within the framework of evolutionary history, Yu Jiaxi and Meng Sen, among others, adopted a textual exegetical style to such an extent that the emphasis on particular details and their connections in textual exegesis enabled an internal frame of reference without a direct and explicit borrowing of Western terms and concepts. The scientific aura of textual exegesis hid these scholars' avoidance of explicit Western criteria in their scholarship. Textual exegesis contributed to the movement for language reform an inductive style of reasoning in the historicization of the Chinese language. Aiming at a phonetic language, many Chinese philologists tried to generalize from examples in Chinese history rules that corresponded to those governing the Western languages. Despite their more linear understanding of the modernity needed for the Chinese language, textual exegesis prevented the language reformers from employing a deductive style of reasoning that would tailor Chinese learning more to Western criteria. Compared to their colleagues who had a less immediate goal of national relevance, the language reformers' concern for practical results sometimes outweighed their historicism to adhere to the nationalist goal of a phonetic language. Tang Lan nonetheless joined with those reforming the Chinese language along phonetic lines. Liu Fu, by contrast, went further to formulate Chinese linguistic rules based on more technical, hence scientific, methods. On the whole, however, these Chinese studies experts' redefinition of approaches to Chinese learning showed on the local level the debate carried out by Cai Yuanpei and others at a more philosophical level: how to situate Chinese learning in a more universal framework while maintaining a degree of freedom from Western values and approaches.

# 6

# Grasping for Permanence in Historical Change

The historical approach taken by many Chinese scholars toward Chinese history paved the way for a new relationship with the past. But the emphasis on change in historicism clashed with a desire for a historical continuity, as

> the more the difference between the individual phases of an entity's history is emphasized, the less plausible it will be to go on considering it one and the same thing through all the phases of its development. . . . [T]he suggestion of diachronicity that is implied by the definition of historicism . . . will have the effect of ungluing the successive phases a historical entity passes through in its history; this will result in synchronicity.[1]

Textual exegesis, widely practiced along with historicism, while avoiding a completely Western approach because of its claim of equivalence with a scientific approach, accentuated the particular characteristics of historical events and eras. A greater historical continuity called for a more transcendental framework that allowed both change and continuity. Moreover, neither a historical nor an objective treatment of history could assign value and meaning to anything in history beyond what was transient and specific. As Confucian values were being discredited, more scholars searched for alternative, perennial values in Chinese history. The result, just as in the case of German historicism, was a tendency toward developing a transcendental historical idea or framework that was embodied in all phases of history despite changes. German historicism saw the birth of the historical idea by Wilhelm von Humboldt and Ranke, the characteristics of which included an embodiment of what was unique to both a historical entity and a historical period, giving coherence to them not to be reduced entirely to the kind of knowledge expressed by social-scientific laws and only to be defined on the basis of unbiased historical research.[2] Ranke followed Herder's belief that in a higher reality made possible by God behind the outward appearance of the historical events, persons and institutions studied, there was always a totality, an integrated, spiritual reality and the task of a historical understanding would begin with total immersion in the subject matter and be completed by spiritual apperception.[3]

Many Chinese scholars were directly or indirectly influenced by German historicism. Chen Yinque and Fu Sinian studied in Germany, Liu Shipei was influenced by the German philosophy of history via Japan, and Tang Yongtong read Herder, Ranke, and Windelband while a student at Harvard. But a wider audience, which had not been exposed to German philosophy, also fell under its influence. Unlike the German historical idea, however, the transcendental historical framework developed by Chinese scholars was trans-cultural, and it was not antagonistic to science, as the German historical idea was. This transcendental framework enabled Chinese scholars to continue in their combination of textual exegesis and historicism, which linked their work to greater, more universal meanings aligned with Western values and justified an avoidance of a linear, progressive framework. Such a framework was sometimes used by Hu Shi, who became famous for applying Western individualism and humanism as the criteria for evaluating Chinese philosophers in "An Outline of the History of Chinese Philosophy," one of the first courses Hu offered at Peking University in 1917.[4] After Hu's book based on the lectures of this course was published, Liang Qichao in two lectures at the university attacked Hu for neglecting the religious and ethical aspects of Chinese thinkers like Confucius and Zhuang Zi.[5] Although Liang's call for a balance between the Western scientific approach and metaphysics resembled the cognitive framework suggested by Cai Yuanpei, it was these textual exegetics' connection between this transcendental framework and textual exegesis that gave uniqueness to their scholarship.

In addition to learning from German historicism, this group also drew on French and American transcendental cultural theories. Members of this group, such as Liu Shipei and Huang Jie, borrowed from the nineteenth-century French orientalist Albert Etienne Jean Baptiste Terrien de Lacouperie (d. 1894). Terrien de Lacouperie, as discussed below, offered a racial theory of China that proved useful in reconstructing Chinese history and historical values.[6] Others were also heavily influenced by the culturalistic view of history of Irving Babbitt, a professor of French literature at Harvard University, who presented himself as the valiant Horatius defending cultural values in a commercialized turn-of-the-century America.

## Chinese Intellectual History, Textual Exegesis, and a Transcendental Historical Framework

An exemplar of a textual exegetical and a transcendental historical approach to Chinese intellectual history was the work of Tang Yongtong, professor of philosophy at Peking University beginning in 1931. Tang studied philosophy at Harvard (M.A., 1922), where he came under the influence of Babbitt, Herder, Ranke, and Windelband. He often quoted Windelband and discussed Herder in his student papers. In the 1940s, while at the Southwestern Associated University in Kunming, he tried to write a metaphysical history of the Wei and Jin dynasties based on Windelband's philosophical framework. The Kantian, and later Rankean, belief in the ultimate ethical goal of human cultural development coincided with Tang's belief in the ultimate ethical purpose of individuals and society.[7] Although I have found no evidence that he took any courses with Babbitt, he became well acquainted with Babbitt's work through his friendship with Chinese students who did, as well as through direct conversations with Babbitt himself. His choice of courses in Pali, Sanskrit, and Indian philosophy while at Harvard could all have been the result of Babbitt's influence.[8]

Despite the differences among the German scholars and between them and Babbitt, Tang found important common denominators. For one thing, although their attitudes toward history varied greatly, all of them upheld a transcendental value system. Babbitt was distressed by the influence of individualism, science, and empirical and statistical approaches to scholarship on the humanities. Despite his hostility to scientific methods, Babbitt believed in the universality of human nature and sought a synthesis of European, Indian, and Chinese cultures that would support what he deemed the fundamental elements of a viable society: a humanist mean of sobriety and temperance to be achieved by balancing the material West and transcendentally peaceful Orient. Babbitt's was an ethic that "employed scientific or Socratic means for humanistic, quasi-transcendental ends."[9] Babbitt's loyal Chinese followers wished to fashion in China a similar transcendental moral system, based on a synthesis of Chinese and Western moral values that placed priority on humanity and self-restraint, rather than individualism and over-reliance on sensual experience. Thus, in their minds, Confucianism became grounded in a humanistic tradition on a par with Western humanism and Confucius the man coequal with the ancient Greek philosophers.[10]

Irving Babbitt presented to Tang a comparative approach to values and ideas and eventually helped Tang develop transcendental and universal patterns of human behavior that were a synthesis of science and metaphysics. Although this influence had a belated impact on Tang—as Tang remained a cultural relativist and did not believe in the synthesis of cultures through the 1920s—by the 1930s, Tang had established a trans-cultural historical framework. Tang often conducted comparative studies of thinkers across cultures to show a similarity of human thinking under similar circumstances, which strongly echoed Cai Yuanpei's transcultural framework of the 1910s to 1920s. In his lectures at Peking University on the spread of Buddhism in China, he often asked students to compare and contrast philosophers across cultures.[11] At the same time, Tang Yongtong was careful to differentiate each individual philosopher's thought. He consciously followed the Qing textual exegetical methods and never indulged in grand generalizations. Textual exegesis, combined with historicism, enabled him to value the specific aspects of Chinese culture in his writings. It also supported his view of nationalism in the description of China as a specific entity. Cultural functionalism—that each culture was an organic entity and followed its own rules of development, and that foreign cultures needed to adapt to these rules before assimilation—was extensively employed by Tang to describe the interaction between Chinese and foreign, especially Buddhist, cultures, in China.

Tang's greatest scholarly achievements dealt with the growth of Buddhism during the Wei and Jin dynasties to the Tang dynasty, a period, as Prasenjit Duara has pointed out, that attracted the attention of many Chinese scholars. Chinese historians wished to integrate this era, when a unified empire gave way to small contending kingdoms established by Chinese or by invading outsiders, into a picture of unified and continuous Chinese history.[12] This agenda was especially prominent in the 1930s, when many of Tang's works on Buddhism in China were written and when China faced a national crisis. Although in his publications Tang discussed the underlying similarities between Chinese and Indian practices that ultimately enabled the Chinese to absorb Indian culture, he emphasized the organic character of Chinese culture: specific practices in Chinese culture mattered, and if Indian culture had not conformed to these practices, it could not have been grafted onto Chinese culture. Tang often used a functionalist approach that maintained an a priori connection between specific social phenomena with certain more underlying variables.

Tang was convinced of the specificity of each culture and believed that cultural changes occurred gradually in all societies. Culture was the accumulation of many generations in history, and each culture had its own specific rules. Therefore, after the introduction of Indian culture to China, although changes did occur in Chinese culture, Indian Buddhism constantly had to adapt to Chinese cultural practices, initially mingling with Daoism, then mixing with Chinese metaphysics, and finally emerging in the Sui and Tang dynasties as sinicized Buddhism. Certain breathing practices in Zen Buddhism probably came from breathing practices of Daoists. The Tiantai (Land of Heaven) denomination of Buddhism, however, related its practice to the popular worship of gods and goddesses, so that Buddhist deities, such as Avalokitesvara, replaced the popular Chinese ones in solving everyday problems. Transmigration in Indian Buddhism did not involve ghosts, but ghosts were added when it was transplanted to China. Tang also showed that, to adapt to the particular environments of different regions of China, the formation of denominations, not a salient characteristic of Buddhism in India, came to characterize the spread of Buddhism in China. These denominations promoted their interests through control of property (monasteries); this was not so in India and hence represented an adaptation to the Chinese soil. Those denominations adapted to China had a greater vitality than those introduced directly from India.[13]

By the 1930s, Tang was able to formulate the rules governing cultural borrowings. Tang often criticized people who looked for superficial similarities between cultures, for this denied the specificity of cultural practices and the transcendental truth of each cultural practice. But he also believed that all truth was connected, though the connection would have to come from a very deep intuition. In his scheme, real cultural borrowing would pass through three stages. In the first stage, the most superficial level of learning, foreign concepts would be explained using familiar terms drawn from the existing, native vocabulary. This is precisely what happened when Buddhism began to spread in China. In the second stage, and continuing with the example of Buddhism, after significant contact with Buddhist culture, Chinese Buddhists came to realize the limitations that Chinese concepts placed on a full understanding, so they abandoned these concepts in favor of intuition alone. In the third stage, after understanding foreign elements intuitively, through locating the similarity between the foreign and domestic in the realm of consciousness, the Chinese absorbed elements of Indian Buddhism where they conformed, not in superficial practice but at the level of human consciousness, to the basic orientations of the transcendental rules governing Chinese culture.[14]

The uniqueness of a culture came from its detailed history. Like Herder and Ranke before him, Tang proclaimed empathy to be the key to comprehending historical truth: to understand the true intentions and actions of the ancients, one must use specific historical facts and documents and, through an act of intuition, attempt to experience exactly what the ancients had experienced. In short, the historian must go beyond merely accumulating words to fathom the desires and actions of a people.[15] His specific, textual exegetical approaches to Chinese, Indian, and European thought and practices were guided by the assumption of universal human reason that imparted more universal, trans-historical meanings to the particular practices and thoughts.

Like Tang, many scholars such as Yao Congwu, Wang Guowei, Chen Yinque, and Chen Yuan, in early twentieth-century China studied the patterns of historical interactions between Chinese and foreign cultures. In various ways, they shared with Tang the need to "discover" universal commonalities while honoring the specific contours of Chinese culture and ideas. Yao Congwu, a Peking University graduate sent to study history in Germany in the 1920s who returned there to teach history, focused on the history of Sino-Mongol relations. Wang Guowei was interested in both frontier studies and the interaction between Chinese culture and Buddhism. Chen Yinque, who studied extensively in Japan, the United States (Harvard), France, and Germany (University of Berlin), developed a solid foundation in the study of Chinese interactions with foreign influences, including Buddhism and the non-Chinese tribes that conquered and were later assimilated into Chinese society before the Sui and Tang dynasties.[16] Chen Yuan extensively studied the introduction of foreign religions to China, including Christian strains like Nestorianism and Manicheanism, and the Persian religion Zoroastrianism.[17]

Although this transcendental framework gave meaning to detailed exegetical work, by its very nature, it assumed only the broadest possible universal values, including the universality of human reason, and thus proved insufficient to some academics, who wanted a more tangible and even cultural specific set of values to guide and justify their historical research.

## The Reification of the Historical Idea

For many scholars, segments of Chinese history and culture were direct embodiments of certain values and therefore acquired a timeless quality, which F.R. Ankersmit called the reification of the historical idea. Ankersmit discusses two ways to conceptualize change. One is based on Aristotelian entelechy and the belief that the essence of a nation, state, people, and so on, change according to an inherent principle that causes them to evolve over time but such essence or principle cannot be reduced to any unchanging properties in historical events. The other is a position often taken by historicists who could not resist the temptation to conceive of the historical idea as reducible to concrete events or practices in the past.[18] The latter conception of change was very popular among many Chinese scholars. This popularity was partly due to Chinese tradition, where the highest level of thought was for thought to manifest itseof in specific historical events and processes. In Chinese history, intellectual thought and history are intertwined: thought should be able to manifest itself in historical events. Thought separate from history would be considered abstract and unreal.[19] After overthrowing the authority of Confucian learning, many Chinese scholars searched for alternative values. Although transcultural value systems, which Tang and others tried to build, were one alternative, others sought more intrinsic values, and identified particular historical experiences as embodiments of values that were essential to Chinese culture. As Huang Jie—one of the leading champions of the national essence movement, who later joined the CLLD at Peking University—pointed out, national essence was not a historical relic, but embodied in the long history of Chinese culture, like vapor in the air and salt dissolved in water. It was viable and developing, and its preservation by no means represented a rigid adherence to tradition.[20]

Scholars found different forms of concrete embodiments of transcendental historical ideas. Some supported Confucian values as expressed through certain styles of literary expression, while others advocated an intersubjective communication with the past—relying on subjective experience as at least part of the new value system and to identify expressions of subjective experience in history as trans-temporal truth. They often did this while treating other parts of the past as devoid of intrinsic truth and reflections of their sociopolitical context. The treatment of their own and historical subjective experiences as truth was in line with neo-Confucian thinkers such as Wang Yangming and the greater affirmation of the human being apart from a Confucian definition in twentieth-century China; as reflected in the writings of both more radical reformers like Hu Shi and the more moderate ones such as Liang Qichao and Liu Shipei.[21] Another reason to treat subjective experience as transtemporal value is perhaps that the vast social and political changes between the past and the present in China, and between China and the West, made identification with specific social practices across space or time much more difficult than an identification with human subjective experiences.

Zhu Xizu, who initially tried to create explicit and objective universal standards for history, found it easier to establish a universal framework of history based on intercultural subjective experience than an objective framework of truth. Zhu regarded Western historical classifications and methods as objective and universal and struggled to pattern Chinese history after them. A native of Zhejiang province, Zhu studied history at Waseda University in Tokyo starting in 1904. He became involved in anti-Manchu activities while there, met Zhang Taiyan in 1907, and became Zhang's student. He became secretary at the Educational Bureau of Zhejiang province after the 1911 revolution and was active in promoting the standardization of Chinese pronunciation before assuming a teaching position at Peking University.[22] Zhu was the first to introduce historical methodology to the History Department and wanted to find objective historical stages across cultures. When this proved difficult, he turned to categories describing universal human subjective experience. Following Lamprecht, Zhu argued that the stages of historical narrative comprised a dual process: the first began from genealogy and developed into chronicles, while the second began with epics and developed into biographies. But Chinese history could not neatly fit into this framework. In China, history began with the writing of poetry, followed by biography, genealogies, and ultimately chronicles, such as the *Spring and Autumn Annals*, in the Warring States period, and then moved on to the thematic narratives of the Song dynasty, which marked the highest achievement of Chinese history writing. The highest stage of historical writing, analyzing causal relationships, simply did not develop in China. Zhu also contrived, with little success, to fit Chinese histories into the pattern of Western topical histories: political, cultural, economic, military, intellectual, religious, literary, and business histories.[23]

The difficulty of drawing an exact parallel between Chinese histories and the "objective" historical criteria meant that Chinese history could not be made to reflect the "universal" characteristics of history. To solve the dilemma, Zhu again turned to Lamprecht, who had tried to introduce scientific positivism into historiography but retained a distinctively German subjective emphasis on history. A psychological description of history, fashionable in Germany, especially among neo-Kantians, argued that historical rules could be discovered in human consciousness. According to this approach, historical rules were objective, but objectivity existed only insofar as life objectified itself in the family, society, and so on.[24] Lamprecht was among the few who fought against an intuitive approach to history and championed the introduction of causal relationships. But he did not discard the subjective historical experience. Therefore although he could not use Lamprecht's description of historical stages, Zhu could identify with the subjective experiences that Lamprecht described, for instance, that history consisted of personal memories, especially those bearing on ancestry,[25] which Zhu applied to early Chinese poems devoted to ancestors before the Spring and Autumn period. Lamprecht's description of naturalistic history as growing from genealogy to chronology helped Zhu connect the early eulogies for ancestors with the later Spring and Autumn chronicles.[26] Although the gulf between feelings and the historical forms that expressed them seemed unbridgeable, a subjective identification with feelings *sans* the historical forms was indeed possible and helped to build a trans-cultural historical framework.

Chinese historiography also contains an identification with feelings expressed in history, especially literary history, with or without a necessary correlation with their historical forms of expression. Historically, literary appreciation had been treated as a means of perpetuating Confucian values, as literature did not have any independent value and was regarded as a vessel of Confucian standards. Generations of Chinese poets and essayists worked on rhetoric and rhyme and other matters of literary form. Many twentieth-century Chinese scholars also continued the study of literary expression but, instead of using literature to perpetuate Confucian values, they detached literary sentiment from Confucian values and tailored those values to individual personalities to accommodate human temperaments and natural tendencies. Even one of the most conservative faculty members, Huang Kan—professor of Chinese language and literature at Peking University from 1914 to 1919, an excellent textual philologist, and a student of literary criticism who staunchly fought against the creation of a vernacular—adhered to traditional literary forms and Confucian values, tempered by humanism and sometimes historicism. A Hubei native, Huang had a grandfather and father who were famous classicists. In the late Qing dynasty, he became an ardent nationalist, took part in anti-Manchu activities and fled arrest by the Qing government by going to Japan, where he became a student of Zhang Taiyan.[27] While there, Huang wrote extensively on Chinese culture in the journal *Tiger*. After his arrival at Peking University, Huang turned his political nationalism to cultural nationalism, combined with a cultural elitism that refused to bow to the popularization of culture. Huang vigorously attacked the vernacular movement, calling it the language of the rickshaw pullers and porridge sellers.

Huang offered a course on literary criticism in the form of commentaries on Liu Xie's *The Literary Mind and the Carving of Dragons* (*Wenxin diaolong*), a work written during the Northern and Southern Dynasties (420–589). Historically, literary criticism was of low status since literature, like history, was regarded as a vessel of the sages' wisdom and as such was not something to be analyzed dispassionately. In such an environment, literary criticism never developed into an independent subject of study. Huang's course thus represented something quite novel. Feng Youlan, who was to become a prominent Chinese philosopher, recalled that, as a student at Peking University, he found Huang's course an eye-opening experience.[28] Another of Huang's students, Gu Jiegang, reminisced that, during his student days at Peking University, one of the courses from which he benefited most was Huang Kan's course on the *Literary Mind and the Carving of Dragons*. The course was offered in an atmosphere where Confucian teachings were increasingly treated as documents of history that reflected the past, but Huang's close attention to literary form continued the traditional approach to literature. For men like Liu Xie, literature embodied the rules of the universe as revealed by Confucius. The proper writing technique facilitated the expression of these rules. Rhyme, for instance, was central to poetry because it aided memorization and conveyed sentiments that could not be grasped by unadorned writing alone. Clarity, beauty, and harmony of poetic styles all would contribute to the delivery of the message. Pomposity and grandeur, which originated from the life force of the poets, gave writing form and life that could be compared with the trajectory of a shooting arrow and the contours of a quickly running stream. Since writing was a reflection of the human heart and mind, parallelism was also natural to writing, just as parallels existed in nature, in human eyes and limbs.[29] Because of the moral importance of poetic expression, forms of expression were more or less static and deviations from them often meant a degradation of writing. Historical variations on the form were often criticized as a result. Despite the emphasis on form, Liu sought a greater merger between the individual poets and the morals expressed in these forms.

Like Liu, Huang was attentive to literary form and openly acknowledged admiration for Liu's endorsement of Confucian values. In choosing to identify with Liu Xie's classification of literary forms, however, Huang immortalized the act of literary appreciation, a subjective experience that acquired universal and transcendental meaning because of its linkage to particular literary forms. In his discussion of literary appreciation, Huang gave play to the influence on literary expression of individual personalities, local conditions, natural human tendencies, and so on. This allowed different uses of the same literary form. For instance, Huang argued that form in writing was premised on the author's personality. Thus a soft and gentle personality could not generate a harsh style, nor could courageous warriors write dark and pessimistic poetry. His concept of human nature also prevented Huang from consistently applying Confucian values as an absolute standard for judging poetry. In contrast to Liu Xie, who treated the poem "Encountering Sorrow" (*Li sao*) from the *Elegies of Chu* (*Chu ci*) as a paragon embodying the sages' morals and as a timeless example for all, Huang justified variations in poetry over time as natural. For instance, in his discussion of *yuefu*, which Liu Xie thought had been canonized in the *Book of Songs*, Huang agreed with Liu Xie that the *yuefu* in the *Book of Songs* were models of moderation and restraint. Yet Huang found Liu overcritical of *yuefu* that did not praise virtues but catered to more vulgar tastes. After all, Huang commented, it was human nature to like the vulgar and dislike the excessively refined. On this particular point, Huang sounded almost like a liberal in his championing of free expressions according to the writer's natural inclinations and in his rejection of a rigid ethics that dictated the sublimating sentiments. Such inconsistencies occurred several times in his commentary on the *Literary Mind and the Carving of Dragons*.[30]

In commenting on literary genres, Huang criticized Liu for overestimating the moral intent of the poetic form known as the *song* (颂, hymns and eulogies sung at sacrifices to gods and ancestral spirits of the royal house). Liu Xie believed that the *song* represented in the *Book of Songs* were composed in praise of the virtue and majestic appearance of the Zhou king. Although the precise content of the praise later varied, the purpose and the form remained unchanged. The form was abused starting from the poetry of such Han poets as Han Yu and Fu Yi, and Ma Rong from the Three Kingdoms period, when the moral message was not appropriately conveyed.[31] Huang disagreed with Liu that the *song* had to carry this strict moral purpose. Instead of treating *song* as a static form of poetry, Huang historicized its development, broadening its range from rhymed poetry to include satirical poems and even rhymed prose, all of which substantially departed from the ancient meaning of *song*. For Huang, each form of the *song* was legitimate and could not be ignored. Huang thus connected historical changes in poetic expression with changes in human experiences arising from environmental vicissitudes and human nature.[32]

Whereas Western schools of thought such as naturalism and individualism may have found their way into Huang's writings and encouraged a more historical treatment of the literary forms, Huang's focus was the eternity of literary expressions in certain forms. His historicism enabled him to allow different uses of the same literary forms while they still embodied the same transcendental values.

Unlike Huang, who idolized literary forms, Liu Shipei (professor of Chinese literature at Peking University from 1917 to 1919) immortalized individual poetic experiences in history. Like Huang Kan, Liu Shipei treated Liu Xie's *The Literary Mind* as a canon of literary expression. He shared with many Confucians throughout history the belief that literary forms conveyed a trans-historical Dao and that the literati's responsibility was to express himself fully in these forms. Literary writings, however, were not mere emotional expressions that followed set formats, but were based on many different elements, including one's temperament.[33] In other words, the writer of literature should carefully delineate things around him and, employing established literary formats, merge himself with his surroundings. A relationship between the author and his environment according to heavenly principles would follow as a matter of course. Literary expressions were thus configurations of relationships between humans and their social and natural environments. Unlike Huang Kan, who was preoccupied with literary forms and their definitions, Liu hardly discussed the forms per se but focused, instead, on how literary styles meshed with their sociopolitical contexts and those who used them. Liu historicized literary forms rather than trying to give each a set definition.

Liu's lack of attention to a strict definition and adherence to literary forms was corroborated by his radical attitude toward Confucian culture. Like Huang, Liu had been a radical and a nationalist, yet, unlike Huang, he borrowed from Western science and intellectual ideas from philosophers like Plato and

Rousseau and tried to fashion a national revival through a synthesis of these elements. Born in 1884, he was part of a family near Yangzhou that had long produced well-respected literati. After achieving *juren* status in 1902, he joined radical revolutionaries in Shanghai the following year and contributed to various journals, attacking the Qing government for, among other things, its failure to neutralize a Russian threat to northeastern China. One of his works, titled *Rangshu* (Treatise to Expel the Manchus, 1903), was on the expulsion of the Manchus from China.[34] In 1907, he joined the revolutionaries in Japan, where he worked with Zhang Binglin as coeditor of *People's Magazine* (*Ming bao*) and met Huang Kan, Lu Xun, and others. Liu championed gender equality and was married to a feminist.

Opposed to the Qing government, Liu sought a revival of Han history and literature. He and Huang Jie, joined the Southern Society (*Nanshe*), a patriotic poetry society established in 1909 to oppose the Qing government.[35] Liu Shipei also wrote many political treatises. His articles in the journal *Natural Justice* (*Yongyan*, a journal sponsored by Liang Qichao and based in Tianjin early in the twentieth century) illustrated his social vision of an ideal community that resembled Plato's *The Republic* and Rousseau's *The Social Contract*.[36] Except for the absence of Plato's social classes and their immutable division of labor in society, Liu's society resembled Plato's republic with respect to childrearing and shared Plato's goal to gear individual life to the goal of the state. As with Rousseau's general will in *The Social Contract*, Liu sacrificed individual liberty to gain absolute equality in order to form authentic general will of the people. This, in turn, would strengthen the people and protect them from despotism. Liu's concern with strengthening the people reflected his assessment that China's weakness lay in its economic inferiority relative to other countries. Liu also sought to reform China by using history. He was aware of the tremendous power of historicism to rid China of a Confucian past. Liu wrought precisely such a change by dismissing the Confucian style of history and the Confucian idols—the Zhou dynasty kings—and by associating a historical golden age with the pre-Confucian Yellow Emperor. In his articles on national essence written between 1905 and 1907, Liu delineated an idealized Chinese past in the age of the Yellow Emperor, when people were equal, wealth was shared, and land belonged to all. This ideal society disintegrated when the rulers became more self-interested and the majority of people became lazy.[37] Patterned after Huang Zongxi's glorification of the Yellow Emperor in his *Plan for the Prince* (*Mingyi daifanglu*), Liu's historicization of the Yellow Emperor actually resembled the historical myths of ancient China constructed by both Confucius and Terrien de Lacouperie, who located the beginning of China in the person of the Yellow Emperor. In Terrien de Lacouperie's history, the Yellow Emperor became someone who had moved his tribe from Mesopotamia. Thus the Chinese culture established by the Yellow Emperor was non-Chinese in origin. By this fiction, Terrien de Lacouperie denied the ability of indigenous Chinese to construct a glorious civilization. Liu Shipei, as well as Zhang Binglin and many others, accepted his theory out of a desire to find an authoritative alternative to Confucianism: if the Confucians proclaimed the Zhou dynasty the ideal society, Liu and others had to select, or conjure up, a different ideal society for emulation, although Liu tried to downplay the point that Chinese culture was not created by the Chinese.[38] Terrien de Lacouperie was useful for having pointed the way toward inherent virtue in Chinese culture despite its decline. Liu and those who thought like him believed that this decline was due to the intervention of Confucian learning toward the end of the Zhou dynasty, when the Yellow Emperor's social order was swept away. In this scheme, Confucius became the culprit for the immutability and sterility of imperial China. By contrast, other ancient Chinese philosophers became paragons of virility and spirit, equivalent to their contemporaries, the classical Greek philosophers. Through such a history, Liu intended to uncover the true past and thus to stimulate a cultural renaissance.[39]

In many of his writings, Liu Shipei treated history and literature as reflections of their historical contexts. One example is his *A History of Medieval Chinese Literature* (*Zhongguo zhonggu wenxueshi*). The subject of Liu's book, the history of Chinese literature from the Wei and Jin dynasties to the end of the Southern dynasty (roughly from the early third century to the end of the sixth century), was the same as the topic later researched by Tang Yongtong and others, including Hu Shi. The external environment for writers had a tremendous impact on their writing styles. The preference of the Ling emperor of the Han dynasty for parallel prose led countless writers to churn out works in this style. Although Daoist writings influenced literature during the Wei kingdom, the severe legal rule by the Wu king of Wei kingdom gradually reduced that metaphysical frivolity in literary writings, making the latter clear and simple. A sophist writing style developed in poetry writing during the time of the Xiandi emperor in the Han dynasty, when ambitious commoners who wanted to commend themselves to the emperor's service started the style of sophist arguments. In addition to emperors' policies and personal preferences, society also influenced writing styles. The social disintegration and decline of social customs and habits during the Three Kingdoms period (220–280), for instance, stimulated writings lamenting what had been lost. Intellectual currents also played an important role in shaping writing styles. For instance, Daoist and Buddhist metaphysics not only guided the content of philosophical writings of men such as Wang Bi, He Yan, Qi Kang, and Ran Ji but also influenced their writing styles. Wang Bi and He Yan, influenced by Daoists and by Legalists, were clear and concise and employed both clear thinking and literary frills. Ji Kang and Ran Ji, by contrast, wrote in a grand and powerful style that elaborated on

Daoism but actually more closely resembled the sophists.[40] Despite political fragmentation during the Wei and Jin dynasties, in Liu's view, China continued to enjoy great continuity with the past.

This continuity, however, lay more in subjective experience than anything else: faced with similar circumstances, people responded in similar ways. Thus people who came later could readily understand and identify with sentiments of their forebears. Liu premised his focus on human feelings on the universality of human nature, a notion, he believed, that could be found both in Confucianism and in Western social science from the Enlightenment to nineteenth-century positivism. His respect for his own subjectivity and his own moral judgment related to his affirmation of the individual with its own space, although Liu believed as well that the individual was also linked to other individuals in the universe into a larger self.[41] Thus despite changes in society over time, the permanence of human feelings and their expression created a continuity that cut across time and space. The correlation between personality and form of expression was also trans-temporal, making possible its repetition in history. Liu closely examined such correlations in his historical narrative of the writers of the Three Kingdoms period: Wang Can was "sharp and impatient" (*zao rui*), thus his writing style was "quick and his talent shot through it" (*ying chu er cai guo*); Liu Zhen was "narrowminded" (*qi bian*), thus his words were "grand and his feelings overwhelming" (*yan zhuang er qing hai*); and Lu Ji was "prudent and careful" (*jin zhong*), thus his "feelings were sophisticated and words shifty" (*qing fan er ci yin*); his brother, Lu Yun, was "easy and quick" (*qing min*), thus his "words were sharp and his style smooth" (*feng fa er yun liu*).[42] Each individual, in his own style of expression, embodied rules that also governed the universe. The importance that Liu attached to individual experience led him to conclude that an understanding of one's own nature would provide a moral compass for guiding behavior.[43] Similar personalities and correspondingly similar self-expressions in history perpetuated certain moral themes despite changes in society and politics.

If Liu's history reflected the subjective experience of poetry writing, Huang Jie's history of poetry reflected how that subjective experience was perpetuated in history. A professor of Chinese literature at Peking University (1916–26, 1928–35), Huang was one of the cofounders of the *National Essence Journal* (*guocui xuebao*) in 1904 and of the Southern Society, and a radical revolutionary first opposed to the Manchu regime and then against Yuan Shikai's restoration of the empire. After the Manchurian Incident of 1931, in addition to what he regularly offered, Huang often taught patriotic poetry by early Qing scholars such as Gu Yanwu to inspire his students. Having expended his energies in the cause of China's future, he died in 1935.[44] Huang's historicism was permeated with a concern for the subjective poetic experience in history, which he saw as a product of environment and temperament. Huang discussed the perpetuation of the poetic styles of Han Yu and Du Fu of the Tang dynasty by Ouyang Xiu, Wang Anshi, and Su Shi during different stages of the northern Song, and the style of Yang Wanli during the Tang by Lu You during the Song dynasty. Poetic characteristics were associated with individual poets who passed them along.[45]

Huang's depiction of a linear passage of poetic styles showed his preoccupation with poetic forms. Compared to Liu Shipei, who was concerned with the timelessness of certain poetic experiences, however, Huang noted how those experiences were preserved and perpetuated, often through random events. His focus on the specific passage of these experiences showed a different emphasis: not Liu's display of faith in them, but a greater concern for their precarious existence, which implied the need for an agenda of action to consciously preserve certain historical experiences through their reenactment. Huang believed that poetry was to teach temperamental cultivation through classics like *The Elegies of Chu* and application of moral messages in the poetry to oneself.[46] He found those moral messages in individual poets' writing styles that suited their temperaments.

If Liu Shipei depicted the applicability of the past to the present by a subjective identification achieved through literary appreciation, Qian Mu (professor of Chinese history at Peking University beginning in 1931) portrayed subjectivity as a more distinctly historical process, considering it a gradual deepening of identification with historical experience. Compared to the iconoclast Liu, Qian paid more attention to the historical changes in Confucian moral experience. From the beginning of his tenure at the university, Qian taught a course called "Three Hundred Years of Qing Intellectual Thought" on the progress of the moral experience of conscience in Qing history. The course was a response to one with the same name at Qinghua University offered by Liang Qichao. In his course, Liang had dismissed the importance of moral experience in his discussion of the Qing scholars' development of the idea of *liangzhi* (innate knowledge, conscience) or a historical continuity in subjective moral experience. In fact, the intellectual histories of both Liang Qichao and Qian Mu were teleological: both described a natural and inevitable development of Chinese history, and both aimed to chart an autonomous history for China. They differed principally in the degree of autonomy that they assigned to Chinese history. Liang argued that this autonomy did not exclude a historical interchange between Western and Chinese historical ideas, nor did it exclude analogical historical developments. Thus he analyzed Qing intellectual history in the framework of the European Renaissance, seeing the rise of Qing thought as a reaction to the metaphysical learning of the Song and Ming dynasties that aimed to restore antiquity and acquire knowledge from the outside world. Qing thought gathered momentum along the way and established itself as the new orthodoxy, although it ultimately declined and yielded to the ideas of Western science.[47] Qian Mu, by contrast, maintained that intellectual development in the Qing dynasty was completely autonomous. The rupture between Song and Qing learning that Liang described did not exist; Qing scholars only perfected Song learning, using the traditional framework of Confucian moral experience.

Liang and Qian arrived at different conclusions largely because of their different handling of Confucian moral experience. Liang treated moral experience in Chinese history more from the detached point of view of an observer: it appeared to him as a form of knowledge rather than something he could identify with in his work. Qian, however, used moral experience as his frame of reference. The moral experience in question, *liangzhi,* lay within human nature and needed only to be cultivated in order to be realized. In Liang's view, however, it became more of an objective concept resembling external knowledge, rather than human conscience. Acquiring *liangzhi* meant searching for truth not from within one's heart but in historical materials. Many Qing scholars, Liang argued, departed from the Ming tendency toward moralization and decided that knowledge should be sought in facts. Huang Zongxi and Gu Tingling, for instance, were exhaustive in their search for historical materials. Others even adopted a critical approach to learning by comparing different historical texts. On the whole, Qing scholarship represented a departure from the empty moralization of the Ming dynasty.[48]

Qian Mu took a fundamentally different position: he regarded *liangzhi* as a part of daily experience, rather than as objective knowledge. His was a history of how Qing scholars adopted the concept of *liangzhi* from Mencius and perfected it. Mencius, Lao Zi, and Zhuang Zi had interpreted the Dao as something still, the essence of the universe. The Dao was not, Qian claimed, something within human nature, but was a quest for *liangzhi.* In Qian's history, Qing scholars who emphasized the exertion of moral efforts progressively relocated *liangzhi* from human nature to somewhere outside human nature. Qian tried to show that morality, rather than being an innate quality, should be approached in terms of actual moral experience. Huang Zongxi, an early Qing scholar, described striving to lead a moral life as closely intertwined with the essentially good human character. Wang Fuzhi carried the argument further, contending that human nature itself did not matter as much as human efforts. Good deeds constituted human character. Dai Zhen defined Dao as constant movement between heaven and earth and man. Dai located *li* (reason) within this movement, although he later abandoned this position and argued that both reason and conscience would lie within human nature. But Zhang Xuecheng eliminated the idea of *liangzhi*: there was no set or particularly desirable innate knowledge or conscience. The sages did not set the criteria because they were not naturally good and had their own constraints. The Dao was something that came naturally to everyone, not necessarily after the sage, for everyone faced different constraints in self-cultivation.[49]

Although Qian set out to defend the Chinese moral experience of conscience, his description of the progressive development of conscience in Qing thought culminated in something that had no set definition at all. While upholding the importance of conscience as moral experience, Qian left open the content of conscience. Moreover, the historical examples he offered of the various definitions of conscience, despite the specificity of each, all pointed to the definition championed by Zhang Xuecheng. Each individual's experience contributed to a progressive transformation of conscience from innate nature to moral experience as an end in itself. Qian adhered to the historically Confucian theme of conscience, yet his emphasis on experience allowed for the existence of different expressions of the concept, as understood by each individual. This emphasis also allowed for a greater identification with the historical experience of conscience by Qian and his contemporaries.

In fact, Qian's own life story consisted of constant experiments with moral themes. In this respect, he could identify with the Qing thinkers that he wrote about in terms of the change in their progressive development of the definition of conscience, from an internal to an external quest. The intellectual landscape changed enormously in Qian's lifetime, and he reacted accordingly. As Jerry Dennerline has described it, Qian spent the first half of his life in the tumultuous China of the early twentieth century while trying to adapt, in his own way, to the sweeping changes around him. Qian graduated from a modern high school in southern China in the first decade of the twentieth century. Afterward he taught primary school and high school near his hometown for around twenty years. Throughout those years, he closely followed trends in Chinese historical studies, going so far as to obtain history textbooks from Peking University in the hope that he might study there one day. It was in these textbooks that he first encountered Zhang Xuecheng, whose writings said that all Confucian classics were records of the history of the sage's time. At one point in his teaching career, when he learned of Dewey's visit to China and his educational theories, he even started an experiment in a primary school to see how it would affect the pupils if he encouraged them to do their work on their own initiative. It was also during his years as a primary school teacher that he read other avant-garde Qing scholarship, including Yan Fu's translation of Western works and Sun Yirang's philological works, which incorporated such studies as tortoise-shell engravings and engravings on bronze and stone stalae into the textual analysis of the classical works. Such works inspired Qian to rethink ancient Chinese history. The publications that flowed from this rethinking caught the attention of Gu Jiegang, then one of China's leading historians, to the point that Gu helped Qian Mu locate a job teaching history first at Yanjing University and then at Peking University.[50]

Although Qian was not a thoroughgoing historicist, he used history to build greater identification between his personal experiences and historical moral experiences. His history of Qing intellectual development served a double purpose: to show an autonomous and historically continuous Chinese intellectual development and to build experiential continuity between himself and the people about whom he wrote. The transtemporal moral experience that Qian fashioned seemed to negate the historically unique experiences of each individual. Nevertheless, historicism played an important role in Qian's transtemporal experience, allowing variation in the definition of moral conscience. Furthermore, by allowing for changes in the expression of morality, historicism revealed how the moral concept of conscience withstood the onslaught of dramatic changes in Chinese society: despite their variety, all the expressions of morality that Qian depicted revolved around the exercise of conscience.

## Conclusion

This chapter addresses the issue of finding permanent values in the largely concrete, textual exegetical-style histories in early twentieth-century China. The extensive, textual exegetical and historical approaches to Chinese history threatened to present a fragmented Chinese history. Some historians sought a transcendental universal value system to impart meaning to the concrete histories that they wrote. Western, especially German, philosophy provided the theoretical justification for such a transcendental value framework. Tang Yongtong's writings were an example. Unwilling to accept Confucian values as they were, or Western values in their direct and concrete form as universal, a transcendental value system seemed to provide room for both free exploration of history and justification for the meaning of history. Others chose to reify values in the literary or philosophical experiences in history to prevent an atomization of history. There was a tendency, on the whole, to focus on subjective historical experiences, using them to create historical continuity or compatibility. In the case of Zhu Xizu, the greater similarities between human experiences than their historical forms of expressions enabled him to borrow from German historical concepts about human experience to analyze Chinese historical genres. In the cases of Liu Shipei, Huang Jie, and Qian Mu, a similarity of subjective experience through time and individual reenactments of literary or historical expressions over time maintained historical continuity despite change. In their search for permanent values through a reification of ideas in history, these historians' writings were influenced by individualism, humanism, and historicism, so the new values that they shaped were indelibly stamped with a mixture of Chinese and Western influences.

# 7

# Confucian Moral Cultivation, Science, and Social Relevance

## The Search for an Organizing Principle for the Disciplines of Education and Psychology (1910s–1930s)

Cai Yuanpei's university system was premised on a body of pure/theoretical knowledge, which ultimately would aid nationalism and benefit society through the creation of a non-utilitarian culture that avoided the biased political focus on material prosperity and other more tangible results. This university system suffered from a failure to define a meaningful relationship between the university and society, a problem that would become prominent in the 1920s, when new departments based on a rationale of social relevance were developed. This chapter deals with two such departments, education and psychology, and how they struggled to find their niche at the university.

Significant changes began to occur in the Philosophy Department in the mid-1920s, when education and psychology broke away to form independent departments in 1924 and 1926, respectively. The rationale for the splits came from new educational theories in the United States in the 1920s. Americanization swept through Chinese education in the early 1920s especially during and after a lecture tour by John Dewey from 1919 to 1921. This occurred at a time when many students who had studied in the United States returned to China and assumed teaching positions in leading Chinese universities. A high proportion of them had studied at the Columbia University Teachers' College, where Dewey taught, and they were responsible for introducing Dewey's ideas in China as well as making possible his tour in China. American education was distinguished by a single-track system, in contrast to the dual-track European system that China employed until 1919. Nor did it have a hierarchical educational structure that distinguished between state and local universities or limited the number of universities in a given region, as the French educational system did. Fired by the possibility of raising their own status, many Chinese educators embraced the American educational system and pushed the Ministry of Education to approve its adoption, which took place in 1919. Many provincial senior high and normal schools were upgraded to universities. Before 1921, because of state restrictions there were only five state universities and eight private universities. But by 1926, the number of state universities had increased to thirty-seven, most as a result of upgrades of secondary schools, and private universities also mushroomed.[1] European influence on the Chinese educational structure seemed to be overshadowed by the American educational system, although the European influence never completely disappeared.

The American educational system was adopted because of its claim to social improvement. Following the emphasis on social service was that on educational methods, which led to the emergence of educational departments at almost all major universities. In 1922, the Department of Philosophy at National Peking University divided its curriculum into three fields: philosophy, psychology, and education. Compared to the philosophy section, education focused more on servicing society in practical ways. One of the goals of the field of education was the training of schoolteachers. Courses in education, in addition to those on methodology shared with the other two fields—such as scientific methods and effects, biology, and evolution—included educational history, educational methods in middle schools, school administration, rural education, elementary education, and educational testing.[2] The practical orientation of these courses contrasted with the classical approach in the philosophy courses. It was not surprising that it was decided the following year that education would become independent from the Department of Philosophy. Even before Chen Daqi, the Philosophy Department chair, announced the split, the students in the department had suggested in June 1923 the addition of more specific educational courses, such as educational administration, statistics, teaching methodology, elementary, rural, and tertiary education, secondary school organization, discussions of Chinese education. They also suggested education internships and that a newly established experimental high school in Beijing, called Kongde School (named after Auguste Comte), be affiliated with Peking University so that experimental education could be conducted there.[3]

The Department of Education was formally initiated in 1924. In addition to requiring some of the same courses as the philosophy curriculum, the education curriculum required specialized courses such as education and child psychology, educational methods, educational administration, and testing.[4] More courses were added to the curriculum for the academic year 1926–27, and the course on educational statistics, which was previously an elective, became required, as did a new course on experimental education.[5] In 1926, the Psychology Department became independent, which was related to the experimental orientation increasingly assumed by the curriculum and pushed psychology farther from its classical moorings in philosophy.

The separation of education and psychology from the Department of Philosophy not only indicated a greater specialization of knowledge but also instilled in the university direct social service that Cai Yuanpei had not anticipated. However, this introduction occurred toward the end of his tenure at the university, when he was mostly absent, residing in Germany, France, and elsewhere. Jiang Menglin took the changes more in stride. Yet he did not resolve an inherent problem in the introduction of these two Western and applied disciplines. For all his attempts to build a transcendental level of knowledge uniting the specific areas of learning, Cai Yuanpei had inherited Zhang Zhidong's definition of Chinese learning, not in content, but in structure: subjects of learning traditionally associated with Confucianism, including the classics, history, philology, literature, and philosophy. Zhang's instrumental excision of practical subjects, such as traditional Chinese science and technology, in favor of practical branches of Western learning led to the impression that Western practical learning was introduced not to elevate the practical but to achieve a Western-style social outcome and precisely because it was Western. In his defense of a body of pure knowledge to serve as the rationale for the university's autonomous authority in society, Cai had not intended to introduce any form of applied learning, either Chinese or Western.

Therefore, when the departments of education and psychology came into being, they lacked support from the university's cultural milieu, which endorsed pure learning. They struggled to develop their own identity, from an early association with moral cultivation to a later objective rationalization of human behavior through hardcore science.

## Psychology and Moral Cultivation: The Case of Yang Changji

Western psychological theories were initially introduced in China to enhance the self-cultivation of scholars' temperaments. Historically, Confucians had always explored the workings of the mind in order to regulate emotions and behavior. They believed that positive emotions were important in helping one achieve correct perceptions of the world. Self-cultivation through music, poetry, painting, and calligraphy could help eliminate negative emotions (such as anger, confusion, and jealousy) and avoid provocation by external circumstance.[6] Psychology, by providing one with greater self-knowledge, became appealing to many scholars as a method of avoiding the negative emotions. As early as 1903 Zhang Zhidong had introduced to Peking University courses in psychology, taught initially by two Japanese instructors.[7] Then they were not taught again until 1918. From 1918 to 1919, ethics courses taught by Yang Changji, professor of education, incorporated elements of Western psychology. Yang believed that the study of psychology helped both with self-cultivation and with expanding his understanding of the world, and in 1915, he translated a portion of Herbert Spencer's writings on feelings.

Born in 1871 in a village in Hunan, Yang came from a family of a long line of scholars. His great-great-grandfather and great-grandfather were both graduates from government schools, and the former was a bookkeeper of records of learning (*xuelu*) at the Qing Imperial College (*Guozijian*).[8] Beginning in his early childhood, Yang was taught Confucianism and neo-Confucianism, as well as studying the writings of the contemporary Confucian statesman Zeng Guofan—who represented the ideal scholar-statesman, a practitioner of self-cultivation.[9] In 1898, while studying at Yuelu College (*Yuelu shuyuan*) specializing in Confucian studies, he joined the Southern Society (*Nan she*) in Hunan, where he discussed ideas regarding the masses and the fundamentals of ethics with Tan Citong, a fellow Hunanese and a cofounder of the Southern Society, and with others. In 1903, having witnessed the Qing government's suppression of reform and execution of those who supported it, including Tan, he went to Japan, where he hoped to find the right approach to reforming China.[10] This trip was the beginning of his ten-year sojourn abroad, in Japan (six years), Britain (three years), and Germany (nine months).[11] He returned to China in 1913 and from then until 1917 taught ethics, psychology, and education at the Higher Normal School in Changsha, Hunan, where he befriended the young Mao Tse-tung, then a student there. A fellow student of Yang's at the University of Edinburgh and later a senior lecturer of logic at Peking University, Zhang Shizhao, in 1917, recommended to Cai Yuanpei that Yang be invited to teach ethics, which Cai did.[12]

Psychology remained Yang's prime interest after his return to China, as reflected in his lectures on ethics and personal cultivation. In his diary entry for 1915, he gave a systematic reading of Western works on psychology, such as those by Herbert Spencer and Alexander Bain, especially their sections on emotions. In April of that year, he began translating sections of Spencer on feelings—the first time he had translated anything from English, which he termed "transmitting civilization." From then on, his diaries for both 1915 and 1919 documented his readings of psychology, ethics, and philosophy by English, American, and German writers. He believed that psychology supplemented ethics in contributing to better human self-cultivation. Like any good Confucian scholar, Yang sought a rational explanation for human behavior, and psychology helped rationalize religious emotions. Yang commented in one entry that religion, as explained in psychology, developed as a response to fear: ancient savages, fearing storms and thunder, made up rituals to worship those things in order to escape harm.[13]

In the two years before his death in early 1920, Yang taught ethics, a required course for the Humanities Division, and the history of ethics, an elective course.[14] In an October 1919 diary entry, he pondered the improvement of his lectures on ethics but did not live to put his new approaches into effect. In an outline of lectures, He used ethics as arena for delivering observations on a wide range of topics, including:

> sanctity of labor, part-time work during study, saving the country through material means, science, administration by the people, mutual help, liberty, equality, and fraternity, democracy . . . , no visit to prostitutes, no permitting of concubines, no gambling, far-sightedness, solid work, industriousness, benevolence and kindness, the definitions and boundaries of ethics, the rules of morals, responsibility, conscience, . . . , freedom of will, virtue, the relationship between individual and society, the relationship between men and women, the issue of women, . . . the theories of materialism, absolute idealism, . . . life, broad learning, . . . the criteria of good and bad, appreciation of self, . . . practice, courage, . . . personality, respect for the old, affection for the young.[15]

Topics relating to psychology could be spotted in several places on this rambling list of the areas of ethics that Yang intended to cover in his course and contributed to building the ideal Confucian gentleman's worldview. His focus on ethical behavior was similar to that of ethics committees established in Beijing in the early twentieth century, including the Morality Promotion Committee, established by Cai Yuanpei in 1918.

## Evolution, Behaviorism, and Educational Tests in the 1920s

When Yang Changji was ruminating over Western writings on psychology in terms of self-cultivation, in the late 1910s and 1920s, experimental psychology and hardcore behaviorism were getting a warm reception in China, which also affected the Peking University campus. Experimental psychology focused on the connections between human behavior and tangible, observable factors such as physiological processes and the environment. Its successor, the various behaviorist schools, applied a positivist approach to psychology. Inspired by the Darwinian evolutionary theory that the development of living organisms depended on their adaptation to the environment, behaviorism treated human thinking as a function of the environment. Developed to the extreme, this approach treated the external world as the source of stimuli to which the mind responded by adaptation. Such an approach represented an attempt to trace the genetic development of certain mental powers, memory, and imagination through external or externally induced stimulation and human response.[16] From 1926 to 1927, in the first year after the Department of Psychology became independent, both behavioral and quantitative methods were more extensively employed than before. The required courses, besides those in philosophy, now included a greater emphasis on physiology, physiological psychology, psychological experiments, and educational testing. Even the survey course on psychology, taught by Fan Jichang, an advocate of behaviorism, focused more than before on the physiological basis of behavior and stimulus-response. The course on social psychology, which previously favored the theory of instinct, now, taught by Xie Xunchu, was refocused to take a more stimulus-response approach on how society changed human nature and shaped personalities. The course on IQ testing, employing American educational testing methods and models, covered topics ranging from students' IQ, alternative testing methods, and regular examinations to studies in the correlation between personality and moral behavior.[17]

Many in China sought to use experimental psychology as a means of exerting the social authority of Chinese scholars in a different way from that of Confucian moral and ethical practices. Behaviorism, by virtue of its external observation of the mental processes, seemed to offer objective accountability. That experimental psychology and stimulus-response theory were championed not just by university educators but also by many primary and secondary school teachers indicated the appeal of those theories, often perhaps as pedagogy and ideology, to the educators of the new schools. Historically, Confucian scholars combated Buddhism and Buddhist interpretations of Confucian learning with what they conceived of as a rational explanation of the world. In the twentieth century, finding a rational explanation for human behavior continued to be an important task for Chinese scholars, who now used experimental psychology to combat religion and superstition, just as Confucianism had been used earlier.

One of the first Chinese translators of Western experimental psychology was Chen Daqi, a professor of philosophy at Peking University in the late 1910s. Chen used theories of experimental psychology to deal with supernatural worship and practices, which were popular in the 1910s because of political instability and a spiritual vacuum in the wake of the downfall of the imperial system. Chen believed the superstitious practices would harm China's future and wanted to eliminate them with scientific explanations.[18] In particular, he battled divination and the worship of ghosts in various forms. Experimental psychology provided Chen Daqi with a means of attacking such practices by observing the physiological movements of the diviners during their practices and thus discovering what was attributed to supernatural intervention in these people's own movements.

Chen used the idea of bodily functions or movements, such as digestion, the heartbeat, and the movement of muscles—which are not directly perceptible or, in some cases, subject to conscious control—to explain away what was assumed by the man in the street to be communication with supernatural beings. Chen cited the example of divination, wherein a person inquiring about his fortune through "randomly" picking up a bamboo chip was not aware that it was the movements of his own muscles, which he did not directly perceive, that helped him make the selection.[19] Chen's point was that the human unconscious followed definable rules that were rooted in the world of human physiology.

Born in 1887 in Haiyan, Zhejiang province, Chen Daqi was tutored in the traditional Chinese style as a youth. In 1900, he entered the language school attached to the Jiangnan Manufacturing Company that had a modern curriculum on Chinese and English. In 1903, moved by *The Revolutionary Army* (*Geming jun*) by the radical Zou Rong, which attacked the Chinese imperial government for having lost control of China to foreign countries, Chen went to Japan. From 1903 to 1909, he studied, first, Japanese and the science subjects in Tokyo, and, then, English, German, law, and economics at the Second High School in Sendai, a preparatory school for university study. In 1909, he entered the Imperial Tokyo University philosophy section in the humanities division and learned the difference between the East and West in philosophy. Influenced by a psychology professor, Chen became intensely interested in psychology, choosing it as his major, and logic and sociology as minors. He graduated from Imperial Tokyo University with a bachelor's degree in psychology in 1912 and shortly thereafter returned to China to head Zhejiang High School. He was not there long before he joined the preparatory school division of the Beijing Institute of Law and Politics (*Beijing fazheng zhuanmen xuexiao*) to teach psychology and logic. In the summer of 1914, at the invitation of President Hu Renyuan, Chen went to Peking University to teach philosophy, psychology, logic, and, later, epistemology and narrative psychology. In 1921, he left for a year's study at the University of Berlin. Upon his return, he became chairman of the Department of Philosophy. In 1927, he became the university provost (*jiaowuzhang*). In 1929, after the Nationalist government grouped universities in Peking into a district system headed by Beiping University, an amalgamation of universities in and near the city, Chen was made deputy president of Beiping University. The following year, after Peking University was revived, he became the deputy president for a year before he resigned to assume a job he had held earlier in his career as secretariat of the State Examination Institute, which administered examinations for the selection of civil servants in the Nationalist government.[20]

Chen turned to experimental psychology because modern psychology challenged the human ability of observation. Since this human ability lay at the very basis of the Confucian ethical description of the human being, a new rational explanation of human thinking and behavior needed to be found, and experimental psychology, with its scientific rationality, seemed to be the answer. Modern psychology's depiction of the fallible human mind shook Chen's belief in the ethical human mind as preached by Confucius. Chen employed contemporary psychological theories to illustrate how human physiology limited human sensations and perceptions—for example, the perception of a moving light and of distance. Chen warned for awareness of the limitations of the human mind. For instance, Chen commented on two kinds of judgments: one based on values and the other on facts. Qualities derived from sensual experience, such as smell, sound, color, heat, and cold, as John Locke pointed out, were not innate qualities of things but human experience. Human perceptions were correct, Chen believed, to the extent that they corresponded to reality.[21]

Elsewhere, Chen defined truth as the relationship between thought and reality, corresponding but not identical. Human experience of heat and cold and other phenomena were largely a result of external stimuli and did not reflect external reality. Thought, although deriving from such sensation and perception, was several levels removed from them. Thus two people subjected to the same external stimuli could have very different responses.[22] He also laid out criteria that could measure whether an external object of human experience actually existed: whether it was confirmable either by directly perceiving it or by indirectly proving its existence; and whether its existence was confirmed by all objective criteria so that it did not just represent subjective opinion.[23]

He differentiated between objective judgments based on different degrees of conviction. A higher degree of conviction would often lead one to an absolute judgment.[24] Here, Chen emphasized the need for personal awareness of the subjective elements infused in one's seemingly objective judgments. His awareness of the limitations of human observation and thinking made Chen turn to experimental psychology to fulfill what ethical Confucian learning could no longer accomplish. A Chinese scholar's moral responsibility drove him to find a new way to implement human moral behavior. Moral concern prevented Chen from giving a full account of the result of his questionnaire in a 1918 survey at girls' higher primary schools in Beijing on child awareness of moral standards. In the charts that Chen made, he listed only what he thought were correct answers; all the rest he classified as ambivalent or incorrect. He listed the percentage of the latter in the answers, but did not give their content at all.[25] Apparently, Chen felt that since they did not need to be imitated, the "wrong answers" did not need to be known.[26]

Constant moral behavior depended on the rationality of human thinking. The Confucian and Mencian emphasis on the ethical nature of the human heart guaranteed the moral basis of human behavior. If human behavior were inherently irrational, it would be hard to regulate it or demand moral behavior. Experimental psychology, by providing a rational explanation of human behavior from a physiological point of view, provided Chinese scholars like Chen Daqi with a means of understanding human behavior and therefore devise ways to regulate it for moral purposes. First championed by physiologists such as Wilhelm Wundt at the University of Leipzig in the late nineteenth century, and based on the study of the connection between the mind and physiology, experimental psychology differed from another influential school of behaviorism—social psychology—that placed greater emphasis on the a priori existence of complex emotions like fear and love that motivated human behavior. By the 1920s, the uncertainty of innate thoughts turned many psychologists away from social psychology. The best-known experimental psychologist was Wundt, whose perspective emphasized that human consciousness was caused by external stimuli of the sensory organs. These elements were then transformed into an organized and coherent experience through conscious perception and creative synthesis, often accompanied by physiological processes.[27] Wundt's emphasis was on the diversity of external stimuli and how they caused different sensations and perceptions.[28]

Embracing Wundtian theory, Chinese scholars failed to notice its fine distinction between hypothesis and factual statement. Because the degree of complexity of human consciousness could not be completely revealed in his experiments, Wundt described the dimensions of consciousness that he defined as more metaphorical descriptions of what was happening than what really happened. There was never a time when one could actually see the operation of those dimensions, which he believed always acted in combination with one another.[29] Chen Daqi, by contrast, disregarded the uncertainty and hypothetical tone of Wundt's description and posited a definite and fixed relationship between the stages from sensation to thought. Feelings were rooted in various sensations; emotions comprised a compound of feelings. Perceptions were the result of a process of compounding sensations, and conceptions were associations of perceptions. All were rooted in and affected by the human biological processes.[30] Although Wundt tried to *explain* thinking in physiological terms, Chen sought to *root* thinking in physiology and external stimuli.

Chen's pursuit of a definite connection between external stimuli and inner mental processes, as mentioned earlier, represented his search for the certainty of thought prompted by his moral concern for human ability to grasp truth and to regulate human behavior for moral purposes. That truth is within human grasp and that there is absolute certainty to human thinking are paramount conditions for making Confucian morality possible. Confucian morality not only referred to specific moral conduct but also was premised on a belief in an almost "omnipotent" moral being. This belief in the "moral omnipotence" of human beings not only made many Chinese shun Christianity but also was cause for the heated debates within the Confucian school of thought in the Song and Ming dynasties because some Song Confucians, influenced by Buddhism, relied on a more transcendental interpretation of truth instead of rooting it directly in the human heart, as Mencius did earlier.

Chen's attempt to conceive of human thinking as a certainty through experimental psychology preceded the widespread welcome given to American behaviorism in China in the 1920s, when many Chinese students started to return to China from their studies in the United States. These students favored the stimulus-response school of behaviorism and played down or attacked other branches of psychology, such as Freud's psychoanalysis, as well as soft-core behaviorism, such as social psychology, that did not depend on experiments and external observation. Stimulus-response (S-R) attributed almost all inner-thinking processes to observable, humanly manipulated external stimuli. In this it differed from Wundtian psychology, which still acknowledged the validity of introspection and did not insist on such a close relationship between external stimuli and human response. The S-R school in the United States combined a scientific positivism and a zeal for social engineering. John Watson and other members of the school treated thinking as a function of external stimuli completely manipulable by psychologists, hence susceptible to social control.[31] Many scholars who subscribed to this view were able to conduct experiments because of the Wundtian streak that permeated their thinking. Many American physiological behaviorists, such as Edward Thorndike and Lewis Terman, were students of G. Stanley Hall, Hugo Munsterberg, and William James, among others, who had been trained in physiology under Wundt in Leipzig. It has been said that these physiologists turned themselves into psychologists, in both Germany and the United States, because of an oversupply of doctors at the turn of the century.[32] Thus physiology strongly influenced their study of psychology. Their primary work was in the technical process by which a stimulus is translated into a response.

To the Chinese propagators of these ideas—such as Guo Renyuan, a Columbia-trained professor of education and psychology at National Southeastern University, and probably the most famous behaviorist in China in the 1920s—the virtue of stimulus-response experiments lay in their observability. Experimentation, they believed, not only would widen the understanding of innate processes but also would put the study of the latter on a surer basis, since experiments could be replicated.[33] Behavior arising from instinct, however, was less fathomable. Guo criticized the American champions of S-R, such as John Watson, for attempting to explain the behavior of children with instinct theory and for otherwise failing to abandon the concept of instinct theory.[34]

To make thought completely observable, many Chinese psychologists viewed thought as a demonstrable physiological process. Gao Zhuo, an editor of the *Encyclopedia of Education* (*jiaoyu baike quanshu*) (who changed his name to Juefu in 1928), tried to explain dreams using a behaviorist approach. A translator of Freud's works, Gao called for an objective evaluation of Freud,[35] yet criticized his dream theory as subjective, since Freud saw everything as a symbol of male or female sexual organs, a contention that could not be confirmed with actual external experiments. Gao argued that thought was simply speech without sound, a view that originated with Watson. Even dreams were based on speech, he claimed, since in dreams people talked, though during sleep speech was controlled by the lower central nervous system.[36]

Along the same lines, Fan Jichang, another psychologist at Peking University, mimicked Watson in emphasizing the physiological basis for thought by interpreting it as speech devoid of sound. Just as speech is a result of external stimuli and the working of kinesthetic sense organs, thought follows this S-R pattern, although in the latter case the pattern consists not in a direct stimulus from the outside followed by a response but, rather, in a genetic inheritance formed over many years.[37] Both Gao and Fan avoided discussing the mind's processing of external experience into more abstract speech.

Although returned students from the United States were responsible for the popularity of behaviorism in China, many of its propagators, such as Gao Zhuo and Fan Jichang, had never been to there. Their interest in S-R owed to its emphasis on explicit observability, in which, like Chen Daqi's rendition of Wundt's theory, the explanation of thought processes shifted from introspection to external factors. Gao Zhuo at first had been a champion of William MacDougall's social psychology, but after several heated debates with champions of hard core behaviorism was converted to Guo Renyuan's perspective. Gao's reaction to Watson's experiments on children's mood reactions was that McDougall did not base his arguments on reality and experiments.[38] Contrasting experimentation with a Confucian intuitive approach to human behavior, many scholars saw the introduction of behaviorism as a means of eliminating Confucian influence on the understanding of human thought and behavior. However, Confucian learning did not simply disappear because it was denounced. Because the rejection of Confucianism was categorical and not critical, Confucian learning continued to haunt the champions of behaviorism in the complete accountability of human behavior, only now not from an intuitive but an external point of view.

In addition to embracing S-R theory, many Chinese educators found attractive the educational tests or surveys designed by American educators. Like

S-R theory, these instruments appeared to offer public accountability. They were a scientific means of gauging public opinion allowing educators to quickly grasp how to frame their position on certain social or professional issues for the public. The tests and surveys also offered them a way to demonstrate their credibility to society and academia. Their motives closely resembled the educational professionalization movement in the United States in the early twentieth century, when the educators wanted to pose as social engineers and impress society with quantitative data on students' mental development as well as to treat educational criteria as a science with demonstrable results. Edward Thorndike and Lewis Terman, the champions of the IQ test, for instance, were students of physiologists turned psychologists. Both Thorndike and Terman were familiar with medicine but shared an aversion to medical instruments; hence they decided to apply the medical methods of physical examination to the psychological examination of school children.[39] Their quantitative approach to intelligence made them appear socially accountable.

In introducing educational testing to China, Chinese educators seemed to be more concerned about public demonstrability than its inner validity. Almost no Chinese psychologists or educators who championed S-R had a medical or scientific background. Many educators conducted statistical surveys of schools to obtain firsthand observation of the process of education. The educational tests designed by Lewis Terman and Edward Thorndike became popular in China. Lectures on educational testing were sponsored by the China Educational Improvement Association, one of the most important educational organizations in China in the 1920s, to introduce its use in class placement, graduation, educational efficiency, methods and teaching materials, as well as criteria of teacher evaluation.[40] With little modification, educators applied these tests to Chinese schools hoping to establish their social accountability through quantitative results. This attempt by the Education and Psychology Departments at Peking University and other Chinese universities to establishing their social relevance and possible utility in social reform had a dismal outcome. Unlike in the United States, where behaviorism developed into a viable profession by connecting itself to actual social services, in China professions in the social sciences developed late and slowly, and college graduates had a hard time finding jobs in their specialty except in teaching and government service, the largest sources of employment in the 1920s and 1930s. Moreover, in additon to the absence of gainful employment in their field, the psychologists found that the attempt to find a completely rational explanation of human behavior through hardcore behaviorism did not result in enhanced status, for, unlike the experience of their American counterparts, their potential to be social engineers was not welcomed.

Attempts at spreading education, including university education, came at a time when China was experiencing great political instability, and the state education budget was not only tight but often unavailable.[41] In 1933, half of the graduates from Central University (formerly National Southeastern University), a prestigious university in Nanjing, could not find jobs befitting their education.[42] It is clear that without the flourishing of professions in China, schools and universities would not have sufficient outlets for their graduates and, with all their rhetoric of pedagogy, the educators could not develop into an influential profession. In this context, the American educational system and its social service orientation came under challenge. Against this background, at Peking University, the promotion of public service and public accountability at an excessively elite university that prided its existence on pure knowledge linked to transcendental realms became a more glaring oxymoron that even the authority of science could not cover up. The Department of Education managed to get by not by virtue of the rigor of its curriculum, but by the market for teachers created by the expansion of the Chinese school system in the 1920s.

## The 1930s: Developing a Greater Internal Rationale for Education

In spite of a momentary flourishing of education in the 1920s, much of the expansion was ephemeral, and educators began to question the applicability of foreign educational methods to the Chinese context. Some of them argued that intrinsic elements of Chinese society had to be taken into consideration. Tao Xisheng, a socialist and professor at Peking University, used a Marxist historical approach to point out the incongruity between European educational goals and Chinese society.[43] Others called for the development of a unique Chinese educational agenda suited to China. Among the critics of Chinese education, Jiang Hengyuan, chairman of the Chinese Professional Education Association, argued that Chinese professional education failed in the first thirty years of the twentieth century because Chinese educators lacked an overall perspective on Chinese educational reform.[44]

The hindrances to educational expansion such as lack of jobs for graduates led many educators to search for intrinsic rules to guide educational development. Behaviorism, though not abandoned, was now blended with several other theories. Theories of the faculties of the mind, including cognitive and moral faculties in the learning process, regained attention. Xiao Encheng's *Child Psychology*, (*Ertong xinlixue*) published in 1934, typified this trend. Xiao, who had earned a Ph.D. in psychology at an American university and joined the faculty at Peking University in 1930, synthesized social psychology and behavioral psychology based on the study of biology and physiology. In discussing children's mental development, he combined genetics and inheritance with the role of the operations of human physiology and with external stimuli on the body.[45]

Although hard science was used as the rationale for psychology and education in the 1920s, it was not really scientific—as the moral need for a rational explanation of the human mind or social accountability, rather than observance of necessary rules and procedures in reaching their conclusions, dominated the concerns of many psychologists and educators. Nor did it provide the social credibility for the psychologists and educators for robust professional development. In other words, the services of professional educators and psychologists were not needed; it was not that China did not need education, but simply that it was not ready for educational professionals. Educators began to search for educational philosophies that could flourish in the current environment. One of them was Wu Junsheng, professor of education at Peking University beginning in 1931.[46] Since the introduction to China of Western knowledge, Wu argued, the Chinese educational community had responded to various strands of Western thought randomly. In ethical education, for instance, Chinese secondary schools had swung from Confucian ethics focusing on individual cultivation to Western ethics emphasizing public virtue, and then returned to Confucian ethics.[47] Educational philosophy was a relatively new topic in the 1930s, and nothing systematically dealing with that topic had yet been written. Yet Wu felt impelled to publish a book on it despite the fact that he had not taken even a course on it at the University of Paris, where he earned his Ph.D. He would later claim that the first book in English on the topic, *Modern Philosophies of Education*, by John S. Brubacher, at Yale, was published four years after his meaning he had the foresight to discern the need for a work on educational philosophy.

Wu's educational philosophy was a teleological picture of the internal dynamics of Western philosophies and educational theories from ancient times to the 1920s.[48] The polarity between the champions of faculty psychology and a completely materialistic approach prepared the way for Dewey's educational philosophy, which would be the Golden Mean avoiding the excesses of both. Applied in education, Dewey's educational theories focused on the spontaneity of experience and the development of students' individual goals.[49]

This tidy image of the development of ideas, however, eliminated all the details of philosophers' arguments as well as the background to these ideas: ideas seemed to develop in isolation in an ahistorical dialectical relationship, finally culminating in synthesis. Wu did not show that Dewey drew inspiration from sources as diverse as Hegel, Darwin, and Leibniz, who could not be easily classified as spiritualists or materialists, and from his mother who was a traditional pious Christian. Wu presented a linear progress chart of Western educational philosophy as the backdrop for the development of Chinese educational philosophy. The problem with Wu's philosophy was similar to that which caused an identity crisis for the Education Department at Peking University: the absence of a viable rationale in Chinese society. Wu's pessimism about Chinese society was reflected in his comments in 1933 that the Chinese educational community should be wary of the constraints in educational reform because of the slow economic and social developments in China, especially in the countryside, and the limited impact education could have on society.[50] His views on Chinese society could be an important reason why he turned away from the social determinism of Emile Durkheim.[51] At first complaining that Dewey overemphasized individualism, Wu now found Dewey's individualism a means for remaining pro-active in a society that did not inspire great hopes.

The Department of Education managed to survive despite an absence of a viable educational philosophy. Professional training of teachers and school administrators remained an important part of the education program at Peking University in the 1930s. The department's curriculum at the time required courses in school administration, teaching methods, educational psychology, and educational testing. Elective courses included education from rural, popular, and kindergarten, to normal schools.[52] In 1931, students were able to specialize in one of four fields: politics/economy, philosophy/psychology, English/mathematics, or history/geography.[53] As Yang Lianggong, first a student and after 1931 a professor in the Department of Education, put it, the department was to prepare students for one of three professions: high school teachers, school administrators, or researchers in education. Despite the department's continued orientation toward the practical, it no longer had a uniform focus. On the one hand, some faculty members actively sought to build a meaningful connection between education and Chinese society through contributing to newspaper columns. Yang Lianggong, Wu Junsheng, Ni Liang (Wu's wife), Liu Tingfang, his wife Liu Wu Zhuosheng, Qiu Chun, and Xiao Chengen organized a short-lived association called the Society for Tomorrow (*Mingrishe*), an organization to improve the connection between education and society made up largely of Peking University faculty, and established a weekly page in the Tianjin newspaper *Dagongbao* between 1932 and 1934 called "Tomorrow's Education" (*Mingri zhi jiaoyu*). Arguing that Chinese education should become more specialized and follow Chinese social norms, they stressed socially demonstrable methods, such as statistics, the use of educational tests, and other surveys. Ni Liang taught courses at Peking University in the Department of Education on statistics and educational testing in the 1930s. Educational psychology and educational methods were also important topics of discussion in "Tomorrow's Education." Yang Lianggong compiled a questionnaire for all the heads of the provincial, prefectural, and municipal education bureaus on their definition of their position in 1932, the first time such a questionnaire was distributed to heads of education bureaus in China. And the results were published in "Tomorrow's Education" in 1932.[54]

The Department of Education also tried to build a greater internal rationale for education through comparative studies. The department curriculum increased the number of courses on comparative education,, including "Comparative Education," offered by Xiao Encheng and Wu Junsheng (1931–32); "Comparative Education: Germany," by Dai Xia (1931–32); "Comparative Education: The United States," by Yang Lian (1931–32); "Curriculum Compilation," by Xiao Encheng (1932–33); "Modern Educational Thought," by Qiu Chun (1935–36); and "Educational Institutions in Various Countries," by Qiu Chun, Wu Junsheng, and others (1935–36). Wu Junsheng and Xiao Encheng explained that their course would systematically compare the various European and American educational institutions, including the emphasis on individualism in the English system, the democratic spirit in the American system, the centralization in the German system and its reforms after the end of World War I, the democratic and centralized French system, and the new educational system of the Soviet Union.[55] In 1934, Qiu Chun compared the educational structure in China to that of seven other countries, especially with regard to the single-track versus dual-track system.[56] Even if they did not provide a viable internal rationale for Chinese education, comparative education courses would offer a perspective for the educational courses offered at Peking University and therefore serve to some extent as the rationale for the department.

Unlike the Education Department, the Psychology Department did not move into new territory. Its curriculum from 1930 to 1932 continued to stress behaviorism and publicly demonstrable knowledge for social accountability. Gestalt psychology, a school of thought that tried to break away from S-R and spread from Germany to the United States in the 1920s, was first offered in 1930, but only as an isolated course.[57] This predominant focus on the socially demonstrable curriculum, however, was not able to save the department. By the fall of 1934, insufficient student enrollment forced the closure of the department. Its curriculum was combined with that of the Departments of Philosophy and Education.[58] Its closure signified the irrelevance of professional psychologists *qua* social engineers in a pre-industrialized China, where the influence of science remained superficial in a few big cities among a handful of middle-class professional Chinese.

## The Department of Education Experiences Greater Emphasis on Moral Education and Identification with the State

Without support from the wider public or compatible Chinese social values to endorse a Dewey-style educational philosophy, Wu and many other Chinese educators searched for an external moral authority to bolster their efforts and found it after 1928 in the Chinese state. Educators came to identify the goal of education as serving state interests for several reasons. The Nationalist government established in 1928 was the chief financial supporter of education. Beginning in 1930–31, the state covered about 71 percent of all educational costs, out of revenue from both central and local governments.[59] Several university faculty members worked full or part time for the Nationalist government. Chen Daqi became chairman of the newly founded Examination Yuan.[60] Jiang Menglin, before assuming the presidency of Peking University in 1930, served as education minister, and Cai Yuanpei became the head of Academia Sinica. This close connection between state and education and resources owned by the state gave many education faculty hope that they could implement their goals through state established channels. Lacking a viable connection to society, educators again found their social relevance in moral education, and this time, often through the compulsory moral education classes implemented by the Nationalist government called *xunyu* (political tutelage), which was an eclectic combination of Confucian morals and teachings on loyalty to the Nationalist party and the nation. Instead of resisting it as political indoctrination, many educators welcomed the course addition as complementing high school moral cultivation. This was especially so in the 1930s, when some of them blamed the failure of Chinese education on the low quality of the students, not academically, but morally. Moral cultivation, to them, directly contributed to the quality of higher education. Liu Tingfang, professor of education at Peking University, for instance, criticized high schools for failing to shape the character of students, a problem that he believed could be redressed through political tutelage. The high school stage was crucial, Liu said, for it established the basis for character cultivation among college students.[61]

To the educators, political tutelage did not mean just the agenda set by the Nationalist government. Xia Qian, one of the editors of "Tomorrow's Education," considered the Nationalist government's definition of *xunyu*—cultivating loyalty among youth, filial piety, humanity, kindness, faith, justice, peace, courage, and neatness—too narrow. Middle schools, as the place to cultivate both the mind and body of future citizens, should include also the cultivation of physical fitness, public morality, national culture, life skills, a foundation in science, a habit of physical labor, and interest in the arts. Xia suggested that *xunyu* and regular classroom teaching should be fully integrated.[62] His suggestions for the implementation of *xunyu*, however, stood in contrast to the goals of the Nationalist government. The government's regulations relied primarily on traditional Chinese values with a few Western elements, indicating its use of political education as a form of social control. But Xia, in his amendments, focused on cultivating the students' receptivity to the new knowledge required of citizens in a republic. He saw a continuum between the two views. Although he might genuinely have believed in both, it was likely that he thought it was the government's responsibility to make schools into a place to propagate values. In this case, he included both values that were actually championed by the state and those that the state was supposed to profess. Other educators concurred with Xia in asserting the importance of *xunyu* in middle schools, by implementing educational theories from the West. Zhang Huai, another editor of "Tomorrow's Education," defined oral education as cultivation of aesthetic and social feelings by eliciting students' instinctual development in the positive aspects, and decreasing training student discipline through repression.[63]

A deepening sense of national crisis motivated many educators to petition for integrating political and moral education with regular classroom teaching. Feeling responsible for the future of the nation, they criticized the Nationalist government's exclusion of *xunyu* from regular classes, emphasized the cultivation of physical fitness, which would lead to psychological health, accurate information about sex, a habit of achieving success, life skills, continuous motivation, and fair play,[64] an amalgam of values based largely on American educational theories.

The professional knowledge from educational theories that many educators had was directly applied to the cause of national salvation. The program on moral education was systematic, with an emphasis on eliciting spontaneous student acceptance and forming habits, made possible by a child-centered education based on children's internalization of knowledge. Quoting Dewey and Kerschensteiner's approaches to knowledge, Zhang Huai discussed how to elicit students' instinct to start the moral cultivation process, and evoke interest and enjoyment from students in implementing a sense of responsibility. Zhang Huai also argued the actual approaches to students' moral education should be based on a thorough observation of students.[65] Western educational theories on teaching, in other words, were seen as the guide to implementing moral education. This marked the full academization of moral education, making it little different from professional education in its need for special training. Educational professionalism blended with a moral vision found its strongest reinforcement in the government stipulated compulsory political tutelage classes. It showed that educators, despite the disparity between their agendas and the government's, found the political tutelage classes an effective means of transmitting their moral vision in a programmatic way.

The institutionalized *xunyu* classes in high schools were criticized by some educators, but others, as mentioned above, found it a useful way to instill in the students an eclectic combination of Confucian moral cultivation, Western educational theories, and nationalism, therefore fulfilling their social relevance. It is not without irony that this lengthy discussion of moral education took up a significant amount of the space in "Tomorrow's Education." The social service orientation of the Education and Psychology Departments in the 1920s and 1930s was largely confined to a scholastic discussion of social service in terms of impeccable scientific methods, moral cultivation, and other scholastic issues, instead of a vigorous introduction of socially relevant programs. Their lack of success reflected the nationwide failure to actually implement education in daily life. The only success stories were isolated cases of individuals such as James Yen and Liang Shuming, isolated educators/social reformers dedicated to the countryside.[66]

In conclusion, the Peking University educators' introduction of Western educational and psychological theories was faced with dual obstacles from the start. First, the social relevance that the education and psychology faculty members tried to establish deviated from the pure knowledge orientation of the university, thus they could not attract much institutional support and were often criticized. Second, their use of science to create that social relevance had little connection to their social context, which itself was unfertile ground for establishing their authority. In the absence of a viable philosophy for the disciplines of education and psychology, the faculty engaged in an internal dialogue about the certainty of human thinking. Strict behaviorism guaranteed a fully rational explanation of human thinking while offering social accountability. But when this social accountability did not garner social status for the educators or psychologists in the 1930s, many of them returned to an emphasis on moral cultivation and seemingly resumed their old role as shaping human thinking via moral guidance; this time, they relied not just on Confucian values but an eclectic combination of Confucian morals, Western educational theories, and nationalism. Lacking the proper means to implement this new moral system, many found the *xunyu* class enforced by the Nationalist government in high schools a useful venue for doing so. In view of the absence of funding, an unresponsive society, and imminent national crisis, many educators identified with the Nationalist government's Three Principles of the People—nationhood, people's rights, and people's livelihood, and decided that being co-opted by the state was their best option for survival as academics.

# 8

# Western Legal and Political Theories as Agents of Social Reform

## The Development of the Law and Political Science Departments (1920s–1930s)

Like education and psychology, law and politics were two potentially practical and socially oriented fields of learning. Precisely for these reasons, Cai Yuanpei had attempted to separate the field of law from the university in 1917 and was stopped by strong protests from the faculty. Unlike other applied subjects of learning, however, law and politics, because of their historical connection with government office, were regarded by Zhang Zhidong as of a higher level than practical education with a technological bent. And precisely because of the special historical connotation of law and politics, Cai Yuanpei related them more with government office in history than the actual laws and political practices from the Chinese past. Although he did not succeed in cutting the law program, Cai did succeed in reducing the connection between the study of law, politics, and government office. The curriculum of law and politics from 1912 to 1937 demonstrated a gradual progression from the training of lawyers and candidates in the civil service examinations to a focus on scholarship. The disciplines of law and political science therefore represented a disjuncture with the laws and political practices of the Chinese past.

At their inception, the Law and Politics Departments attracted an inordinate number of students who hoped to use their knowledge in these disciplines to pass the new civil service examinations or to qualify for waiver of these examinations. Following the Japanese example, wherein after the Meiji restoration university graduates who majored in law were often enrolled in the state bureaucracy through a civil service examination, in China after 1912, the republican government circulated the criteria for a senior civil service and a regular civil service examination and implemented these criteria in June 1916. The senior civil service examination consisted of a preliminary and a formal stage, whose contents comprised law and economics: constitutional law, criminal law, civil law, administrative law, international public law, and economics. In addition to these subjects, the candidate had to choose one of the following: finance, commercial law, criminal prosecution law, civil prosecution law, or international private law. Graduates from the preparatory schools affiliated with universities would have their preliminary examinations waived, and university graduates would have the whole examination waived. The regular civil service examination was based on the high school curriculum, and the senior civil service examination on the university curriculum.[1]

Most of the students who enrolled at the university went into the Division of Law and Politics (which consisted of three departments: Law, Political Science, and Economics). Even before the civil service examinations were held, many students who were enrolled in the Division of Law and Politics hoped to find a job in the state bureaucracy after graduation. They often tried to achieve this by cultivating connections with one another, with members of the state bureaucracy, and with the instructors, who were usually government officials or lawyers. Before 1917, in the Subdivision of Law in the Division of Law and Politics, many instructors, while teaching at Peking University, concurrently assumed senior positions in the republican law courts, including serving as assistants and translators for Japanese lawyers who helped the Qing government draft its Chinese criminal and civil laws. Among them was Zhang Xiaoyi. At that time, Japan served as the center of education for much of the law faculty, but after Cai Yuanpei became chancellor that year, he appointed many instructors to the law faculty who had been educated in Europe. To sever the connection between government office and scholarship, Cai ruled that faculty members who concurrently held jobs outside the university could not be appointed as professors, only as lecturers. According to this new regulation, even well-known lawyers such as Wang Chonghui could only be hired as lecturers. In his speeches, Cai encouraged the students to focus on scholarship and not use university education as ladder to office and wealth.[2]

In the 1912 political science curriculum, law figured prominently because of its role in the future civil service examinations. Of the twenty-seven courses, ten were on law: constitutional law, administrative law, the science of constitutional law, international public law, criminal law, civil law, commercial law, legal theories, specific studies in international public law, and international private law. Courses on political science numbered fourteen, of which six were on various government policies. The remaining eight courses, less than a third of the curriculum, dealt with more general issues of political science, including the study of the nation, political science and its history, history of politics, political geography, diplomatic history, and history of political parties. By 1916, the curriculum on law in political science was reduced to seven courses, which, however, almost all coincided with the law topics on the senior civil service examination. In their fourth year, students had to specialize in one of four areas, two of which were constitutional and international public law, and the other two sociology and political science.[3] By 1921, however, changes, although slight, were evident. The Law Department increased the number of courses with perspectives on law in political science and economics. The Political Science Department began to offer courses blending law, politics, and economics. The courses on political science were primarily surveys, such as fundamentals of political science, politics and the study of the state, and political and diplomatic histories, instead of more specialized courses.[4]

From the beginning of his tenure at Peking University, Cai Yuanpei promoted research in the two departments. Before, law had been taught largely in foreign languages (English, German, French, and Japanese) and by country. Cai decided that research should be stressed rather than preparation for the civil service examination or the training of lawyers, and comparative law would best facilitate research. The prohibition on allowing those who concurrently held positions outside the university to become professors made it difficult to implement this reform because the two instructors who were capable of offering comparative law, Wang Chonghui and Luo Jun, were both lawyers and could serve only as lecturers and could not be relied on for the departmental curriculum reform. Research in comparative law became possible only in the 1920s after the appointment as full-time faculty members of returned students from England, such as Wang Shijie and Zhou Gengsheng .[5]

In 1922, Mei Zufen, a third-year student in political science, proposed a series of reforms to the curriculum of the Law, Political Science, and Economics Departments that were obviously a product of Cai Yuanpei's policies. Mei charged that these departments focused too much on specific laws, such as civil and criminal law clauses, and not on the scholarship of law. Mei asked for the creation of more courses on fostering a philosophical perspective, including ethics, psychology, history of Chinese and Western philosophies, as common electives, and more comparative law courses, such as comparative civil and criminal laws. At the same time, he proposed that the number of specific courses on civil, criminal, and administrative laws be reduced.[6]

In 1923, Zhou Jieren, another student in political science, also suggested curriculum improvements. Like Mei, Zhou asked to eliminate the more specific law courses, such as those on civil law regarding debt and property rights, and replace them with more general civil law surveys. The reply from Chen Qixiu, professor of political science, basically concurred with Zhou that the courses required for the civil service examinations should not automatically constitute the required courses in the department, and that the proportion of political science courses should exceed those in law.[7] Beginning in the fall of 1923, a new curriculum with a more comprehensive coverage of sociology, law, and economics was implemented and remained intact until 1926.[8] The curriculum of political science, therefore, became more focused on an academic study of policy-making, in place of law courses in preparation for a career as a lawyer or government bureaucrat.

Unlike the political science curriculum, which experienced some reforms, the law curriculum remained more or less intact from the early 1910s through 1926.[9] The difference between the departments, however, was not as great as it appeared. The Law Department was also quickly becoming more academic. Prominent law professors, such as Wang Shijie, Yan Shutang, Bai Pengfei, and Huang Youchang, who taught in the 1920s, were full-time faculty. The growing academization of the disciplines of law and politics, however, forced the faculty to struggle with the content of these disciplines as theoretical knowledge and as knowledge of immediate social relevance. This struggle was reflected in the research they produced.

## Eliminating the Historical Chasm Between Chinese and Western Politics: Western Law and Politics as Intellectual Choices

Because starting from the earliest curricula for the university, Chinese law and politics in history were treated as statecraft not worth emulating, an academic study of law and politics meant primarily the study of Western law and politics. Without an external reference, the latter became their own reference. The deep chasm between Chinese and Western law and politics as well as society led to a moralistic treatment of Western law and politics, and the Chinese state was often scrutinized for its resemblance to or departure from Western practices. Despite the a priori value assigned to Western legal and political practices, Chinese scholars of law and politics often did not subscribe to a particular school of thought. As reflected in their research, they often adopted a relativistic attitude toward Western law and politics.

Yan Shutang was a leading legal scholar and professor at Peking University in the 1920s and 1930s, after having earned his law degree at Yale Law School. Yan compared Western legal protection of individual rights to the Chinese state's abuse of those rights. Expressing concern that, in dealing with civilian opposition, the Chinese government often enacted curfew laws and subjected most civil cases to police tribunals,[10] Yan explained that the term in Chinese for "rights," an amalgam of words for "power" and "interest," was borrowed from the Japanese translation. Such a term did not exist in traditional Chinese law; there was only "obligation" or "responsibility" (*yiwu*). On the issue of property ownership in civil law, Yan argued its definition in China excluded "rights." Following German and Swiss laws, Chinese civil law stated that possession of something did not mean ownership of it. Although ownership was unconditional, "possession" meant actual possession of something at the moment and was conditional. "Rights," Yan argued, were the law's way of protecting one's interests, therefore if one's possession of something was protected by law, it should be said that one had the right to it, hence, ownership.[11]

In another article, Yan indirectly criticized the Chinese state's mistreatment of political prisoners. Tracing the history of political prisoners' treatment in the West, he stated that after the French Revolution such people were treated differently from ordinary criminals because they did not attack the entire people, only a particular social class. Although some of them, such as anarchists, were still punished severely in some Western countries, most countries treated political prisoners humanely. In contrast, he wrote, the Chinese government killed patriots and never asked for extradition of real criminals, who carried huge sums of state money overseas or were hiding in the foreign concessions in China.[12] Criminal punishment had to follow definite criteria, which were concerned primarily with the individual's responsibility toward himself and society.[13]

Yan seemed to assert individual rights only when criticizing the autocratic Chinese state. In 1922, a year before he wrote the above-mentioned articles, he had defined rights primarily as for the benefit of society, not individuals. Although eighteenth-century champions of moral autonomy, such as Kant, advocated that laws protect individual liberty, beginning in the nineteenth century, Yan argued, more social scientists came to believe that the purpose of legal and political institutions was to achieve, not the maximum freedom for each individual, but freedom for the maximum number of people. Historically, despite various legal theories based on individualism, laws were made to protect not individual rights but society.[14] When some champions of the jury system, a sign of democracy, suggested that China incorporate that practice in its legal reforms in 1924, Yan opposed it, claiming that it had no historical roots in China. He doubted that the Chinese possessed the courage to make independent judgments according to legal standards.[15] The democratic system, Yan believed, was not suited to China in the 1920s.

Yan's discomfort with democracy and the historical chasm between China and the Western countries often divorced his discussion of constitutional government from the social dynamics behind the development of Western society. His discussions of Western political practices were self-referential, as he did not compare them to practices in China or elsewhere. Regarding the conflicting arguments in Western law on what the basis of law should be—social conventions, ethics, or arbitrary external force—Yan presented the pros and cons of each school of thought based on its intellectual content. Those advocating that it be based on arbitrary external force believed that human nature is evil and mere education in peaceful coexistence is insufficient to prevent human conflict. Those who advocated the enforcement of law through social pressure, such as sympathy, public opinion, habit, or ethics, focused more on the historical evolution of the law through social conventions and ethics. All approaches had their drawbacks. Some approaches would not countenance arbitrarily enforced laws. Basing laws on social conventions, however, would easily make the law vulnerable to changes over time in social attitudes, and both the historical and ethical approaches overstated the innate rationality of laws at the cost of the effectiveness of external force.[16]

Yan left unexamined particular social circumstances in these legal arguments as a convenient way of avoiding a confrontation with the incongruity between these laws and the Chinese situation. Yan's tendency to reduce the dynamics of Western legal and political development to an intellectual exercise was shared by many colleagues, such as Wang Shijie. A graduate of Beiyang University (1911), Wang earned his B.S. at the London School of Economics and Ph.D. in law at the University of Paris, and from 1920 to 1927, he was a professor of law at Peking University, teaching courses including comparative constitutions and administrative law.[17] In 1924, Wang established a radical journal, *The Contemporary Review* (*Xiandai pinglun*), which was devoted to comments on both domestic politics, especially the 1924 settlement conference by the Duan Qirui government allegedly to end civil warfare in China, and foreign policy, in particular the state's attempt to eliminate extraterritoriality. In 1926, the warlord government temporarily banned the journal.[18] In *Contemporary Review* and elsewhere, Wang wrote extensively on the legal rights of individuals and limiting the power of the state. After 1927, Wang assumed different positions in the Nationalist government, including director of the Legislative Yuan, president of National Wuhan University, and education minister in the 1930s.

A lawyer by profession who was deeply involved in Chinese politics, Wang took an instrumental approach to his specialty, Western constitutional law: he indicated the intellectual possibilities for Chinese law in terms of the pros and cons of each choice. This approach, while showing Wang's deep interest in Western constitutional laws, also revealed his awareness of the vast differences between the contexts in which they were developed and the Chinese social context. Like Yan, Wang compared the practices of the Chinese state to Western legal practices as an expression of his frustration with Chinese politics. For example, in his criticism of the Chinese state's dismissal of individual freedom, Wang contrasted Chinese and Anglo-American criminal law, which Wang argued was the best guarantee of individual freedom. In English law, private individuals could raise criminal indictments. China, however, absorbed the most conservative elements of continental law regarding the protection of personal freedom. The Chinese constitution contained only one clause on the inviolability of individuals from arbitrary arrest and punishment, in contrast to ten in the U.S. constitution. Moreover, beginning with laws developed during the Qing dynasty, private individuals had limited opportunity to declare criminal indictments, which were mostly the responsibility of the state prosecutor.[19] This comparison between the right of the individual in Anglo-American and Chinese criminal trials was not appropriate. Although the use of grand jury indictment was practiced from time to time in Britain and the United States, it was by no means the major form of indictment in criminal trials there; state prosecutors made most indictments, and even grand jury indictments have often been initiated by state prosecutors.[20] Such a statement was Wang's effort at drawing a moral contrast between Chinese law and Western law.

Wang also sought examples of the state's redressing of its mistakes from European and American law to criticize the low esteem of human rights in Chinese law. In the United States and Britain, the private citizen who incurred harm caused by the state could petition the state for compensation. In continental Europe, the compensation could be made either by the government official who committed the mistake or by the state. In China, however, the Court of Claims (*Pingzheng yuan*) could not hear cases requesting state compensation. The only mention of compensation was that by government officials as private persons, meaning that the state would not make any compensation.[21] Wang also criticized the military regimes of China for placing soldiers above the law. He called for the deprivation of all their political rights, including the right to run for office, and for their being subject to civilian law so that they could no longer avoid legal sanctions by relying on military courts that were often corrupt under the warlord regimes.[22] He criticized China's excessively punitive laws in force since the beginning of Yuan Shikai's regime in 1915, which called for thieves to be executed, denied suspects to the right to appeal, and banned political gatherings in the absence of prior police notification.[23] He discussed various methods tried in the West to restrain central power, such as the federal form of government, and the relationship between the federal constitution and various levels of courts in Switzerland and the United States to prevent the abuse of power by any social group. He suggested a merger of the legislative and the executive branches of government to prevent autocratic behavior and transgression of the law by the executive.[24]

Despite Wang's comparisons and his prescriptions for restraints on the Chinese state, he did not find any particular Western democratic procedure applicable to China because of his conviction that the Chinese were not ready for democracy. In this, Wang suffered from the same predicament as Yan Shutang: while reflecting his genuine indignation over the conduct of the Chinese state, his criticism of the Chinese state did not represent his true opinion of the Western democratic practices he praised. Those practices were used to highlight his despair over the parlous condition of the Chinese state. He was certain that China was not ready for any kind of representative government because of the low level of its people's education. Commenting on the government China was supposed to form in 1924 at the anticipated settlement conference (which did not materialize), Wang stated that it would be difficult to form a democratically elected government in China because neither direct democracy nor professional representation would work: in addition to the low level of education, the lack of sufficient development of the social professions made the exercise of professional representation in Chinese politics impossible.[25] Were it not for the use of Western standards as a reference point for criticism of the Chinese state, Wang, like Yan Shutang, would have championed very different values than individual rights. For instance, he approved of state intervention in Western countries on certain issues, such as the protection of private property. He quoted approvingly from modern opponents of absolute private property ownership in the West to show that it should be subject to social interests. For instance, in 1916 during World War I, France enforced compulsory cultivation of certain plants on all lands, with or without the consent of the (absentee) landowners. Sometimes, confiscation of private property in the public interest was also justified, as in the 1841 French laws. Similar treatment of private property was also found in German laws and, to a lesser extent, in British and U.S. laws.[26] Although noting the evolution of Western legal and political theories, which evolved from an individualistic interpretation of rights in the early nineteenth century to a greater emphasis on social well-being in the latter part of the nineteenth century, in his criticism of the Chinese state, Wang pointed to individualistic democracy as the pinnacle of truth and the practice of government in China as its antithesis.

As in the case of Yan Shutang, Wang's account of Western law as following rational and legitimate developments was relativistic and sounded like a series of self-modifying intellectual principles following an evolutionary path. Wang's interest in Western law and their implementation in China led him to comparative law. One course he taught at Peking University, comparative Western constitutions, resulted in a book that emerged from the lectures *Comparative Law* (*Bijiao xianfa*), which published five editions between 1927 and 1937. Wang demonstrated both the pros and cons of Western legal practices, presenting them as rational and intellectual in contrast to the very irrational Chinese political scene. In discussing basic constitutional formats, for instance, Wang introduced both rigid and flexible constitutions and evaluated the advantages of each format for fulfilling people's rights.

Rigid constitutions could help in maintaining stability and preventing revolutions, but could also suffer from the problem of complicated amendments, which would often obstruct social development. In that respect, flexible constitutions were better because they could be easily amended if the legislature and the judiciary were the same body because the judges on the amendment and implementers would be the same people. But flexible constitutions, precisely because they were flexible and easily amended, suffered from a lack of stability. Therefore the rigid constitution had the advantage.

Such relativistic treatment, especially pointing out the reasonability of all laws, was applied to the political values undergirding Western laws as well. For instance, Wang traced the arguments on human rights, especially the right of suffrage, from being irrelevant to the state to becoming the inherent right of the people before and after the French revolution. In his views on sovereignty, Rousseau argued that suffrage rested with the people. Those advocating this view did so to counter the European situation when suffrage was largely restricted to the aristocracy and the propertied class. Those against it argued for suffrage as a social responsibility of the voter, who was authorized by the state to vote for the sake of the whole society, therefore he had to be from a select group of responsible people. A compromise of these two views was evident in the French constitution of 1791, when citizens were divided into active and passive citizens, and suffrage was limited to the former. After the nineteenth century, German scholars also became increasingly aware that voter' organizations were an important part of the government and that suffrage was a social responsibility of the voters. Following these two contrasting views suffrage organizations were established. Thus all arguments, from those against popular suffrage to those for it, had a credible basis. The discussion mirrored the different possibilities on an intellectual spectrum.

The same kind of relativism was also reflected in many other topics Wang addressed, such as professional representation.[27] Wang's rational and relativistic approach to Western law and politics contrasted with his perception of the Chinese political reality. In commenting on the Chinese government in 1924, for instance, Wang condemned the Chinese "long parliament" of thirteen years from its inception at the founding of the Chinese republic, when its members were often elected through bribery or inserted by warlords, as an illegitimate organization that had destroyed any interest in a parliamentary government in China and could in no way stop autocracy.[28]

The rational approach to Western law and politics, however, showed its limitations with respect to Japanese and Western imperialism in China. Faced with sharp confrontations between Chinese workers and Western and Japanese employers in the foreign concessions in Chinese cities, Wang avoided condemning the foreign companies as imperialistic as many radical nationalists and Communists did. He treated the British companies' abuse of Chinese workers not as an assertion of the power of Western companies in China but as equivalent to Chinese internal labor disputes. In doing so, he denied the authority of the Chinese state over factories on Chinese territory. Concern for the Chinese workers who were beaten up and killed in foreign concessions in Shanghai, Wuhan, and Hong Kong because of their demonstrations for shorter working hours and higher pay prompted him to research legitimate worker demonstration procedures in British laws. For instance, he argued that the Chinese workers in foreign concessions should be allowed to form legitimate labor unions and demonstrations because such organizations were an inevitable product of the industrial revolution. In China, from 1926 to 1927 alone, 107 workers' strikes broke out, of which seventy-three were related to the beating of workers often by foreign police of factory owners, and worker demands for increased pay. Labor unions were especially important in foreign concessions, where state laws of social security and minimum wages would not apply to foreign factories, and only unions could offer a form of self-defense for the workers. This argument against the atrocities of the British and Japanese managements' behavior in China treated the problem as a domestic issue and circumvented the issue of Chinese state sovereignty in China.[29]

Wang would not go as far as his colleague Cao Jie, in the Law Department, who argued for the abolition of extraterritoriality in China. Optimistic about the newly established League of Nations, which proclaimed a new form of diplomacy in the world after World War I based not on power but on cooperation, Cao argued in 1923 that China should raise the issue of abolishing extraterritoriality in China at the League. However, Cao observed that the condition for doing so was the establishment of many local courts to implement uniform laws throughout China so that foreign merchants who traveled to inland China would not be subject to trials relying on different customs and practices, a condition that prompted them to ask for extraterritorial status in the first place.[30] A concession of the power politics that Britain played in China would demolish the rational and intellectualistic depiction he gave of British law and politics. Wang, however, could opt for the alternative of radical politics, condemning Western imperialism, but only when he saw the Chinese state was in a position to enforce effective punishment against imperialism in China. This was demonstrated by his participation in negotiations on behalf of China with the British over the British concessions in Wuhan in early 1927. After the Nationalist government established temporary headquarters in Wuhan, following the Northern Expedition. Clashes between the Chinese celebrating the success of the Northern Expedition and the British in Wuhan resulted in the death of one Chinese seaman and injuries to dozens of others. In response, the Nationalist government overturned British rights to concessions in that city. In need of personnel who could speak English and were familiar with diplomatic procedures, the government invited three faculty members from Peking University—Wang Shijie, Zhou Gengsheng, and Chen Hansheng—to become its advisers. Negotiations with Britain in February 1927 led to an agreement for the return of British concessions in Hankou and Jiujiang.[31] Such confrontation with the British contradicted with Wang's earlier refusal to acknowledge British imperialism in China but showed the condition of his acknowledgment, when the Chinese state, by asserting its sovereignty, was on a par with Western governments.

Like Yan Shutang and Wang Shijie, Gao Yihan (professor of political science at Peking University from 1918 to 1927) found an intellectual ideal in Western political practices. After graduating from Meiji University, Japan, Gao worked as editor of the *Morning Bell* (*Chenzhongbao*) and *Weekly Commentary* (*Meizhou pinglun*) before taking up his post at Peking University.[32] In his articles on history in the 1920s, he discussed historical events in Western politics that showed Western political thought unfold in a rational manner, in contrast to Chinese politics, in which irrational personal rule was rampant. His articles used history to denounce personal rule.[33] One of his targets in Chinese politics was Duan Qirui, a warlord who had control of the Chinese state from 1917 to 1926 and manipulated the constitution to stay in power. As prime minister in 1925, Duan tried to abolish the representative government and set up a traditional censorial bureau to keep an eye on members of the government.

In 1917, Gao provided the government with reference materials on constitutional rule. As compiler at the Bureau of Translation in the Ministry of the Interior, he was authorized to compile a book on comparative local administrations in Britain, the United States, France, and Japan.[34] This project paved the way for Gao's later textbook on different political forms and their origins. This textbook, first published in 1930 and printed in six editions within a year and a half, comprised lectures he delivered at Peking University and at the Shanghai Law and Politics University, where he went in 1927. Gao cautioned that politics should not proceed from the will of an individual ruler and offered rational methods of management.[35] He considered Western-style government managerial, in contrast to the personal style of Chinese rulers, exemplified by President Xu Shichang's proclamation in 1921. Europe, Gao maintained, had experienced personal rule in medieval times, but in the modern era it had evolved out of it. The continuation in China of personal rule would severely stifle people's conscience and individuality.[36]

Gao showed how Western political theories corresponded to particular social conditions, hence, to objective reality. For example, the definition of the state differed at various points in French history. Jean Bodin, a sixteenth-century French lawyer who argued that the highest rights in a state were eternal, above the law, and unalienable, advocated that sovereignty rested with the king in a historically justifiable manner because he wanted to burnish the dignity of the state and eliminate feudal divisions. Léon Duguit, a French lawyer of the late nineteenth century, advocated that sovereignty be based on legal structures at a time when the state had become a managerial device in an industrial society. Different social stages called for different political theories. Monistic sovereignty advocates, such as Bodin, mostly after the sixteenth century during the building of absolute monarchy, often aimed at national unification. Pluralistic sovereignty advocates, mostly after World War I, such as Duguit, by contrast, often wanted to achieve industrial and social autonomy. Political theories reflected the social circumstances of the theoreticians, thus both monistic and pluralistic arguments of sovereignty were historically valid. Gao believed that, as a response to the need for a nation-state, monistic sovereignty had historical validity but ignored the complexity of society and focused on coercive authority, rather than the social forces that constituted sovereignty. In other writings, Gao discussed the development of individualism in Europe in the latter part of the eighteenth century, in which he posited that, like other political theories, individualism was a function of society—a reaction to the adverse conduct of government.[37]

While he cherished Western liberalism's defense of the individual, at heart Gao leaned toward socialism. His vision was of a communal society where the individuals cooperated and were respected by one another, and where the state functioned as a manager, actively intervening for the sake of society's interests, though he was against violent social change.[38] What appealed to him about communism was not the Marxist call for radical revolution but its social and economic equality. Gao quoted John Stuart Mill and a Japanese philosopher to emphasize the importance for everyone of physical labor. even connected labor sharing with justice and ethical behavior.[39] Gao glorified Rousseau's idea of a social contract and mistakenly concluded that this would prevent revolution.[40] Gao had a special penchant for utilitarianism and its call for the pursuit of the entire society's happiness. He contrasted this goal with the Chinese state's suppression of the people, concluding that the responsibility of the state was to promote the greatest social happiness by arbitrating relations between different parts of society.[41] He especially admired Mill, because of Mill's endorsement of happiness not only for society as a whole but also for individuals. Mill's prescription was an antidote to the autocratic rule of China, which enforced individual will on society.[42] In other words, Gao wanted the state, within limits, to play a significant role in improving well-being for all of society. In fact, he sometimes showed a desire for greater state intervention in society than did the guild socialists. The ideal state that Gao wanted to introduce to China was socialistic and federal, with strong guilds, like those championed by British Fabian socialists, with a sharing of sovereignty between guilds and the state. Professions should enjoy a certain degree of autonomy in the state, while the state should become more managerial and its functions more specialized.[43] Like his colleagues Yan and Wang, Gao was looking for an assertive external authority to play an important role to promote social interest. His reliance on Western models as the exclusive criteria of politics led to his depiction of the Western managerial state as an ideal, in contrast to the warlord practices in China.

## Writing Moral Histories of Western Political Science

The legal and political histories written by Zhang Weici (also named Zuxun), a leading faculty member of political science at Peking University in the 1920s and 1930s, reflected a more nuanced approach to Western politics. But Zhang's historicism applied only to those aspects of Western politics that would provide him with guidance for building an ideal Chinese political system. Zhang pointed out that, from 1911, when the republic was founded, to 1930, when Zhang wrote his history of Western politics, various dictatorial governments controlled the Chinese state. The history of Western democratic politics showed that democracy did not develop in a linear and smooth fashion in the West, and even an established democratic system had its limitations. This enabled Zhang to hold on to the hope that, even though not all Chinese political practices were democratic, it did not mean that the entire system was without merit. In his lectures on European political science at Peking University, Zhang focused on the historical origins of modern concepts such as sovereignty, representative government, and the growth of central government power. For instance, he traced the concept of sovereignty to Bodin. Advocating the historical legitimacy of Bodin's argument, Zhang claimed that it coincided with a national aspiration for unity that had been facilitated by the weakening of the nobility. The sanctity of sovereignty that developed during this era lent a mystical aura to sovereignty in a democratic state to elevate the status of the state. Thus, in Zhang's account, sovereignty was a concept with historical connotations that were not democratic and was appropriated by a constitutional government. Historical narratives enabled Zhang to avoid a linear, progressive rationale for Western political developments, thus offering a more nuanced perspective of the Western democratic process. As for representative government, Zhang discussed its practice before and after the French revolution and problems associated with direct representation in history: the representatives directly selected by the people had to rely too much on them for support, hence they were overwhelmingly concerned with their own voting districts. The professional representative system arose where the representatives were not from geographic districts but from professions and served as an alternative form of election to complement the geographically representative system.[44]

Zhang also took a historical approach to the jurisdictional power of European governments. He argued that it took root in a gradual process, made possible only when the state was able to compel people to submit their disputes to the court and accept the court's decisions. Laws, especially those governing civil relations, came about around the mid-nineteenth century, when industry and commerce were highly developed and social life became increasingly complex.[45]

Historicism enabled Zhang to identify the pitfalls in Western politics of those values that survived to the present. He did not look into the histories of all Western political practices, however, only those that embodied modern democratic and constitutional values. His desire was to establish and maintain a representative government with predominant middle-class rule. He consciously sidestepped the political system of the Soviet Union, where the revolution had overthrown the middle class but the regime lacked the management skills to run the country.[46] Similarly, Zhang commented that the decline of living standards of European middle class after World War I, due to rising inflation and workers' movements, would have a deleterious effect on European politics.[47] He saw that the absence of a homogeneous, sizable middle class that could articulate its own interests would lead to the demise of a democratic government or even of a state. Regarding the European states newly established after 1918, such as Poland, Czechoslovakia, and Yugoslavia, Zhang, in 1927, showed concern for their stability because their constitutions were derived from those in Western Europe and the United States, rather than evolving from the traditions of their own countries. Zhang also observed that some of these new states, such as Poland, Finland, Estonia, Latvia, and Lithuania, faced potential destabilization from problems including multi-ethnic groups within their borders and territorial disputes with neighboring countries.[48] He almost foresaw the pact between Poland and Nazi Germany to gain the Polish-speaking territories of Czechoslovakia, and Hitler's invasion of Poland, not least to repossess the former West Prussia, and the instability in the Baltic states, which had had a long history of Russian occupation, a reason that Russia wanted to regain them after World War II.

Zhang's ideal model of the middle-class representative government was the managerial, locally centered American system, where civic protest, such as demonstrations and strikes by labor unions, allowed a moderate venting of dissatisfaction by the lower levels of society and hence avoided the radicalization of dissent. In an article on the rise of unions in the United States from the Knights of Labor in 1869, to the American Federation of Labor (AFL) in 1890, and to the Industrial Workers of the World (IWW, called the Wobblies) in 1905, Zhang compared the policies of the IWW with those of the AFL: the latter, by guaranteeing salaries and job security of its members, co-opted the workers into the middle class and won the support of the majority of American labor. The IWW, with its radical politics and appeal to those excluded by or dissatisfied with the AFL, was always a fringe organization that sometimes inspired fear rather than admiration. The co-optation of labor into the middle class in the United States vitiated the appeal of radical ideologies such as communism.[49] In this article as well, Zhang expressed his belief that a country with a sizable middle class could enforce moderate democratic rule and avoid class struggle.

In his vision of democratic government, Zhang favored the late nineteenth-century Western political theories that advocated government intervention in society for social welfare with a penchant for local rule. He wrote favorably of local rule in medieval European cities and traced the movement toward self-rule by American municipal governments. Affirming the legitimacy of federal laws over cities, Zhang depicted some U.S. cities' attempt at greater self-rule as a move toward a more managerial style of government that could effectively implement federal and state regulations without excessive intervention from the federal and state governments.[50] The "good government" movement in the early twentieth century, in part a reaction by new immigrant leaders to City Hall corruption and the "political machines" and in part a desire for apolitical managerialism,[51] as demonstrated in the municipal government of Galveston, Texas, represented Zhang's ideal.

Zhang Weici's emphasis on a managerial style of government revealed both his ideal for rational politics by experts and his fear that radical, highly ideological politics would only lead to revolutions that would drag China into a situation like that in the Soviet Union. His historical account of the development of Western democratic values indicated his understanding of the tortuous road Chinese politics would have to take in order to reach democracy.

## Going Beyond Intellectual Idealization: Conceptualizing Imperialism in Class, Nationalist, and Legalist Terms

In the 1930s, faced with a deepening sense of national crisis, the Law and Political Science Departments were increasingly criticized as favoring Western learning at the expense of Chinese learning. Consequently, many methodological courses on society were added to the curriculum of both departments. In the Law Department curriculum from 1931 to 1935, the additions included Xu Deheng's two courses on sociology, offering law students a social perspective.[52]

The political science curriculum was refocused to take a more practical orientation, even as it continued to include methodological and theoretical courses. This reorientation was due in part to department faculty such as Chen Qixiu, who suggested the addition of courses on Chinese as well as European economy and society.[53] The 1931–32 curriculum for the Political Science Department followed Chen's recommendations.[54] By 1935, the content on Chinese society reflected in the political science curriculum was even greater, allowing students to specialize in political thought, political institutions, or international relations, all three of which required courses on sociology, the history of Chinese society, the history of Chinese political thought, and the history of Chinese society and economy. Chinese diplomatic history, Far Eastern politics, international trade, modern Sino-European cultural interactions, labor law, Chinese legal history, the labor movement and history of socialism were among the courses offered in the three fields. The senior-year curriculum for the field of political institutions also made its required coursework the history of Chinese finance, the history of finance in republican China and its problems, and issues in contemporary Chinese finance.[55] The *Beiping Morning News* (*Beiping chenbao*) responded that the additions to the curriculum in the College of Law focused on increasing basic student skills in theory and practice. The increase in the courses on finance was especially relevant to the problems in current Chinese economy and finance.[56] Other than the courses on finance, however, the other courses on Chinese society remained largely survey courses and, as such, provided a *Chinese perspective* on the theoretical and methodological courses offered in the department but not in-depth study; therefore, they were not suitable fields for specialization. By 1936, Peking University had increased the common core courses for all students to put the current Chinese crisis in historical and international perspective. Added were three required courses—methods of social sciences, contemporary international relations, and introduction to national defense—and two elective courses—the history of social evolution and sociology, and the history of imperialist invasions of China.[57]

Despite the increase in courses to enhance awareness of Chinese society, only a few professors were aware of the gap between the predominant intellectual idealization of the West and the reality of Chinese society. Like his colleagues, Chen Qixiu (professor of law from 1919 to 1926 and 1930 to 1937) wrote extensively on individual rights, citizenship, and the rationale for government and laws. A graduate of the Law Division of Imperial Tokyo University where he studied from 1913 to 1917, Chen took a teaching position, first, at the Law and Commerce Institute and, then, beginning in 1919, at Peking University.[58] He criticized the state for its unrestrained power and disregarding economic laws. At the same time, however, he recognized the difficulty China faced in its transition from a clan-controlled, self-sufficient economy to a commercial economy based on market forces; no leader was in a position to abolish obstacles to domestic economic development and issue foreign policies that favored the free competition of Chinese products abroad. Because of the absence of state regulation over the economy, productivity in China had declined because of the prevalence of traditional means of production. Over-concentration of capital and a historical legacy of clan-based control of society prevented the effective functioning of free-market competition. The gap between the rich and the poor was growing, with an attendant deterioration of morality.[59] Chen believed that legal and political reform would follow economic reconstruction. He understood that a deteriorating Chinese economy would prevent him and his colleagues from putting into action any of the ideals borrowed from the West, where stronger economies enabled effective government policies and facilitated the careers of professionals such as lawyers and academics.

One of the few law or political science faculty who radically broke away from the practice of an intellectualistic and relativistic approach to Western law and politics was Chen Hansheng. Born in Wuxi, Jiangsu Province, to a family of scholars, Chen attended modern primary and secondary schools in his hometown and Changsha, where he completed his high school education at the Yale-in-China program. After graduating from Pomona College in 1920, Chen Hansheng earned a master's degree in history at the University of Chicago in 1921 and a Ph.D. in history at the University of Berlin in 1924. At the invitation of Cai Yuanpei, Chen taught European and American history and historiography at Peking University beginning in 1924, and later, added a course on American constitutional history in the Law Department. After his return to Peking in 1924 Chen was introduced to communism by Li Dazhao, a colleague in the History Department and one of the founding members of the Chinese Communist Party. After this point, Chen contributed articles to publications of the Communist International and conducted intelligence for it, although he did not formally join the Chinese Communist Party until 1935.

The same social concern that prompted Chen to seek communism as a solution to China's social problems also informed his research. Although trained as a historian, Chen became interested in social research, in particular at the grass roots, after his return to China.[61] One topic that he found engaging was Japanese-owned textile factories in Shanghai, specifically the bond workers (*baoshengong*) there.[62] Chen published pamphlets and distributed them among the workers. The pamphlets called the workers the victims of the industrial contract system (*baoshen zhidu*), forced to work in the factories due to the decline of the Chinese countryside caused by natural disasters, wars, heavy taxes, inflation, and high debts. The pamphlets infuriated members of the Nationalist government, who searched Chen's background for evidence of communist support. The investigation into his research project forced Chen to switch the focus of work from Japanese textile factories in Shanghai to the rural economy.[63] Chen Hansheng was able to pursue this line of research because Cai Yuanpei, who invited Chen to join the Academia Sinica, despite pressure from Chen's detractors, continued to support his work at the Academia Sinica.[60]

In 1933, Chen was made a member of the Commission for Rural Rehabilitation established by the Executive Yuan of the government in Nanjing. The commission sponsored studies of such problems as the availability of credit, taxes, the marketing of major food grains and cash crops, and irrigation, in Wuxi, Hebei, and Lingnan, Guangdong—areas that experienced rapid industrial and commercial development and witnessed rapid economic changes.[64] His ultimate goal was to find a general guideline for Chinese economic development and revive the Chinese rural economy. He explored the problems of land concentration, especially in southern China, where a high percentage of the landlords were absentee ones.[65] In the 1930s, Chen began more consciously to conceptualize the Chinese situation in terms of class struggle.[66] He depicted the sharp tension between not only peasants and landlords but also peasants and foreign companies, pointing out the collusion between the Chinese state, militarists, bureaucrats, local strongmen, landlords, and foreign capitalists in China.[67] Chen viewed the foreign interests in China and China's gentry as irreconcilably antagonistic to the Chinese peasants and workers. This intellectual understanding obviously contributed to his confirmed belief in communism. He joined the Party in 1935 and, performed covert operations for the Communists throughout the 1930s and 1940s, including helping Party members wanted by the Nationalists to escape from Shanghai. Marxism helped Chen to conceptualize the hurdles China faced on the road of westernization and Western and Chinese societies in an unequal power relationship: Western governments and companies, with their superior power, dominated Chinese politics and economy. Yet Marxist social analysis represented another source of foreign influence. In his attempt to understand Chinese society, Chen, like later Chinese Marxists, did not resort to Chinese traditional scholarship or methodologies.

Another faculty member who went beyond an intellectual theorization of China's legal and political future was Zhou Gengsheng, who taught in the Law Department from 1922 to 1926. Zhou was especially interested in a legal solution to extraterritoriality. Zhou was a native of Changsha, Hunan province. As an orphan, he was patronized by local elites and studied politics, law, and economics at Waseda University in Japan in the first few years of the twentieth century. A fervent nationalist, Zhou fought both the Qing government in the 1911 revolution and the Yuan Shikai government. Fleeing arrest in 1913, Zhou went to study politics, law, and economics, at the University of Edinburgh, earning a Ph.D. and a gold medal for his achievements. He subsequently earned a Ph.D. in law at the University of Paris. While in France in 1919, he and Wang Shijie as well as other Chinese students studying in Britain and France, besieged Wellington Koo, the Chinese delegate at the Paris peace conference, to prevent him from signing the Versailles treaty, which was to transfer Shandong province from German to Japanese control. But unlike Wang Shijie, Chen Daqi, and Hu Shi, among others, who ended up working for the Nationalist government in the 1930s and 1940s, Zhou declined a position in the Legislative Yuan offered in the late 1920s.[68] Although critical of the corruption and lawlessness of the various Chinese governments, Zhou was preoccupied with China's weak international status. [69] As his daughter once recalled, his one concern before 1949 was the abolition of unequal treaties between China and other countries.[70] His writings dealt both with issues of international law inspired by specific cases in China and resolutions to some of these cases. For instance, regarding extraterritoriality, Zhou discussed its history in Europe and compared its practice in China with the Western theories on it, emphasizing that China still held sovereignty over leased territories to Russia, Germany, Japan, Britain, and so on.[71]

Regarding the status of the Shanghai and Wuhan international territories where conflict broke out between Chinese workers and foreign police in 1925, Zhou argued that these concessions were allocated to foreigners for residence and commerce, not administration, so they were still Chinese territory by law, thus all political actions of foreign powers were obliged to have the Chinese state's approval. He thus charged the British with being chiefly responsible for the workers' deaths since Britons formed the majority of the staff in the Department of Industry in the international concession in Shanghai that authorized opening fire on unarmed demonstrating workers. He further argued that the International Concessions Police opening fire at Chinese workers in Shanghai was not just a violation of law but an encroachment of Chinese sovereignty. It should not be treated as merely a legal matter, because doing so would acknowledge that Britain maintained a special status. That special status should be chipped away at, beginning with Britain to create a precedent for other foreign countries to follow.[72] Although in the matter of extraterritoriality Zhou believed that the solution went beyond a legalistic approach, he believed that China had to recover its sovereignty by following international law.[73] Zhou's interest extended beyond China to the fight for national independence of British colonies around the world.[74]

## Conclusion

Despite the greater development of the law and political science curricula over the years, a vigorous academic standard guiding the two disciplines was by no means clear. Most of the faculty projected an idealized picture of Western law and politics, presenting Western politics as rational and managerial and the antithesis of the irrational politics and personal rule in China. They often adopted a relativistic approach to the discussion of Western politics, which hid their ambivalence toward the Western values of democracy and individualism. While praising these values and using them as the standard to measure the Chinese state, many of these professors personally preferred a moderately authoritarian state and had doubts about democracy and individualism in China. Yet they predominantly presented an uncritical evaluation of Western democratic politics, a view probably associated more with their perception of Western society, such as greater political stability in general and greater prosperity, than with the values embodied in Western law and politics. The deep social chasm between industrialized West and (partially) industrializing China probably contributed to their failure to identify with Western democratic values and fully embrace ideas like individualism. They created a great dilemma for themselves by fashioning the ideal of a rational and managerial type of state that was so remote from the Chinese reality. They avoided discussing the social dynamics beneath Western legal and political practices because, first, those practices were treated as "iron laws" that China needed to adopt before it could become stronger and, second, the social disparity between China and the West would prevent the implementation of such laws in China. This trend did not change despite the deepening national crisis and the greater social awareness introduced to the curriculum. Those who argued for alternative approaches to the study of Chinese politics and Western politics, such as Chen Hansheng and Zhou Gengsheng, always remained in the minority.

# Conclusion

On July 7, 1937, clashes outside the city walls of Beijing between Chinese Nationalist troops and the Japanese army marked the outbreak of the Sino-Japanese War, which would last for the next eight years. The war had a profound impact on the development of Peking University, leading to the university's merger with Nankai and Qinghua universities and then a long retreat, first, to central China and, then, to the relatively undeveloped region of southwestern China (hence the name "Southwestern Associated University") far from the area under Japanese occupation.[1] Although the spirit of Peking University, foremost of which was Cai Yuanpei's *jianrong bingbao,* would continue, the year 1937 provides a logical place to end the present discussion because of the reorganization of the university that followed and the vast changes from the academic environment to economic conditions that took place at this point.

The history of Peking University in the twentieth century both paralleled and shaped the development of Chinese intellectual culture. Early university structure and curriculum were affected by the imperial government's dramatic change from the imperial examination system to the modern educational system and the subsequent end to a direct linkage between education and politics. As reflected in the university curriculum, a Confucian emphasis on integrated learning was also replaced by academic specialization. Academic specialization, however, did not prevent the various disciplines with Chinese learning content from adopting similar approaches to learning, including a blend of historicism, scientific methods, textual exegesis, and European metaphysics; such approaches integrated the study of Chinese history, literature, philology, and philosophy into the umbrella term "Chinese studies." This newly assembled and integrated body of Chinese knowledge, however, was transformed through the years, from Zhang Zhidong's attempt to recreate a Chinese universe *qua* moral universe to a repositioning of Chinese learning into a more universal discourse of knowledge, of which Chinese learning was a part and on a par with Western learning. The approaches developed in Chinese learning in the first thirty years of the twentieth century, including a textual exegetical style, evolutionary historicism, and inductive reasoning, served as the foundation of the future academic disciplines of Chinese history and philology. Moreover, most of the faculty members discussed here had as their institutional basis the Research Institute of Chinese Studies, part of the graduate school at Peking University where, led by Hu Shi and Shen Jianshi, they conducted their textual exegesis, archaeological studies, collected and studied folksongs and ballads, and discussed language reform. As part of the movement for the scientific reorganization of the national past championed by Hu Shi, they performed an extensive taxonomy of the Chinese national past, which paved the way for the later taxonomy of Chinese knowledge in academic disciplines such as archaeology, anthropology, philology, history, and literature. Furthermore, many of them later joined the newly established Academia Sinica's Institute of History and Philology, which continued the work at Peking University's Research Institute of Chinese Studies to transform Chinese studies into modern academic disciplines.[2] A modern academic transformation of Chinese learning was further facilitated under Cai's *jianrong bingbao* policy, wherein Liang Shuming's division of Chinese and Western cultures into two different stages of universal human development paved the way for an academic separation of the arts and sciences by freeing the arts from the omnipotent grip of a scientific framework.[3] Xiong Shili's subjection of both China and the West to a transcendental, universal spirituality opened up new possibilities for Confucian learning in the twentieth century, enabling it to draw upon the ethical and metaphysical schools of thought of the West in order to develop into a more metaphysical philosophy and adapt to the modern and, later, postmodern era. One can safely say that the development of Peking University led the development of modern academic disciplines in China.

This development was obviously guided by modern nationalism, but nationalism was not the ultimate criterion in deciding the university culture. For Cai, nationalism was secondary to his transcendental framework of knowledge. To Cai and many of his colleagues, academic autonomy meant that the university would develop its own culture, distinct from nationalism or politics, that would in the long run benefit the nation but avoid the utilitarian decisions to achieve immediate national salvation. Against the pressure to replace the Confucian cosmology with scientism, Cai maintained a largely even-handed treatment at the university of the traditional and the modern, the Chinese and the Western. That said, science played a critical role in the methodology and rationale of academic disciplines. It enabled treating Chinese history and literature, or even Confucian classics, as historical documents, facilitating the introduction of a historical approach that replaced cyclical and moralistic history in Chinese learning. Even textual exegesis thrived in the twentieth century by following something like scientific objectivity.

Ultimately, however, the rationale behind the academic disciplines—and the initial motivation behind Zhang Zhidong's 1903 curriculum—was the desire for change, to bring about a new social, cultural, and political reality in China. The motivation for change led to the introduction of historicism, which enabled Chinese scholars to recount change in the Chinese past in order to rationalize change in the present and to introduce scientific methodology to give greater credibility to their documentation of change in the past. It also led to the treatment of Western learning as an agent of change. As reflected in the disciplines of education, psychology, law, and politics, this resulted in a confusion of academic criteria: there was little discrimination of methodology because Western learning was meant to bring about social change, rather than be treated as having intrinsic values. Similarly, Chinese learning was also treated in an instrumental way, hence the reduction in the significance of Confucian learning and classical learning in general over a short period. Take the example of a Chinese textbook Xia Zengyou wrote for high school students in the classical style (without punctuation) when it was first published in 1902–4. When a new edition of the book came out in 1933, it was issued as a college textbook with punctuation, indicating a general reduction in classical literacy only thirty years later.[4] Of course, neither all Chinese learning nor all Western learning was treated in an instrumental way. Western concepts such as evolution and historicism worked their way into the new core of Chinese culture, reminiscent of an argument made by Joseph Levenson of the dichotomy between "history" and "value,"[5] with history referring to Chinese culture now reduced from value to history, and value referring to Western culture. The distinction is by no means that clear, especially because after the destruction of the Confucian paradigm, new values were constantly created with the reification of ideas from Chinese history.

One negative consequence of tying disciplinary studies to social change was the instability and even murkiness of academic criteria. Nationalistic causes, such as spreading literacy or repelling foreign invasion, would all affect university curricula and the research methodology of faculty members. But the impact seemed to be most adverse in the disciplines of education and psychology, which were based on a rationale of social relevance and where wide swings of disciplinary rationales took place when the desired social outcome was not achieved. Treating Western law and politics as agents of social change also led to an idealization of Western legal and political developments in the disciplines of law and politics, but the academic criteria guiding the law and political science faculty's research were not always clear, and there was little discussion of methodology. Western politics remained the antithesis of Chinese politics. In general, social change as a rationale for the various social science academic disciplines prevented a rigorous methodological examination of the disciplinary approaches to scholarship, although it facilitated the introduction of science and historicism.

The intellectual culture that Peking University helped to shape in its early years had a tremendous impact on Chinese intellectual culture during the rest of the twentieth century. First, although Cai Yuanpei and Jiang Menglin did not try to recreate a Chinese moral universe as Zhang Zhidong did, they differentiated between a universe of learning that represented a national culture and a universe of learning that would more directly facilitate actual political and social changes in China. The former universe, which was primarily the humanities disciplines, comprised a synthesis of Chinese and Western learning and a universal knowledge framework. Over time, this sphere of learning became more and more Westernized in content. Communist China not only introduced (Western) Marxism and Leninism (it never occurred to me as a child that I should be surprised at the image of Mao alongside Marx, Engels, Lenin, and Stalin on Tiananmen Square in Beijing) but also, during the Cultural Revolution (1966–76), vowed to stamp out Chinese tradition. This body of knowledge, however, retained moral purpose, even though its content and actual morals changed over the years. Yet, at the same time it also retained an ambivalence toward the other body of knowledge as an agent of social change to bring about national strength and prosperity and perception of it as antithetical to Chinese society.

Despite the ambivalence toward Western learning as the agent of change, the continued Westernization in both realms of learning in socialist China greatly facilitated Chinese acceptance of Western knowledge the second time China opened up to the outside world, in the late 1970s. A significant trend in this round of opening is that the Chinese have been looking both outward into outside cultures for borrowings and back into Chinese history in areas that go much beyond the humanities, especially in the 1990s and after. Although the reasons for this trend are very complex, one of them is certainly the decline of Communist credibility and the relaxation of the Communist government over the control of the tools of social transformation—Western knowledge and technology—now more and more operated through privatized hands on a social scale unprecedented in modern Chinese history. The viable development of professions in China today also enhanced the relevance of Western social and applied sciences in China so that these subjects no longer are just instruments for social transformation, but also impart a more permanent way of looking at things and a system of valuation. A less utilitarian approach to Western learning may lead to a less utilitarian approach to Chinese tradition, so that those parts of the Chinese past beyond moral self-cultivation and not immediately relevant to building national strength may become the object of curiosity and study again.

Administration Building of the current Peking University.

Stone lion in front of the Administration Building.

Details of the front gate of the Administration Building.

The Arthur Sackler Museum of Art and Anthropology, completed in 1993.

Pavilion by Nameless Lake (*weiminghu*) (post-1952 campus).

Water pagoda by Nameless Lake.

Details of the pagoda's interior.

Tomb of Edgar Snow, where some of his ashes were buried. Snow was an American journalist who lectured at Yanjing (Yenching) University between 1933 and 1936, on the site of which sits the current Peking University.

The current Peking University library.

Statue of Cervantes.

Bridge on pond that leads to the front gate of the current Peking University.

Honglou today, as the seat of the New Culture Movement Museum and publishing house on topics of cultural preservation.

The triangle corner (*sanjiaodi*), a part of the campus where news postings about the campus make it one of the centers for student gatherings on campus.

Front gate of Peking University.

Children from kindergarten housed on the campus of Peking University.

Campus street.

# Notes

## Abbreviations used in Notes

| | |
|---|---|
| *BDRK* | Beijing daxue rikan (*Peking University Daily*) |
| *BDSKJK* | Beijing daxue shehui kexue jikan (*Peking University Social Sciences Quarterly*) |
| *DFZZ* | Dongfang zazhi (The Eastern Miscellany) |
| *ECCP* | Eminent Chinese of the Ch'ing Period, 1644–1912 |
| *HDPK* | Beijingdaxue shiliao (1898–1911) (Historical Documents of Peking University, 1898–1911) |
| *LYJK* | Guoli zhongyang yanjiuyuan lishi yuyan yanjiusuo jikan (*Journal of the History and Linguistics Institute of Academia Sinica*). |
| *XDPL* | Xiandai pinglun (*Contemporary Review*) |

## Introduction

1. The use of historicism here relies on the interpretations of Frank Ankersmit, Georg Iggers, and Jeffrey Stout. Although they differ in their definition of historicism, they do agree on some premises upon which historicism exists. Ankersmit and Stout agree to some extent on the conditions on which historicism could develop: the disintegration of an established authority or challenge to traditional authority. Iggers differs from Ankersmit in his view toward Enlightenment historiography—Ankersmit views it as drastically different from the historicist writings that followed, whereas Iggers finds much continuity between the Enlightenment and post-Enlightenment histories. But Iggers concurs with Ankersmit that a historical approach to writing developed especially in nineteenth-century Europe. Despite the variation in their perspectives (Ankersmit is a postmodernist while Iggers is not), Ankersmit and Iggers's descriptions of historicism are similar in postulating that it focused on the concrete and individual, pinning the meaning of historical events to their specific contexts. Here, accepting Ankersmit's premise on the rise of historicism, and borrowing from both Iggers and Ankersmit on their defini-

tions of historicism, one can argue that the conflict between China and Western countries also disrupted the harmony between the individual and Confucian principles governing society in mainstream Chinese thought. The Chinese past, once taken for granted, became an enigma. F.R. Ankersmit, *History and Tropology, the Rise and Fall of Metaphor* (Berkeley: University of California Press, 1994), 76, 78; Jeffrey Stout, *The Flight from Authority: Religion, Morality and the Quest for Autonomy* (Notre Dame: 1981), x–xi, 2–21, 37–61, in On-cho Ng, "A Tension in Ching Thought: 'Historicism' in Seventeenth- and Eighteenth-Century Chinese Thought," *Journal of the History of Ideas*, 54 (1993), 561–583. Geog Iggers, "Historicism: The History and Meaning of the Term," *Journal of the History of Ideas*, 56 (1995), 129–152. F.R. Ankersmit, "A Reply to Professor Iggers," *History and Theory*, 34 (1995), 168–170.

2. Hao Chang, "Zhongguo jindai sixiangshi de zhuanxing shidai" (The era of transition in modern Chinese intellectual thought), *Ershiyi shiji* (The twenty-first century; henceforth cited as *21C*), no. 52 (April 1999), at http://www.cuhk.edu.hk/ics/21c/index2.htm.

3. Jin Guantao and Liu Qingfeng, "Xinwenhua yundong yu changshi lixing de bianqian" (The New Culture Movement and changes in the definition of common sense and rationality), *21C*, no. 52 (April 1999), at http://www.cuhk.edu.hk/ics/21c/index2.htm.

## Chapter 1

1. Benjamin Schwartz, "History in Chinese Culture: Some Comparative Reflections," *History and Theory*, 35(4) (December 1996): 32–33.

2. Li Tiangang, "Qingdai ruxue yuxixue" (Confucian learning and Western learning in the Qing Dynasty), *21C*, 67 (Oct. 2001), 51–56.

3. Sun Banghua, "Xichao chongjixia wanqing shidafu de bianjuguan" (Late Qing Dynasty officials' views on change under the pressure of Western influence), *21C*, 65 (June 2001), at www.cuhk.edu.hk/ics/21c/issue/article/000142.htm.

4. Ruth Hayhoe, *China's Universities 1895–1995: A Century of Cultural Conflict* (New York and London: Garland, 1996), 37.

5. Xiaoqing Diana Chen, "The Chinese Scholars and the Modern University: The Appropriation of Foreign Educational Models, 1900–30," in *History of Higher Education Annual*, 1993: 99–116.

6. Su Jing, *Qingji tongwenguan jiqishisheng* (The School of Interpreters in the Qing Dynasty, including its teachers and students) (Taibei: Su Jing, 1985), 150.

7. Dong Shouyi, *Gongqinwang yixin dazhuan* (The biography of Prince Gong) (Shenyang: Liaoning renmin chubanshe, 1989), 40, 44–45, 67–106.

8. Su, *Qingji tongwenguan jiqishisheng*, 3–4, 11, 13–14.

9. Yang Jialuo, ed., *Zhongguo jindaishi wenxian huibian, wuxu bianfa wenxian huibian*, (Collected documents of modern Chinese history: The Hundred Days Reform, I) (Taibei: Dingwen Press, 1973), 1: 22–23.

10. Su, *Qingji tongwenguan jiqishisheng*, 32–35.

11. Tang Zhijun, *Wuxu bianfa renwu zhuan'gao* (Biographies of the participants in the Hundred Day Reform) (Taibei: Wenhai Press), vol. 2, excerpted in Zhu Chuanyu, ed., *Li Hongzhang zhuanji ziliao* (Biographical materials of Li Hongzhang) (Taibei: Tianyi Press, 1979), 1: 40–41; Qu Lihe, *Qingmo xiyi jiaoyu sichao* (Western education in the late Qing dynasty) (Taibei: Committee to Encourage Scholarly Works in China, 1970), 18.

12. Yang, *Zhongguo jindaishi wenxian huibian, wuxu bianfa wenxian huibian*, 1: 29–31; Wang Zhichun, "Guang xuexiaopian" (On popularizing schools), in *Beijing daxue shiliao* (1898–1911) (Historical documents of Peking University, 1898–1911; henceforth cited as *HDPK*, 1) (Beijing: Peking University Press, 1993), 1: 3; Xue Fucheng, "Xiyang xuexiao zhisheng" (The abundance of schools in the West), in *HDPK*, 1: 3; Min Tu-ki, *National Polity and Local Power: The Transformation of Late Imperial China* (Cambridge: Harvard University, Council on East Asian Studies, 1989), 73.

13. Li Qiang, "Yan Fu yu Zhongguo jindai sixiang de zhuanxing, jianping shihuazi xunqiu fuqiang, yanfu yu xifang" (Yan Fu and modern Chinese intellectual transition, and a comment on Benjamin Schwartz's *In Search of Wealth and Power, Yan Fu and the West*), *Zhongguo shuping*, 9 (February 1996): 93–121.

14. See Timothy B. Weston, "The Founding of the Imperial University and the Emergence of Chinese Modernity," in Rebecca Karl and Peter Zarrow, eds., *Rethinking the 1898 Reform Period, Political and Cultural Change in Late Qing China* (Cambridge: Harvard University Asia Center, 2002), 99–123; Tze-ki Hon, "Zhang Zhidong's Proposal for Reform: A New Reading of the Quanxue Pian," in ibid., 77–98. Both have accepted the *ti-yong* continuum premise argued by Min, *National Polity and Local Power*, 51–88.

15. William Ayers, *Chang Chih-tung and Educational Reform in China* (Cambridge: Harvard University Press, 1971), 17, 23–25, 26, 28–29, 31–38.

16. Zhang Baixi, "Zhang Baixi zouqing tianpai Zhang Zhidong huishang xuewuzhe" (Zhang Baixi's petition to the crown on including Zhang Zhidong to redraft the school regulations), in *HDPK*, 1: 57; Guo Jianrong, "Xuezhe dangyi tianxia weijiren" (The scholar should take as his responsibility all the affairs of the world), in Tang, Yijie ed., *Beida xiaozhang yu Zhongguo wenhua*, (Peking University Presidents and Chinese Culture) (Beijing: Peking University Press, 1998), 35–37.

17. Zhang Zhidong, "Daxuetang zhangcheng" (University regulations), in *HDPK*, 1: 97–98.

18. Chen Qitian, *Zhongguo jindai jiaoyu zhidu* (Modern Chinese educational systems) (Taibei: Zhonghua shuju, 1969), 10–11.

19. On Enlightenment historians, see F.R. Ankersmit, "Reply to Professor Iggers," *History and Theory*, 34 (1995): 168–70; idem, *History and Tropology: The Rise and Fall of Metaphor* (Berkeley: University of California Press, 1994), 76–81.

20. Zhang, "Daxuetang zhangcheng," 98–100.

21. Ibid., 99–101.

22. Min, *National Polity and Local Power*, 75.

23. Zhang, "Daxuetang zhangcheng," 104–105.

24. Ibid., 106–107.

25. Min, *National Polity and Local Power*, 76.

26. Zhang, "Daxuetang zhangcheng," 102–103.

27. The sheer number of people taking the examinations and the millions of examination papers that needed to be graded, prevented attempts to reform the eight-legged essay—the standard format for the imperial examinations, which, with its rigid format, at least facilitated the grading of thousands of papers by a dozen examiners within a few days. The sheer logistics of grading also intimidated any attempt to add more subjects to the examination topics. Benjamin Elman, *A Cultural History of Civil Examinations in Late Imperial China* (Berkeley: University of California Press, 2000), 213–220, 524–536.

28. Yang, *Zhongguo jindaishi wenxian huibian, wuxubianfa wenxian huibian*, 2: 344–345, 466–469.

29. "Yuan Shikai, Zhang Zhidong qing dijian keju" (Yuan Shikai and Zhang Zhidong's petition to reduce the examination system), in *HDPK*, 1: 35.

30. Chen, *Zhongguo jindai jiaoyu zhidu*, 90.

31. Chen Pingyuan, "Xinjiaoyu yu xinwenxue" (New education and new literature), in idem, *Beida jinshen jiqita* (The spirit of Peking University, etc.) (Shanghai: Shanghai wenyi chubanshe, 2000), 249, 250.

32. "Zongli yamen zounijingshi daxuetang zhangcheng" (Proposal for the imperial university stipulations by the Ministry of Foreign Affairs), in *HDPK*, 1: 81–82, 87.

33. Chen, "Xinjiaoyu yu xinwenxue," 251–256.

34. Sun Jianai, "Sun Jianai yifu kaiban jingshi daxuetang zhe" (Sun Jianai's memorial to build the imperial Peking University), in *HDPK*, 1: 23.

35. See Luo Junjun, "Jiaoyu gexin nai qiangguo zhiben" (Educational reform as the foundation for national self strengthening), in Tang Yijie, ed., *Beidaxiaozhang yu Zhongguo wenhua* (Peking University presidents and Chinese culture) (Beijing: Peking University Press, 1998), 18–19.

36. "Zhang Baixi," in *HDPK*, 1: 70; Guo, "Xuezhe dangyi tianxia weijiren," 26–33.

37. "Waiwubu weipaiyuan chuyang kaocha xuewushi zifudaxuetang" (The Ministry of Foreign Affairs in response to Zhang Baixi's request to send staff to inspect schools in Japan), *HDPK*, 1: 132; Zhang Baixi, "Shen Zhaozhi shenbao furi kaocha xuetang qingkuang" (Shen Zhaozhi reports his inspection of Japanese schools) *HDPK*, 1: 133; "Zhumei dashi weisong meiguo geyouguanxuetang shouke zhangchengshi zi jingshi daxuetang" (Letter to the Imperial University from the Ambassador to the United States on American schools and universities curricula and regulations), in *HDPK*, 1: 132.

38. Zhang Baixi, "Qingding jingshi daxuetang zhangcheng," in *HDPK*, 1: 89–90.

39. Ibid., 87, 89–90.

40. Timothy Weston suggests that besides the infighting between conservatives and liberals within the Qing government, Zhang Baixi's resignation was directly triggered off by a student movement in 1903 over Russian encroachments in Manchuria, which the court found unruly. See Timothy Weston, *The Power of Position, Beijing University, Intellectuals, and Chinese Political Culture, 1989–1929* (Berkeley: University of California Press, 2004), 59–64.

41. "Yuan Shikai deng zouqing liting keju yiguang xuexiaozhe" (Yuan Shikai et al.'s petition to stop the examination system and implement the school system), in *HDPK*, 1: 37.

42. Ibid.

## Chapter 2

1. Elman, *A Cultural History of Civil Examinations in Late Imperial China*, 83, 128, 148.

2. Qian Gengsen, "Jingshi daxuetang heyi xingcun" (How to explain the survival of Imperial Peking University After the Hundred Days Reform of 1898), *Zhonghua dushubao*, September 16, 1998.

3. Zhu Ying, "Jingshi daxuetang bingfei bianfa shibaihoude weiyi xingcunzhe" (The Imperial Peking University was not the only survivor of the Hundred Days Reform), *Jindaishi yanjiu*, 2 (2000), 315–317.

4. Chen Pingyuan, *Lao beida de gushi* (Stories of Old Peking University) (Nanjing: Jiangsu wenyi chubanshe, 1998), 43–44, 51–52.

5. Chen, *Lao beida de gushi*, 49–50.

6. Chen, "Xinjiaoyu yu xinwenxue," 251.

7. Sun Jianai, "Xieban daxueshi sunjianai souqing yishuju biancuan geshu qinghou qingding banfa bing qing yanjin beishushi" (Sun Jianai, a scholar in the Hanlin Academy suggested the establishment of a Translation Bureau to translate and compile

textbooks and to petition the crown to stop the circulation of certain books), in *HDPK*, 1: 190.

8. Ibid., 190; Yan Fu, "Jingshi daxuetang yishuju zhangcheng" (Regulations of the Translation Bureau attached to the Imperial Peking University), in *HDPK*, 1: 194–196.

9. "Zouding yixueguan zhangcheng" (Imperially approved regulations of the School of Translation attached to Imperial Peking University), in *HDPK*, 1: 169–174.

10. Richard Rubinger, "Education, from One Room to One System," in Marius Jensen and Gilbert Rozman, eds., *Japan in Transition: From Tokugawa to Meiji* (Princeton: Princeton University Press, 1986), 217–227.

11. Hiroshi Abe, "Borrowing from Japan: China's First Modern Educational System," in Ruth Hayhoe and Marianne Bastid, eds., *China's Education and the Industrialized World: Studies in Cultural Transfer* (Armonk, NY: M.E. Sharpe, 1987), 63–64.

12. *Diyici Zhongguo jiaoyu nianjian* (The first Chinese educational yearbook) (Taibei: Zhuanji wenxue, 1971), 2: 334.

13. Zhang Baixi, "Qingding jingshi daxuetang zhangcheng," in *HDPK*, 1: 91–92.

14. Chen Pingyuan, "Beijing daxue, conghe shuoqi" (Peking University, how to trace its earliest beginning), in idem, Laobeida deguski (Stories of Old Beida) (Nanjing: Jiangsu wenyi, 1998), 50; Liu Kexuan and Fang Mingdong, eds., *Beida yu Qinghua* (Beijing University and Qinghua University) (Beijing: Guojia xingzheng xueyuan chubanshe, 1998), 22–23; Liang, Daxuetang zhangcheng," in *HDPK*, 1: 84.

15. "Yange yilan" (A survey of the changes of the University), in *Guoli Beijing daxue jiniankan* (Commemorative issue of National Peking University) (Taibei: Zhuanji wenxue, 1971), 1:87–88; "Daxuetang shifansheng biye fenshu dengdidan" (List of the grades of graduates of the Normal School attached to the university), in *HDPK*, 1: 393–396.

16. "Xuebu zou jinshiguan biye jianglizhe" (The Ministry of Education's memorial on awards to graduates of the School for Jinshi), in *HDPK*, 1: 411–414; "Wei jinshiguan biye xueyuan shouzhiyu" (Announcement on the positions conferred on graduates of the School for Jinshi), in *HDPK*, 1: 406–407; "Jinshiguan yangelue" (A survey of the changes of the School for Jinshi), in *HDPK*, 1: 158–159.

17. "Xuebu zouchouban jinshi fenke daxue bing xianban dagai qingxing zhe" (The Ministry of Education's memorial on the establishment of university divisions and the current situation of those divisions), in *HDPK*, 1: 200–201.

18. Liu and Fang, *Beida yu Qinghua*, 30.

19. "Xuebu zouqing tingzhi gexuetang biyesheng geiyu shiguanjiang" (The Ministry of Education petitions to stop awarding school graduates at all levels with actual government office), in *HDPK*, 1: 439.

20. Liu and Fang, *Beida yu Qinghua*, 12–13.

21. "Xuantong ernian fenke daxue qingxing jilue"(An account of the university divisions' establishment in 1910), in *HDPK*, 1: 142.

22. Zhang Jiqian, "Diyiren xiaozhang, Yan Fu" (Yan Fu, the first president of Peking University), in Xiao Chaoran, ed., *Weiwei shangxiang, bainian xingcheng* (The stars of Peking University in the past hundred years) (Beijing: Peking University Press, 1998), 15.

23. "Choushejinshifazhengxuetang zhuonizhangchengzhe" (Memorial on draft regulations of the proposed Imperial Beijing School of Law and Politics), in *HDPK*, 1: 158.

24. Xiao Chaoran et al., *Beijing daxue xiaoshi* (Peking University History), *1898–1949*, expanded ed., (Beijing: Peking University Press, 1987), 26.

25. "Xuebu zouqing shefenke daxuezhe" (The Ministry of Education's memorial to establish university divisions at Imperial Peking University), in *HDPK*, 1: 197–198.

26. Luo Junjun, "Jiaoyu gexin nai qiangguo zhiben," 16–17.

27. "Xu Jincheng," in *HDPK*, 1: 70–71; Arthur Hummel, *Eminent Chinese of the Ch'ing Period, 1644–1912* (henceforth cited as *ECCP*) (Washington: U.S. Government Printing Office, 1943), 1:312–313, 2: 343.

28. Chen Pingyuan, "Bubei chengren de xiaozhang" (W.A.P. Martin, the president who was not), 95–113, and "Chidaole shisinian de renming" (The appointment that came fourteen years late), 114–117, both in idem, *Lao Beida de gushi*.

29. Chen, "Chidaole shisinian de renming," 117–123.

30. Ibid., 122.

31. The Yanghu school differed from the Tongcheng school in that, while the latter emphasized the six Confucian classics, it emphasized the writing styles of Han Fei, Li Si, and Su Xun, all famous rhetorical, but non-Confucian, writers during the Warring States period who argued for change and adaptation to change. See Chen Zhiping, *Zhonghua tongshi* (Complete history of China) (Taibei: Liming wenhua, 1979), 225–227.

32. *Qingshi* (History of the Qing Dynasty) (Taibei: Guofang yanjiouyuan, 1960), 6: 4932–4933.

33. *ECCP*, 2: 871.

34. *Qingshi*, 6: 4924.

35. "Li Jiaju" and "Liu Tingchen," in *HDPK*, 1: 71.

36. Chen, "Bubei chengren de xiaozhang," 105–106.

37. Zhang Heling, "Jingshi daxuetang lunlixue jinxue jiangyi" (Lecture notes on ethics and classics at Imperial Peking University) (Peking University library, 1903).

38. Stephen C. Angle, *Human Rights and Chinese Thought: A Cross-cultural Inquiry* (Cambridge: Cambridge University Press, 2002), chaps. 4 and 5.

39. Zhang Heling, "Xiushen lunli jiaoyu zashuo jiangyi" (Lecture notes on a miscellaneous treatment of self-cultivation, ethics, and education) (Peking University Library, 1903).

40.Angle, *Human Rights and Chinese Thought*, chap.5.

41. Zhang, "Jingshi daxuetang lunlixue jinxue jiangyi."

42. Zhang Zhidong, "Xuewu gangyao" (Important points on these studies), in *Qingding xuetang zhangcheng* (The imperial edition of school regulations) (Shanghai: Zhizhong Press, 1904), 7.

43.Angle, *Human Rights and Chinese Thought*, chap.5.

44. "Ke Shaomin," in *HDPK*, 1: 71–73.

45. Lao Naixuan, *Tongcheng laxiansheng yigao* (Posthumous writings of Mr. Lao Naixuan of Tongcheng) (Taibei: Yiwenyinshuguan, 1964), 1: 142–145, 235–244.

46. Wang Zhouyao, "Jingxueke jiangyi" (Lecture notes in the field of Confucian classics) (Peking University library, 1903).

47. Chen, "Xinjiaoyu yu xinwenxue," 256–259.

48. Ma Yue, *Beijing daxue zhongwenxi jianshi 1910–1998* (A brief history of the Department of Chinese Languages and Literature at Peking University, 1910–1998) (Beijing: Peking University Press, 1998), 2–3.

49. Chen, "Xinjiaoyu yu xinwenxue," 259–263.

50. Hattori Unokichi, "Jingshidaxuetang xinlixue jiangyi" (Lecture notes on psychology at the Imperial Peking University) (Peking University library, 1903).

51. Ibid.

52. Tu Ji, "Jingshi daxuetang zhongguoshi jiangyi" (Lecture notes on Chinese history) (Peking University library, 1903); Wu Ze, *Zhongguo jindai shixueshi* (History of modern Chinese historiography) (Shanghai: Jiangsu guji, 1988), 2: 288–291.

53. *HDPK*, 1: 265–271.

## Chapter 3

1. Liu and Fang, *Beida yu Qinghua*, 32.

2. Wang Shiru, "Meiyou daoren dexiaozhang, zhangshizhao" (Zhang Shizhao, the president that never assumed office), in Xiao, ed., *Weiwei shangyang, bainian xingchen*, 28–31.

3. Xiao Chaoran, *Beijing daxue xiaoshi*, 40; Liu and Fang, *Beida yu Qinghua*, 34.

4. A detailed account of the finances is available in Guo Jianrong et al., eds., *Beijing daxue shiliao, 1898–1911* (Historical documents of Peking University, 1898–1911)

(Beijing: Peking University Press, 1993), sec. 8, 511–554. See also, a detailed description of life on campus at Imperial Peking University by Hu Xiansu, "Jingshidaxuetang shiyouji" (Memory of teachers and friends at Imperial Peking University), in Wang Shiru and Wen Di, eds., *Wo yu Beida* (Peking University and I) (Beijing: Peking University Press, 1998), 16–27.

5. Chen, "Chidaole shisiniande renming,", 114–137; Shen Yingmo, "Wo yu beida" (Peking University and I), in Mu Zhou and Mu Xiao, eds., *Beida gushi* (Stories of Beida) (Beijing: Zhongguo wujiachubanshe, 1998), 260.

6. Qu Shipei, "Zhuchi xiaowu zuichangde xiaozhang jiangmenglin" (Jiang Menglin, the president who managed the university the longest), in Xiao, ed., *Weiweishangxiang, bainian xingchen*, 59–60.

7. Yang Cuihua, "Jiang Menglin yu beijing daxue, 1930–37" (Jiang Menglin and Peking University), *Zhongyang yanjiuyuan jindaishi yanjiusuo jikan* (Collection of the Modern History Institute of Academia Sinica), 17 (December ember 1988), 261–305.

8. *Zhongbao*, October ober 3, 1926 (Peking University Archive).

9. The China Foundation of Culture and Education was founded in 1924 to distribute the American returned Boxer Indemnity funds. The United States first decided to return its portion of the Boxer Indemnity funds to China for Chinese education in 1908, effective to 1940. The payments would be monthly installments to China, basicaly a transfer of the Chinese gvernment's monthly deposits of Boxer Indemnity payment to the United States in Citibank's headquarters in Changhai, to the Chinese Ministry of Foreign Affairs via the U.S. consul in Shanghai. A second decision was made in 1924, when the U.S. reassessed the amount of Boxer Indemnity payment Chna was to submit to the U.S. to be returned to China for educational purposes. The reassessment, including principal and interest between 1917 and 1940, was over $12 million, up from $10 million (1908–1940) in the 1908 assessment. And the China Foundation was established with appointments from both China and the U.S. to oversee the distribution of the money. Yang Cuihua, *Zhongjikui dui kexue de zanahu* (China Foundation's patronage to science) (Taibei: Academia Sinica, Modern History Institute, 1991), 1–6. Also, Yang, "Jiang Menglin yu beijingdaxue," 279–281.

10. Yang Cuihua, "Jiang Menglin yu beijingdaxue," 279–281.

11. Chen Pingyuan, "Beidade guangrong yumengxiang" (The glory and dream of Peking University), in idem, *Beida jingshen ji qita* (The Spirit of Peking University, etc.), (Shanghai: Wenyi, 2000), 192.

12. Zhang Juncai, "Linshu nianpu jianbian" (A brief edition of Lin Shu's Chronology), in Xue Aizhi and Zhang Juncai, eds., *Lin Shu yanjiu ziliao* (Research materials on Lin Shu) (Fuzhou: Fujian renmin chubanshe, 1983), 28.

13. Ibid., 30.

14. Chen, "Xinjiaoyu yuxinwenxue," 265.

15. Ibid., 265, 269–270.

16. Ibid., 266.

17. Shen Yingmo, "Shen yingmo zixu jin Beida zhi yuanqi" (Shen Yingmo's account of his appointment at Peking University), in Mu and Mu, eds., *Beida gushi*, 223–225.

18. Kai-wing Chow, *The Rise of Confucian Ritualism in Late Imperial China: Ethics, Classics, and Lineage Discourse* (Stanford: Stanford University Press, 1994).

19. Shen, "Shen yingmo zixu jinbeida zhi yuanqi," 223.

20. Shen Yingmo, "Beida de zhangmen dizi" (Zhang Taiyan's disciples at Peking University), in Mu and Mu, eds., *Beida gushi*, 25.

21. Strictly speaking, some of them were more steeped in *liuchao* prose than others, including Lu Xun, Zhou Zuoren, and Liu Shipei, who were hired at Peking University under Chancellor Cai Yuanpei in 1917 and 1920. But generally, these Zhang Taiyan students, with the exception of Huang Kan, had a tendency to appreciate *liuchao* prose more than that of the Tang and Song dynasties. Most of all, it was Zhang Taiyan himself who first elevated *liuchao* prose above that of other dynasties. See Chen Pingyuan, *Zhongguo xiandai xueshu zhijianli, yi zhangtaiyan, hushizhi weizhongxin* (The establishment of contemporary Chinese scholarship that centered on Zhang Taiyan and Hu Shizhi) (Beijing: Peking University Press, 1998), 387–388, 390–391.

22. Shen, "Shen Yingmo zixu jin Beida zhi yuanqi," 224.

23. Zhou Tiandu, *Cai Yuanpei* (Beijing: Renmin chubanshe, 1984), 2–10; Cao Jian, "Jinian xianshi caijiemin xiansheng" (In memory of my former teacher Cai Yuanpei), in *Guoli beijing daxue* (National Peking University) (Taibei: Nanhai chubanshe, 1976), 323–325.

24. Gao Pingshu, *Cai Yuanpei nianpu changbian* (A detailed chronology of Cai Yuanpei, I) (Beijing: Renmin jiaoyu chubanshe, 1996), 1: 245–250.

25. Zhou, *Cai Yuanpei*, 10–40.

26. William Duike, *Cai Yuanpei, Educator and Reformer* (University Park: Pennsylvania State University Press, 1977), 15.

27. Oswald Kulpe, *Zhexue yaolun* (Fundamentals of philosophy), trans. Cai Yuanpei (Shanghai: Shangwu, 1903).

28. Friedrich Paulsen, *Lunlixue yuanli* (A system of ethics), trans. Cai Yuanpei (Taibei: Heluo tushu chubanshe, 1974), 225–378, 411–13, 543, 598.

29. Sun Changwei, *Cai Yuanpei xiansheng nianpu zhuanji* (Biographical chronology of Cai Yuanpei) (Taibei: Guoshiguan, 1985), 1: 248–249.

30. Ruth Hayhoe, *China's Universities 1895–1995: A Century of Cultural Conflict* (New York and London: Garland, 1996), 7, 29.

31. Jean-François Lyotard, *The Postmodern Condition: The Report on Knowledge*, trans. Geoff Benington and Brian Massumi (Minneapolis: University of Minnesota Press, 1984), 32–33.

32. John Craig, *Scholarship and Nation Building: The Universities of Strasbourg and Alsatian Society, 1870–1939* (Chicago: University of Chicago Press, 1984), 13; Chen, "The Chinese Scholars and the Modern University," 105–6.

33. Xiaoqing Diana Chen, "The Chinese Scholars and the Modern University," 106–107.

34. Liu and Fang, *Beida yu Qinghua*, 33.

35. *Diyici Zhongguo jiaoyu nianjian*, 2: 470; Wang Shiru, *Cai Yuanpei xiansheng nianpu* (Chronology of Cai Yuanpei) (Beijing: Peking University Press, 1998), 1: 145–146.

36. It was true that the university closed briefly during the 1911 revolution, and after it was reopened in 1912, only about a hundred students returned, including four from the Science Division and fourteen from the Engineering Division. But that did not warrant Cai's closing the university.

37. Zhang, "Diyiren xiaozhang, Yan Fu," 22–23.

38. Ibid., 20–23.

39. Ibid., 19.

40. Liu and Fang, *Beida yu Qinghua*, 34.

41. Ibid., 35.

42. Wang, *Cai Yuanpei xiansheng nianpu*, 1: 150–174.

43. Shen Yingmo, "Wohe Beida" (Peking University and I), in Wang and Wen, eds., *Wo yu Beida*, 76–77.

44. My interview with Tan Bolu, son of Tan Xihong, at Peking University, May 8–9, 1988.

45. Shen Yingmo, "Wohe Beida," 76.

46. Interview with Tan Bolu, son of Tan Xihong, Peking University, May 8–9, 1998.

47. Li Zhonghua, "Shengming buxi, xinhuo chengchuan," 728.

48. "Liu Shipei yu Cui Shi" (Liu Shipei and Cui Shi), in Zhang Zhongxing, *Honglou diandi* (Brief memories of Peking University), excerpted in Mu and Mu, eds., *Beida gushi*, 218.

49."Beijing daxue zhexuexi jianshi," 6–7.

50. Excerpts of Zhu Haitao, *Beida yu Beidaren* (Peking University and those who have been there), in Chen Pingyuan and Xiao Xiaohong, eds., *Beida jiushi* (Reminiscences of Peking University) (Beijing: Sanlian shudian, 1998), 362–367.; Liu Cunren, "Zai Beida shangke" (Attending classes at Peking University), in Li Hong, ed., *Beida yishi* (Miscellaneous memories of Peking University) (Shenyang: Liaohai chubanshe, 1999), 308–311.

51. Xiao Chaoran et al., eds., *Beijing daxue xiaoshi, 1898–1949*, 192, 199.

52. Li Jun, "Gu Jiegang," in Li, ed., *Beida yishi*, 115–121.

53. Xiao Chaoran et al., eds., *Beijingdaxue xiaoshi, 1898–1949*, 236–237.

54. Yang, "Jiang Menglin yu beijing daxue," 266–267.

55. Xiao et al., *Beijingdaxue xiaoshi, 1898–1949*, 243–253.

56. "Beidade gonggou" (Peking University's prize dog), in Jiang Menglin, "Yi mengzhen" (In memory of Fu Sinian), in Mu and Mu, eds., *Beida gushi*, 177.

57. It seems that Cai Yuanpei was the only president of Peking University who used the word chancellor in English translations of his title, after the German style. Also, see Zhang Ruide, "Jiang Menglin zaonian xingli shangde jiazhi chongtu yu pingheng" (The early value conflicts and equilibrium of Jiang Menglin), in *Jiang Menglin zhuanji ziliao* (Biographical materials of Jiang Menglin) (Taibei: Tianyi chubanshe, 1979), 1: 27–33.

58. Barry Keenan, *The Dewey Experiment in China: Educational Reform and Political Power in the Early Republic* (Cambridge: Harvard University Press, 1977), 63.

59. Ibid., 78.

60. Xiao Chaoran et al., *Beijing daxue xiaoshi*, 235–249.

61. Yang, "Jiang Menglin yu beijing daxue," 274, 284–285.

62. Ibid., 287, 297.

63. "Beijingdaxue xueze, guicheng, 1932–36, wenxueyuan kecheng yilan, 1932–33" (Rules and regulations at Peking University from 1932–36: a survey of the curriculum of the College of Arts, 1932–33) (Peking University Archive, 1933).

64. Yang, "Jiang Menglin yu beijing daxue," 296–297.

65. Xiao et al., *Beijing daxue xiaoshi*, 284.

66. Ibid.

67. Qu, "Zhuchi xiaowu shijian zuichangde xiaozhang, Jiang Menglin," 65; Yang, "Jiang Menglin yu beijing daxue," 279–281.

68. Between 1931 and 1936, the research professors included, from the College of the Arts: Tang Yongtong, Chen Shouyi, Zhou Zuoren, Liu Fu, Xu Zhimo, Zhang Yi, Liang Shiqiu, Ye Gongchao; from the College of the Sciences: Feng Zuxun, Wang Shoujing, Liu Shuqi, Zeng Shaolun, Xu Rang, Wang Jingxi, Ding Wenjiang, Li Siguang, Jiang Zehan, Sa Bendong, Xie Jiarong, Zhang Jingyue, Rao Yutai, Zhu Wuhua, A.W. Grabau, E. Sperner, W.F. Osgood; from the College of Law: Zhao Qiubo, Liu Zhi, Zhang Zhongfu, Wu Dingliang. See Yang, "Jiang Menglin yu beijing daxue," 286.

69. Although in the 1930s Peking University was under greater political control of the university by the Nationalist government, academically, compared with the 1910s and 1920s, between 1930 and 1937, the year the Sino-Japanese war started, it reached a

golden age in both teaching and research thanks to the funding from the China Foundation and Jiang Menglin's capable administration.

## Chapter 4

1. F.R. Ankersmit, "Contemporary Anglo-Saxon Philosophy of History," in idem, *History and Tropology*, 69–70.

2. "Beijing daxue zhexuexi dashiji, 1914–1994" (Important events in the Department of Philosophy, Peking University, 1914–1994), in *Beijing daxue zhexuexi jianshi 1914–1994* (A brief history of the Department of Philosophy at Peking University, 1914–1994) (Beijing: Department of Philosophy, Peking University, 1994), 89–90.

3. *Beijing daxue rikan* (Peking University Daily, henceforth cited as *BDRK*), *BDRK*, September 12, 1922; October 9, 1922.

4. *Yanyuan lunxueji* (Collection of papers on scholarship at Peking University) (Beijing: Peking University Press, 1984), 32; "1935 nian wenxueyuan zhexuexi kecheng yilan" (Bulletin of the curriculum of the Department of Philosophy of the College of Arts in 1935) (Peking University Archive, 1935); "Guoli beijing daxue zhexuexi kecheng zhidaoshu, 1931–32" (Bulletin of the curriculum of the Department of Philosophy at National Peking University, 1931–32) (Peking University Archive, 1932); "Wenxueyuan kecheng yilan, zhexuexi kecheng" (Bulletin of the curriculum of the College of Arts: the Department of Philosophy, 1932–33) (Peking University Archive, 1933).

5. Lu Xun, for instance, criticized Chinese culture metaphorically as sick with hereditary syphilis. Lung-kee Sun, "The Presence of the Fin-de-Siècle in the May Fourth Era," in Gail Hershatter et al., eds., *Remapping China: Fissures in Historical Terrain* (Stanford: Stanford University Press, 1996), 194–209. Also, despite the skepticism toward Freud among many Chinese, Lu Xun employed a Freudian method in several of his stories and showed the conflict between the human conscious and subconscious.

6. Ban Wang, *The Sublime Figure in History*, (Stanford: Stanford University Press, 1997), 22–24.

7. See Laurence Schneider, *Ku Chieh-kang and China's New History: Nationalism and the Quest for Alternative Traditions* (Berkeley: University of California Press, 1971).

8. Wang Hui, "Cong wenhua lunzhan daokexuan lunzhan, kexuepuxi de xiandaifenhua yu dongxi wenhua wenti" (From a cultural debate to one on science and metaphysics, the modern taxonomy of science and the issue of Eastern-Western cultures), *Xueren*, 9 (1996), 132–134, 136.

9. Ibid., 143.

10. Cai Yuanpei, "Yu shidai huabao jizhe de tanhua" (Talk with a journalist from *Contemporary Pictorial Journal*), in Gao Pingshu, ed., *Cai Yuanpei meiyu lunji* (Cai Yuanpei's writings on aesthetics) (Changsha: Hunan renmin chubanshe, 1987), 214.

11. Nie Zhenbin, *Cai Yuanpei jiqi meixue sixiang* (Cai Yuanpei and his aesthetics) (Tianjin: Tianjin renmin chubanshe, 1984), 224–226.

12. Lewis White Beck, "From Leibniz to Kant," in Robert Solomon and Kathleen Higgins, eds., *The Age of German Idealism* (London & New York: Routledge, 1993), 14.

13. Cai Yuanpei, "Kangde meixueshu" (Kant on aesthetics), in Gao, ed., *Cai Yuanpei meiyu lunji*, 37–39.

14. Ibid., 41.

15. Ibid., 39.

16. Anthony La Vopa, "Specialists Against Specialization: Hellenism as Professional Ideology in German Classical Studies," in Geoffrey Cocks and Konrad Jarausch, eds., *German Professions, 1800–1950* (London and New York: Oxford University Press, 1990), 32–33.

17. Cai, "Duiyu jiaoyu fangzhen de yijian" (My views on the educational policies), in Gao, ed., *Cai Yuanpei meiyu lunji*, 5.

18. Nie, *Cai Yuanpei jiqi meixue sixiang*, 239–241.

19. Daniel Bonavae, "Kant's Copernican Revolution," in Solomon and Kathleen, eds., *The Age of German Idealism*, 46–56.

20. Patrick Gardiner, "Kant: Critique of Judgment," in Solomon and Higgins, eds., *The Age of German Idealism*, 103–124.

21. Quoted in ibid., 125–126.

22. Ibid., 119–126.

23. Zheng Jiadong, *Tradition in Disintegration* (*Duanlie zhongde chuantong*) (Beijing: Zhongguo shehuikexue chubanshe, 2003), 65-68.

24. He hardly differentiated between Kant, Friedrich Schiller, and the Italian philosopher Benedetto Croce, for instance, subjecting them all to a pursuit of the transcendental truth. In reality, the latter two emphasized much more than Kant an immanent representation of truth through art. Katharine Everett Gilbert and Helmut Kuhn, *A History of Aesthetics*, (New York: Macmillan, 1939), 359; see also Cai Yuanpei, "Meixue de quxiang," in Gao, ed., *Cai Yuanpei meiyu lunji*, 132–136.

25. Guy Alitto, *The Last Confucian* (Berkeley: University of California Press, 1979), 18–69.

26. For Liang's early life and the reception of his *East West Philosophies*, see ibid.

27. Wang Hui, "Cong wenhua lunzhan dao kexuan lunzhan, kexue puxi de xiandai fenhua yudong xiwenhua wenti" (From culture debate to the debate about science and metaphysics in 1923: the taxonomy of science in modern China and the division of east/west cultures), *Xueren*, 9 (1996): 171–175.

28. Kathleen Higgins, "Arthur Schopenhauer," in Solomon and Higgins, eds., *The Age of German Idealism*, 330–362.

29. Jacques Maritain, *Bergsonian Philosophy and Thomism*, (New York: Greenwood Press, 1968), 67–68.

30. Higgins, "Arthur Schopenhauer," 334.

31. Maritain, *Bergsonian Philosophy and Thomism*, 42.

32. Ibid., 71, 74–77.

33. Liang Shuming, "Zishu zaonian sixiang zhizai zhuanzai bian" (On the changes in my early thought), *Zhongguo zhexue nianjian* (Chinese philosophy annals) (1982), 1, 340; quoted in Yong Ma, *Liang Shuming wenhualilun yanjiu* (A study of Liang Shuming's cultural theories) (Shanghai: Shanghai renmin chubanshe, 1991), 23.

34. Jing Haifeng, "He er butong liang dashi, xiongliang bian nansuo yinfa de wenti yu sikao" (Complementing yet differing from each other, the two philosophers Liang Shuming and Xiong Shili, their questions and our reflections), *Xueren*, 7 (1995), 198.

35. Maritain, *Bergsonian Philosophy and Thomism*, 41.

36. Liang Shuming, "Dongxi wenhua jiqi zhexue" (The cultures and philosophies of the East and the West), in *Liang shuming quanji* (Complete works of Liang Shuming) (Jinan: Shandong renmin chubanshe, 1989), 1: 409–414.

37. Jing Haifeng and Li Yeming, *Liang Shuming Pingzhuan* (A biography of Liang Shuming) (Nanchang: Baihuazhou wenyi, 1995), 53–55.

38. Liang, "Dongxi wenhua jiqi zhexue," 452, 464–465.

39. Ibid., 452–454, 458.

40. In his preface to the third edition of "Dongxi wenhua jiqi zhexue," (1922), in *Liang Shuming quanji*, 1: 321–323; see also Liang's preface to "Renxin yu rensheng," in *Liangshuming quanji* (Jinan: Shandong renmin chubanshe, 1990), in which he mentioned Confucian psychology differed from Western psychology, and his borrowing of Western psychological terms in "Dongxi wenhua jiqi zhexue" was wrong, and so he needed to redo a book on Confucian psychology. See "Zixu" (Preface), in *Liang Shuming quanji*, 1: 327–329. In his 1929 preface to the eighth edition of "Dongxi wenhua jiqi zhexue," he mentioned that he was wrong to use Western psychological terms and that he hoped to use *Kongzi shizhi* (An interpretation of Confucius) to redress his mistakes.

41. Liang, "Renxin yu rensheng," 3: 592–594.

42. Ibid., 599.

43. Jing, "Heerbutongliangdashi, xiongliang biannansuoyinfade wentiyusikao," 205–206.

44. Guo Qiyong, *Xiong Shili sixiang yanjiu* (An intellectual study of Xiong Shili) (Tianjin: Tianjin renmin chubanshe, 1993), 1–18.

45. Jing, "Heerbutongliangdashi, xiongliang biannansuoyinfade wentiyusikao," 203.

46. Maritain, *Bergsonian Philosophy and Thomism*, 76.

47. Ibid.

48. Tu Wei-ming, "Xiong Shi-li's Quest for Authentic Existence," in Charlotte Furth, ed., *The Limits of Change: Essays on Conservative Alternatives in Republican China* (Cambridge: Harvard University Press, 1976), 269–270.

49. Xiong Shili, *Xinwei shilun* (New exposition of consciousness only) (excerpt from the vernacular edition), in Huang Kejian et al., eds., *Xiong Shili ji* (Selected writings of Xiong Shili) (Beijing: Qunyan chubanshe, 1992),124, 132–138, 145–148; Feng Qi, "Xinwei shilun de yipi chengbian yi yu xingxiu buer shuo" (The concepts of "the contraction and extension of life force lead to change" and "human nature and its use cannot be differentiated" in *The Exposition of Consciousness Only*), in Xue Chufu, ed., *Xuanpu lunxueji* (Papers in the garden of metaphysics) (Beijing: Sanlian, 1990), 117; Guo Qiyong and Li Minghua, "Shilun xiongshili zhexue de xingzhi" (On the nature of Xiong's philosophy), in ibid., 262–263; Ran Yunhua, "Xiong Shili dui fojia de pipan" (Xiong Shili's critique of Buddhism), in ibid., 139–140.

50. Jing, "Heer butong liang dashi, xiongliang biannan suoyinfa de wenti yu sikao," 190, 196.

51. Maritain, *Bergsonian Philosophy and Thomism*, 78–79, 120–121, 152.

52. Xiong, *Xinweishilun*, 91.

53. Ibid., 84–85.

54. Tu Wei-ming, "Xiong Shi-li's Quest for Authentic Existence," 264–266.

55. Xiong, *Xinweishilun*, 81–82, 145.

56. Ibid., 150–151, 173, 175, 183.

57. Maritain, *Bergsonian Philosophy and Thomism*, 77–78.

58. Guo, *Xiong Shili sixiang yanjiu*, 302.

59. Zheng Jiadong, Tradition in Disintegraton (*Duanlie zhongde chuantong*), 87.

60. Zheng Shiqu, *Wanqing guocuipai wenhua sixiang yanjiu* (A study of the culture and thinking of the National Essence group in late Qing China) (Beijing: Beijing Normal University Press, 1997), 240–241.

61. Ibid.

## Chapter 5

1. Luo Zhitian, "Zouxiang guoxue yushixue de saixiansheng" (Mr. Science as applied in national learning and history), *Jindaishi yanjiu*, 3 (2000), 73–74.

2. Ankersmit, "Historicism: An Attempt at Synthesis," *History and Theory*,34 (3) (1995), 146–147, 152.

3. Jerome Grieder, *Intellectuals and the State in Modern China* (Cambridge: Harvard University Press), 246.

4. F.R. Ankersmit, "The Sublime Dissociation of the Past: or How to Be(come) What One Is No Longer," *History and Theory*, 40 (3) (October 2001), 315, 317.

5. Tao Menghe, "Xin lishi" (New history), *Xin qingnian* (New Youth), 8(1) (1920), 32, 35.

6. Ankersmit, "Historicism," 143–144.

7. Iggers, "Historicism,", 133, 134, 141, 178–182.

8. *BDRK*, November 29, 1917.

9. The field of history in the Division of the Arts in Zhang Zhidong's curriculum was implemented in 1910, upon the initial operation of the university divisions. History as a field resumed a brief existence after the 1911 revolution but, after the graduation of its twenty-nine students in the summer of 1913, the field of history was closed. It did not enroll students again until the fall of 1917, and its reopening was related to its role in facilitating the state's writing of national history. At Peking University in November 1917, the state Bureau of National History was incorporated into the Humanities Division and renamed the Office of National History Compilation (*guoshi biancuanchu*), with Cai Yuanpei as its head. The office's responsibilities included collecting all relevant historical materials and compiling republican and earlier Chinese histories. Because of the installation of this office, in the summer of 1917 a History Subdivision was created in the Humanities Division, where the office would be located. In 1919, the Office of National History Compilation was moved out of Peking University and attached to the State Council. Niu Dayong, "Beijing daxue shixuexi yange jilue" (A brief review of the development of the History Department at Peking University), *Beida shixue* (History at Peking University), 1 (June 1993), 257–258; Sun Changwei, ed., *Cai Yuanpei xiansheng nianpu zhuanji* (A Biographical chronicle of Cai Yuanpei) (Taibei: Guoshiguan, 1986), 2: 62–65; *BDRK*, March 25, 1919, 3–4; "Guoshiguan tuoli daxue" (The National History Bureau has separated from Peking University), *Chenbao*, August 27, 1919.

10. "Guoli beijing daxue jiangshou guoxuezhi kecheng bing shuomingshu" (Courses on national history and explanations at National Peking University), *BDRK*, October 19, 1920.

11. *BDRK*, December 2, 1917, 3; Prasenjit Duara, *Rescuing History from the Nation, Questioning Narratives of Modern China* (Chicago: University of Chicago Press, 1995), 37–38.

12. Duara, *Rescuing History from the Nation*, 38–39.

13. History curriculum at Peking University for the 1925–26 academic year, *BDRK*, October 9, 1925.

14. History Department curriculum, *BDRK*, October 19, 1921, 2; October 12, 1925, 3.

15. Lao Gan, "Lun luxi huaxiang sanshi, zhuweishishi, kaotangshan, wushici" (Notes on three western Shangdong sculptures in the Han Dynasty), in *Guoli zhongyang yanjiuyuan lishi yuyan yanjiusuo jikan* (Collected papers of the Institute of History and Linguistics, Academia Sinica) (henceforth cited as *LYJK*), 8(1) (1939), 93–127.

16. "Wenke gaiding kecheng huiyiyi jue'an xiuzheng ruzuo" (The final revised version of the meeting to revise the curriculum in the Humanities Division), *BDRK*, December 9, 1917; "1918 wenbenke kecheng" (Curriculum for the Humanities Division for 1918) *BDRK*, September 26, 1918, 2–3; "Guoli beijing daxue jiangshou guowen shuomingshu" (Explanation of Chinese studies instruction at National Peking University), *BDRK*, October 19, 1920, 3–4.

17. Curriculum of the Chinese Languages and Literature Department, *BDRK*, April 30, 1918.

18. "Guoli beijing daxue jiangshou guowen shuomingshu," , *BDRK*, Oct. 19, 1923, 4.

19. Chen, *Zhongguo xiandai xueshu zhijianli*, 202–210.

20. Wang Wenbao, *Zhongguo minsuxue fazhanshi* (History of Chinese folklore studies) (Shenyang: Liaoning daxue chubanshe, 1987). On Gu Jiegang, see Laurence Schneider, *Ku Chieh Kang and China's New History* (Berkeley: University of California Press, 1971). For an overall view of the project as a nationwide phenomenon, see Hong Chang-tai, *Going to the People* (Cambridge: Harvard University Press, 1980). Also, Chen Yi'ai, *Zhongguo xiandai xueshu yanjiu jigou de xingqi—yibei jindaxue guoxue menwei zhongxin de yantao 1922–1927* (The rise of research institutions in modern China: a case study of the National Learning Institute at Peking University, 1922–1927) (Taibei: Zhengzhi daxue, 1999).

20. Chen, *Zhongguo xiandai xueshu zhijianli*, 200–202; Hu Shi, "Lishi de wenxue guannianlun" (A historical approach to literature), *Xin qingnian*, 3(3) (1917), 233–237.

21. Chen, *Zhongguo xiandai xueshu zhijianli*, 202–207.

22. Luo Zhitian, "Xueshu yu guojia, guocui, guogu yu guoxue de sixianglungzheng" (Scholarship and the state, the intellectual debate between national essence, national past, and national learning), *21C*, (Aug. 2001), 103.

23. Luo Zhitian, "Xinsongxue yu minchu kaoju shixue" (Neo-Song dynasty learning and textual exegesis in early republican China), *Jindaishi yanjiu*, 1 (1998), 8–10, 17, 19.

24. Zhang Yue, "Wusishiqi duixinshiliaode jieshou yurenshi" (Unearthing and understanding of the new historical sources during the May Fourth era), *Lishi yanjiu*, 3 (2000), 67–68.

25. Luo Zhitian, "Shiliao de jinliang kuochong yu bukan ershisishi" (The maximum expansion of primary sources of history and the phenomenon of bypassing the 24 dynastic histories), *Lishi yanjiu* 4 (2000), 156.

26. In the curriculum for the academic year 1922–23, freshman Chinese majors would take two courses in literary history and selected works of poetry and prose; the other two required courses would be philology, including a survey, and a course on reading ancient texts. Almost half the elective courses were on philology, including pronunciation, morphology, Old Text, New Text, and mixed Old and New Text readings, theories of music and ancient Chinese music. Furthermore, philology was one of the three special fields to major in, the other two being pure literature (prose, poetry, drama, and novels,) and literature that did not belong to these categories. "Zhongguo wenxuexi kecheng zhi daoshu" (Instructional guide to the curriculum of the Department of Chinese Language and Literature), *BDRK*, October 13, 1921, 4. Although philology was only one of the five courses for freshman Chinese majors in 1923–24, it occupied a very important position in the elective courses. See "Curriculum of the Chinese Language and Literature Department," *BDRK*, September 18, 1923, 3.

27. Curriculum of the Chinese Language and Literature Department, *BDRK*, October 13, 1925, 3.

28. The 1925 specialization was brought about by the need to balance the required and elective courses students took following Chancellor Cai Yuanpei's curriculum reform in 1919, when Chinese Language and Literature became an independent department and, like other departments on campus, required 80 units of credit hours to graduate (one hour per week of class for a year was considered one unit of credit hour), of which half were in required and half in elective classes.

29. "Yuyan wenxue, Zhongguo wenxuexi kecheng yilan" (Language and literature: bulletin of the curriculum at the Department of Chinese language and literature, 1932–33).

30. Luo, "Shiliao de jinliang kuochong yu bukan ershisishi," 160–161.

31. Wang Fan-sen, *Fu Ssu-nien: A Life in Chinese History and Politics* (Cambridge and New York: Cambridge University Press, 2000), 199. On Fu Sinian's patronage of archaeology, also see Q. Edward Wang, *Inventing China Through History: The May Fourth Approach to Historiography* (Albany: SUNY Press, 2001), 121–130.

32. Hao Chunwen, "Dunhuang wenxian he lishi yanjiu de huigu he zhanwang" (A retrospect and prospect of the excavation and historical study of Dunhuang documents), *Lishi yanjiu*, 1 (1998), 112–136; Sang Bing, "Boxihe yu jindai Zhongguo xueshujie" (Paul Pelliot and modern Chinese scholarly community), *Lishi yanjiu*, 5 (1997), 115–138.

33. Zhang Qizhi, ed., *Zhongguo jindai shixue xueshushi* (A History of Modern Chinese Historiography) (Beijing: Zhongguo shehui kexue chubanshe, 1996), 373–457. Sang Bing, "Wanqing minguo shiqide guoxueyanjiu yuxixue" (Chinese studies and Western learning in late Qing and Republican China), *Lishi yanjiu*, 5 (1996), 32–33.

34. Zhu Fenghan, "Jinbai nianlai de yinxujia guwen yanjiu" (On the research on the tortoise shell engravings from the Ying Shang Dynasty ruins in the past hundred years), *Lishi yanjiu*, 1 (1997), 115–116, 127–136.

35. He argued that, before the discovery of the Shang tortoise shells, the vertical and horizontal bars in the *Book of Changes* were often attributed to legendary figures such as Fuxi and Huang Di. But the discovery confirmed speculation of another kind, i.e., the bars actually came from these tortoise shell inscriptions. The *Book of Changes* was but the philosophizing of these divination practices. Rong Zhaozu, "Zhanbude yuanliu" (The origin of divination), *Zhongyang yanjiuyuan lishi yuyan yanjiusuo jikan* (Journal of the History and Linguistics Institute of Academia Sinica), 1(1) (1928), 47–95.

36. Fu Sinian, "Lun suowei wudengjue" (On the so-called five noble rankings), LYJK, 2(1) (1930), 110–128.

37. Dong Zuobin, "Wudengjue zai yinshang" (The five aristocratic ranks in the Yin-Shang Dynasty), in Wang Tianyou et al., *Beijing daxue bainian guoxue wencui* (National essence in the past hundred years at Peking University) (Beijing: Peking University Press, 1998), volume on history, 98–112.

38. Hu Shi, "Shuoru" (On Confucians), LYJK, 4(3) (1934), 233–284.

39. Besides lending credible, scientific evidence to a historical study of Chinese learning, archaeological excavations sometimes also led to the study of the ancient past quite unrelated to Confucian learning. In the case of Huang Wenbi, an archaeologist who had graduated from Peking University as a philosophy major in 1918, it led him to the study of ancient topography. Huang Lie, "Huang Wenbi zhuanlue" (A brief biography of Huang Wenbi), in *Zhongguo xiandai shehui kexuejia zhuanlue* (Biographies of Contemporary Chinese Social Scientists) (Taiyuan: Shanxi renmin chubanshe, 1982), 8: 325–330; Zhang Qizhi, ed., *Zhongguo jindai shixue xueshushi*, 416–417; Huang Lie, "Huang Wenbi xiansheng zhuanlue" (A brief biography of Mr. Huang Wenbi), in idem, ed., *Huang Wenbi xiansheng lishi kaogu lunji* (Collection of Mr. Huang Wenbi's papers on history and archaeology) (Beijing: Wenwu chubanshe, 1989), v–xi.

40. *BDRK*, September 29, 1923, 3; October 2, 1924; October 9, 1925, 1; October 12, 1925, 1; December 3, 1926, 2; December 4, 1926, 2; January 12, 1927, 2; January.15, 1927, 2; January17, 1927, 2; January 19, 1927, 2; Zhu Xizu, "Bianbo beijing daxue shixuexi quanti xuesheng quzhu zhuren zhuxizu xuanyan" (A rebuttal to the "Announcement to expel Zhu Xizu, chairman of the History Department, by all the students of the History Department"), *BDRK*, December 9, 1930, 3–4.

41. *BDRK*, September 29, 1923, 3.

42. Wen-hsin Yeh, *The Alienated Academy: Culture and Politics in Republican China, 1919–1937* (Cambridge: Harvard University Asia Center, 1990), 33, 34.

43. John Henderson, *Scripture, Canon, and Commentary: A Comparison of Confucian and Western Exegesis* (Princeton: Princeton University Press, 1991), 73–74.

44. Chen, *Zhongguo xiandai xueshu zhijianli*, 161–179, 191–193.

45. See Luo Zhitian, "Gujin yu zhongwai de shikong hudong, xinwenhua yundong shiqi guanyu zhengli guogu de sixiang lunzheng" (The interchanges of time and space of the traditional and the modern, and the Chinese and the foreign: the intellectual

debates of sorting out national learning during the New Culture Movement), *Jindaishi yanjiu*, 6 (2000), 80–83, 104–105.

46. Chen, *Zhongguo xiandai xueshu zhijianli*, chaps. 5 and 6.

47. "Beijing daxue shixuexi kecheng zhidaoshu," 1931–32.

48. *Beiping zhoubao*, February 26, 1933.

49. Lu Xun, "Zhongguo xiaoshuo shilue" (A history of Chinese novels), in *Lu Xun quanji* (Complete works of Lu Xun) (Beijing: Renmin wenxue chubanshe, 1973), 7: 149. What Lu Xun meant was perhaps that the classical language could express the same meaning in fewer words than the vernacular could.

50. Ibid., 211–237, 248–49, 281–294.

51. Ibid., 183–200, 248–258, 238–247, 295–322.

52. Fu Shizhong, "Yi yujiyu xiansheng" (In memory of Mr. Yu Jiaxi), in Dong Ding, ed., *Sili Furen daxue* (History of Private Furen University) (Taibei: Nanhai chuban, 1982), 124–129.

53. See Lao Gan, "Zhongguo danshazhi yingyong ji yanbian" (The application and change of use of dansha, or red sand, in Chinese history), *LYJK*, 7(4) (1938), 519–531.

54. Yu Jiaxi, "Hanshisan ji" (Textual analysis of the medicine Hanshisan), *Furen xuezhi* (Scholarly journal of Furen University), 7 (1938), 1969–2003.

55. Yu Jiaxi, "Xiaoshuojia chuyu baiguanshuo" (Textual analysis on the saying that novelists came from the position of petty officials), *Furen xuezhi*, 6(1937), 1683–1695.

56. Mo Runsun, "Xuejian hansong de yujiyu xiansheng" (The Mr. Yu Jiaxi whose scholarship encompassed both Han and Song learning), in idem, *Haiyi zazhu* (Miscellaneous writings, remnants from the sea) (Hong Kong: Xianggang zhongwen daxue chubanshe, 1990), 132.

57. Yu Jiaxi, "Taishigong shuwang piankao" (An exegesis of the missing chapters from Sima Qian's History), in Zhou Zumo, ed., *Yu Jiaxi lunxue zazhu* (Miscellaneous scholarly writings by Yu Jiaxi) (Beijing: Zhonghua shuju, 1963), 10–11; see also Mo Runsun, "Xuejian hansong de yujiyu xiansheng," 131.

58. See Meng Sen, *Mingqingshi jiangyi* (Lectures on the history of Ming and Qing) (Beijing: Zhonghua shuju, 1981), 1–6, 363–381; Wu Xiangxiang, "Mingqingshi quanwei Meng Xinshi" (Meng Sen, authority on Ming and Qing history), in idem, *Mingguo bairenzhuan* (A hundred biographies of the republic) (Taibei: Zhuanji wenxue, 1971), 1: 237–240; Meng Sen, "Qingshi gaozhong jianzhouwei kaobian" (An exegesis of Jianzhouwei in the *History of Qing Dynasty*), *LYJK*, 3(3) (1932), 331–344.

59. Zhu, "Bianbo beijing daxue shixuexi quanti xuesheng quzhu zhuren zhuxizu xuanyan," 3–4.

60. There was relatively little coverage of new literature in the field of Chinese literature except for a course on how to lecture on literature organized by Hu Shi, Zhou Zuoren, and Xu Zhimo, three forerunners of the new literature movement, a course on new literature writing by Hu Shi and his colleagues Zhou Zuoren and Yu Pingbo, and a course on poetry by the new poet Xu Zhimo, in 1931–32. See Xiao et al., eds., *Beijing daxue xiaoshi*, 286.

61. Q. Edward Wang, *Inventing China Through History: The May Fourth Approach to Historiography*, 111–121.

62. *Jingbao*, Apr.25, 1934 (Peking University Archive).

63. "Beijing daxue shixuexi kecheng zhidaoshu," 1931–32. "Wenxueyuan shixuexi kecheng yilan" (Bulletin of the History Department curriculum in the College of Arts) (1935) (Peking University Archive).

64. Wang, *Inventing China Through History*, 171–173; Wang, *Fu Ssu-nien*, 202.

65. Luo Zhitian, "Xueshu yu guojia, guocui, guogu yu guoxue de sixiang lunzheng" (Scholarship and the state, the intellectual debate between national essence, national past, and national learning), 21C, (Aug. 2001), 102–111.

66. "Dengyun" (Equal rhymes), in *Zhongguo dabaike quanshu* (Chinese Encyclopedia) (Beijing: Zhongguo dabaike quanshu chubanshe, 1988), Linguistics Section, 51.

67. Li Jinxi, *Guoyu yundong shigang* (A history of the standard vernacular movement), 3rd ed. (Changsha: Shangwu, 1940), 157–158.

68. "Qieyinzhi" (Phonetic Chinese alphabet), in *Zhongguo Dabaike quanshu*, Linguistics section, 315.

69. H.H. Wu, "Qian Xuantong yu guoyu yundong" (Qian Xuantong and the national vernacular movement), in idem., *Minguo renwu liezhuan* (A history of various people in Republican China) (Taibei: Zhuanji wenxue, 1986), 117–128. On Peking University philologist Mao Yuzao's contribution to the 38 phonemes based on ancient characters finally decided upon by the Ministry of Education in 1913, see Kong Gang, Yang Kangshan, "Beida wuma diyiren Ma Yuzao" (Ma Yuzao, the first of the five "Ma"s at Peking University), in Xiao Chaoran ed., *Weiwei shangyang, bainian xingchen, mingren yu beida* (Stars of the past hundred years—famous people and Peking University) (Beijing: Peking University Press, 1998), 384–385. A popular argument goes that Zhang Bing lin, former teacher to many philologists at Peking University, played an instrumental role in identifying the suitable ancient Chinese charactes as phonemes.

70. Li, *Guoyu yundong shigang*, 160–177, 191–193, 199–306.

71. Luo Zhenyu, "Yesu huishi zaiying yunxueshang de gongxian" (The Jesuits' contributions to phonetics), in *Zhongyang yanjiuyuan lishi yuyan yanjiusuo jikan* (Journal of the History and Linguistics Institute of Academia Sinica), 1(3) (1930), 267–358.

72. Wei Jiangong, "Guyinxueshang de da bianlun—gege yuyu mogu dukao yinqi de wenti" (A big debate on ancient phonetics, caused by the article on the ancient pro-

nunciation of ge, ge yu, yu), in *Beijingdaxue yanjiusuo guoxuemen yuekan* (Monthly of the Institute of Sinology of Peking University), 1(1) (1926), 49–108.

73. Wei Jiangong, *Lun qieyunxi de yunshu* (On pronunciation books that belong to the type of *Qieyun*), in *Beijing daxue bainian guoxue wencui* (National essence in the past hundred years at Peking University) (Beijing: Peking University Press, 1998), volume on language, 87–127.

74. Wei Jiangong, "Zhongguo guying yanjiushang xiege xianjue wenti" (Some pre-eminent issues in the study of ancient Chinese phonetics), *Guoxue jikan*, 3(4) (1932): 612–69.

75. A. Von Stael-Holstein, "Yingyi fanshu yu zhongguo guyin" (Phonetically translated Buddhist books and ancient Chinese pronunciation), in *Guoxue jikan*, 1(1) (1923): 47–56.

76. Wei, "Zhongguo guying yanjiushang xiege xianjue wenti," 640–687.

77. Shen Jianshi, "Zhengli guogude jige timu" (Several topics we can work on to systematize the Chinese past), *Beijing daxue rikan* (Peking University daily), February 18, 1922, 3.

78. Shen Jianshi, "Wenzizhi gexin yanjiu zixingbu"' (Search for language reform from studying word parts), *Beijing daxue yuekan* (Peking University monthly), 1(2) (1919): 35–37.

79. Shen Jianshi, "Guangyun shenxixu jifanli" (On words in the phonetics book Guangyun and examples), *Beijing daxue yuekan*, 1(8) (1921): 73–74.

80. Shen Jianshi, "Guoyuwenti zhilishide yanjiu" (A historical study of the issue of a standard language), *Guoxuejikan*, 1(1) (1923), 57–79.

81. Shen Jianshi, "Youwenshuo zaixunguxue shangzhi yange jituichan" (The evolution and propagation of the "right part" theory in Chinese phonetics), in Academia Sinica, History and Philology Institute, *Qingzhu Cai Yuanpei xiansheng liushiwu zhounian lunwenji* (Papers in celebration of the 65th birthday of Mr. Cai Yuanpei), 777–854.

82. Wei Jiangong, "Huida" (Response [to Shen Jianshi]), in *Qingzhu Cai Yuanpei xiansheng liushiwu zhounian lunwenji*, 847–849; Li Fanggui, "Huida, (response)," in ibid., 849–851.

83. Tang Lan, *Guwenzixue daolun* (Introduction to ancient philology) (originally published in 1935) (Jinan, Shandong: Qilushushe, 1981), 25–294.

84. Zhu Fenghan, "Jin bainian lai de yinxujia guwen yanjiu" (On the research of tortoise-shell words from the Ying Shang ruins in the past hundred years) in *Lishiyanjiu* (Historical Research), 1 (1997), 120.

85. Liu Bannong, "Shi yuxiaoshuo jingshenshang de gexin, jieshao yuehansheng fandai keshi zhi wenxue sixiang" (Spiritual innovations in poetry and novels, on the literary thinking of Johnson and Van Dyke), *Xin qingnian*, 3(5), 421–429; Liu Bannong,

"Wo zhi wenxue gailiangguan" (My views on literary reform), *Xinqingnian*, 3(3): 219–231; Bao Jin, "Liu Bannong zhuanlue" (Biography of Liu Fu), in Bao Jin, ed., *Liu Bannong yanjiu ziliao* (Research materials on Liu Bannong) (Tianjin: Tianjin renmin chubanshe, 1981), 1–10.

86. Liu Bannong, "Ji wafu jigao gei Zhou Qiming" (Sending my collection of poems "Earthern crock" to Zhou Zuoren), in idem, *Bannong wenxuan* (Selected works of Liu Bannong) (Taibei: Zhengwen chubanshe, 1968), 2: 106–109.

87. Liu Bannong, "Guoyu wentizhong yige dazhengdian" (A big contention point on the issue of a national dialect), in idem, *Bannong wenxuan*, 2: 1–6; Liu Bannong, "Guoyu yundong lueshi tiyao" (A brief history of the movement for a national dialect), in ibid., 2: 13–16; Liu Bannong, "Hanyu zisheng shiyanlu tiyao" (An outline of the experiments on the different pronunciations in the Chinese language), in ibid., 2: 7–12.

88. Wei Jiangong, "Zhonghua minguo guguoli beijing daxue jiaoshou Faguo guojia wenxue boshi liuxiansheng xingzhuang" (Life and acts of Mr. Liu, Ph.D. from the state of France, formerly professor of National Peking University of the Republic of China), *Guoxue jikan*, 4(4) (1934): 18–31.

89. Liu Fu, "Zhongxiaozidianxu" (Preface to the dictionary of primary and middle school students), *Guoxue jikan*, 4(4) (1934): 1–15.

## Chapter 6

1. Ankersmit, ""Historicism, An Attempt at Synthesis," 153.

2. Ibid., 154.

3. Georg Iggers, *The German Conception of History; The National Tradition of Historical Thought from Herder to the Present* (Middletown, CT: Wesleyan University Press, 1968), 35–133.

4. Hu Shi, *Zhongguo gudai zhe xueshi dagang* (An outline of ancient Chinese philosophy) (Shanghai: Shangwu, 1918), 1: 11, 34–35; 2: 75.

5. Liang Qichao, "Ping hushizhi Zhongguo zhexueshi dagang" (On Hu Shi's Outline of Chinese Philosophy), in idem, *Yingbingshi wenji* (Collections of the master of the ice tea house), 63 *ce*, 4: 27.

6. Lydia Liu, *Translingual Practice, Literature, National Culture, and Translated Modernity—China, 1900–37* (Stanford: Stanford University Press, 1995), 242–243; see also Martin Bernal, "Liu Shipei and National Essence," in Furth, ed., *The Limits of Change*, 90–112. On a synthesis of national essence and historicism, see Theodore Huters, "A New Way of Writing: The Possibilities for Literature in Late Qing China, 1895–1908," *Modern China* 14(3) (July 1988), 243–258.

7. Sun Shangyang, "Tang Yongtong xueshu fangfa lunshulue" (A brief discussion of Tang Yongtong's scholarly methods), in *Journal of Peking University (Humanities and Social Sciences)*, 35 (2) (1998), 136.

8. Sun Shangyang, "Tang Yongtong de wenhua sixiang" (Tang Yongtong's views on culture), in Zhang Dainian, Tang Yijie, et al., eds., *Wenhua de chongtu yu ronghe* (The clashes and reconciliations of cultures) (Beijing: Peking University Press, 1997), 130.

9. Thomas Nevin, *Irving Babbitt, An Intellectual Study* (Chapel Hill and London: University of North Carolina Press, 1984), 15–47, 89–110; Sun Shangyang, "Tang Yongtong de wenuhua sixiang," 135.

10. Liu, *Translingual Practice*, 247–251.

11. Deng Aiming, "Tang Yongtong xiansheng sanyi" (Miscellaneous reminiscences of Mr. Tang Yongtong), in *Yanyuan lunxueji*, 64.

12. Prasenjit Duara, *Rescuing History from the Nation* (Chicago: The University of Chicago Press, 1995), chap. 1.

13. Tang Yongtong, *Suitang fojiaoshigao* (Lecture notes on the history of Buddhism in China during the Sui and Tang Dynasties) (Beijing: Zhonghua shuju, 1982), 204–208, 212–218. Ren Jiyu, "Tang Yongtong xiansheng zhixuede taidu hefangfa" (Mr. Tang Yongtong's attitude toward scholarship and his methods) in *Yanyuan lunxueji*, 40–41; Tang Yongtong, "Wenhua sixiang zhi chongtu yu tiaohe" (The conflict and reconciliation of cultures), *Xueshu jikan* (Scholarship quarterly) (January 1943), reprinted in idem, *Wangri zagao* (Miscellaneous writings of the past) (Beijing: Zhonghua shuju, 1962), 119–124; Sun Shangyang, "Tang yongtong de wenhuasixiang," 138–143.

14. Zhang Qizhi, "Tang Yongtong guanyu zhongwai wenhua bijiao de guandian he fangfa," 117–118; Tang Yijie, "Changming guocui, ronghua xinzhi" (Clarify and promote the national essence and absorb new knowledge), 102–103; both articles in Zhang Dainian et al., (eds.), *Wenhua de congtu yu ronghe* (The clashes and reconciliations of cultures) (Beijing: Peking University Press, 1997).

15. Sun Shangyang, "Tang Yongtong xueshu fangfa lunshulue," 136–137; Iggers, *The German Conception of History*, 79.

16. On Gu Jiegang, see Laurence Schneider, *Ku Chieh-kang and China's New History*. On Chen Yingque, see Wang Rongzu, *Shijia chenyingque zhuan* (Biography of Chen Yingque, the historian) (Taibei: Lianjing, 1984). On both Chen Yingque and Yao Congwu, see Qingjia Edward Wang, "Chinese Historians and the West: the Origins of Modern Chinese Historiography" (Ph.D. diss., Syracuse University, 1992).

17. Chen Yuan, "Tang ruowang he muchennai," (Johannes Adam Schall von Bell and Mu Chennai) in *Furen xuezhi* (Scholarly journal of Furen University), 7 (1938), 1–28. Idem., "Yongqiañqian feng tianzhujiao zhizhongshi," (Those royal families who were converted to Catholicism during the reigns of Yongzheng and Qianlong) in *Chenyuan xueshulunwenji* (Collection of Chen Yuan's scholarly writings) (Beijing:

Zhonghua shuju, 1980), 156–79. Chen Yuan, "Huihuijiao ruzhongguo shilue," (A brief history of the spread of Islam in China) in *Chenyuan xueshulunwenji*, 542–561. Idem., "Yuanyelikewen jiaokao," (An exegesis on the religion of yelikewen during the Yuan Dynasty) ibid., 1–59. Idem., "Huoaojiao ruzhongguokao," (The study of the spread of Zoroastrianism in China) ibid., 303–28. Idem., "Monijiao ruzhongguokao," (A study of the spread of Manicheanism in China) ibid., 329–97.

18. Ankesmit, "A Reply to Professor Iggers," 168–173.

19. Zheng Jiadong, *Tradition in Disintegration*, 35.

20. Zheng Shiqu, *Wanqing guocuipai wenhua sixiang yanjiu* (A study of the culture and ideas of late Qing champions of National Essence), 2nd ed. (Beijing: Beijing shifan daxue chubanshe, 1997), 112.

21. On the discussion of human rights, see Angle, *Human Rights and Chinese Thought*, chaps. 6–8.

22. "Zhu Xizu xiansheng nianpu" (Chronology of Mr. Zhu Xizu), in *Zhu Xizu xiansheng wenji* (Collected writings of Mr. Zhu Xizu) (Taibei: Jiusi chuban youxian gongsi, 1979), 6: 581–590; see also Luo Xianglin, "Zhu Tixian xiansheng xingzhuang" (Life and history of Mr. Zhu Xizu), in Zhu Xizu, *Shiguan lunyi* (On building a library of national history) (Taibei: Xuesheng shuju, 1978), 236–239.

23. Zhu Xizu, *Zhongguo shixue tonglun*, 2nd ed., (Chongqing: DuLi chubanshe, 1944), 49–69.

24. Iggers, *The German Conception of History*, 109–145.

25. Zhu, *Zhongguo shixue tonglun*, 18–21.

26. Ibid., 19–29.

27. Chen Xinxiong, "Mingguo guyinxue yanjiu kaichuangren Huang Kan" (Huang Kan, the pioneer researcher in archaic speech sounds), *Shidaxuebao* (The scholarly journal of National Taiwan Normal University), 31 (1986): 367–419.

28. Feng Youlan, *Sansongtang zixu* (Autobiography of Three Pine House) (Beijing: Beijing daxue chubanshe, 1984), 37.

29. Huang Jinhong, ed., *Yushi xiangzhu wenxin diaolong* (Annotated edition of *The Literary Heart and the Carving of the Dragon*) (Taibei: Hongdao wenhuashiye, 1976), 108–109, 430–431, 480–481.

30. Huang Kan, *Wenxin diaolong zhaji* (Notes on *The Literary Mind and the Carving of Dragons*) (Shanghai: Zhonghua shuju, 1962), 20, 31–34; Huang, *Yushi xiangzhu*, 66–68.

31. Huang, *Yushi xiangzhu*, 122–123.

32. Huang, *Wenxin diaolong zhaji*, 68–69.

33. Liu Shipei, *Zhongguo zhonggu wenxueshi* (A history of medieval Chinese literature) (Hong Kong: Shangwu, 1958), which is based on Liu's lecture notes at Peking University, 1917–19.

34. Peter Zarrow, *Anarchism and Chinese Political Culture* (New York: Columbia University Press, 1990), 2–19, 37–38.

35. I am grateful to Peter Zarrow for pointing out this paradox to me. On the other hand, Liu was famous for his pendulum-like swings in political position largely because of his pursuit of political fame.

36. Zarrow, *Anarchism and Chinese Political Culture*, 83–86.

37. Ibid., 40.

38. Bernal, "Liu Shipei and National Essence," 96–98, 104–105.

39. Ibid., 106.

40. Liu, *Zhongguo zhonggu wenxueshi*, 8–9, 33.

41. Zarrow, *Anarchism and Chinese Political Culture*, 43–45.

42. Liu, *Zhongguo zhonggu wenxueshi*, 13, 33–64.

43. Hao Chang, *Chinese Intellectuals in Crisis* (Berkeley: University of California Press, 1987), 151, 154, 159.

44. "Huang Jie," in Zhong Bike and Sun Caixia, eds., *Minguo renwu beizhuanji* (Collection of tombstone notes and biographies of Republican China) (Chengdu: Sichuan renmin chubanshe, 1997), 750–751.

45. Huang Jie, *Shixue* (Poetics) (Beijing: Guoli beida chubanbu, 1918), 17–26.

46. Ibid., 1.

47. Xiaobing Tang, *Global Space and the Nationalist Discourse of Modernity: The Historical Thinking of Liang Qichao* (Stanford: Stanford universityPress, 1996), 198–202.

48. Liang Qichao, *Zhongguo jin sanbainian xueshushi* (Chinese intellectual history in the past three hundred years) (Shanghai: Fudandaxue chubanshe, 1985), 140–145, 179–182.

49. Qian Mu, *Zhongguo jin sanbainian xueshushi* (Chinese intellectual history in the past three hundred years) (Chongqing: Shangwu yinshu, 1946), 6–10, 76, 294–306; see also Wu Xiangxiang, "Qian Mu chanyang chuantong wenhua" (Qian Mu's elaboration on traditional Chinese culture), in idem, *Minguo bairenzhuan* (Biographies of a hundred people in republican China) (Taibei: Zhuanji wenxue, 1971), 4: 189–199; Jerry Dennerline, *Qian Mu and the World of Seven Mansions* (New Haven: Yale University Press, 1988).

50. Qian Mu, *Bashiyi shuanqin, shiyou heyi* (Reminiscences of my parents, teachers, and friends at eighty) (Taibei: Dongda tushu, 1983).

## Chapter 7

1. Liu and Fang, "Beida yu Qinghua," 109.

2. *BDRK*, October 9, 1922.

3. "Zhexuexi quanti tongxue tanhuahui jilu" (Record of the conference of all students from the Philosophy Department) *BDRK*, June 12, 1923, 2.

4. *BDRK*, September 27, 1924.

5. *BDRK*, November 25, 1926.

6. Peter Bol, *This Culture of Ours: Intellectual Transitions in Tang and Sung China* (Stanford: Stanford University Press, 1992), 100.

7. According to an anecdote about a class that Zhang audited, the Japanese instructor declared that, as one ages, one's memory also declines. Zhang almost banished the course from the curriculum because he thought the instructor was implying that he was too old to remember anything. Recounted in Zou Shuwen, "Beijing daxue zuizaoqi de huiyi" (Memories of the earliest days of Peking University), *Zhuanji wenxue*, 3(6) (1963), 38–39.

8. Wang Xingguo, *Yangchangji de shengping ji sixiang* (The life and thought of Yang Changji) (Changsha: Hunan renmin chubanshe, 1981), 7–8.

9. Yang Changji, *Dahuazhai riji* (Diary from Dahuazhai) (Changsha: Hunan renmin chubanshe, 1981), 9–11.

10. Wang, *Yangchangji de shengping ji sixiang*, 30–43.

11. Ibid., 49–67.

12. Ibid., 174.

13. Yang, *Dahuazhai riji*, 161–63, 165, 169–173, 175–205.

14. Wang, *Yangchangji de shengping ji sixiang*, 174–175; see also, Guo Tingyi and Shen Yunlong, "Cong gaoxiao dao beida de qiuxue shengya" (My schooling from higher primary school to Peking University),, an interview with Tian Peilin recorded by Winston Xie (Hsieh), Taibei, February 18 and 27, 1960, *Koushu lishi* (Oral history), 2 (1991).

15. Yang, *Dahuazhai riji*, 196–97.

16. Ralph Blake, *Theories of Scientific Method* (Seattle, University of Washington Press, 1960), 276.

17. "Xinlixuexi kecheng zhidaoshu" (Bulletin of the curriculum of the Department of Psychology, 1926–27), *BDRK*, April 14, 1927, 2; April 15, 1927, 2; April 16, 1927, 2; April 18, 1927, 2; April 20, 1927, 2; May 9, 1927, 2.

18. Zhou Jinhua, *Jingshi renshi, chenda qizhuan* (Teacher of classics, and teacher of man: a biography of Chen Daqi) (Taibei: Shangwu, 1986), 64–67.

19. Chen Daqi, *Mixin yu xinli* (Superstition and psychology) (Beijing: Peking University Press, 1922), 5, 64–65.

20. Zhou, *Jingshi renshi, chenda qizhuan*, 1–12.

21. Chen Daqi, "Shishipanduan hejiazhipanduan" (Judgments based on facts and on values), *BDRK*, 1(3) (1923), 447–460.

22. Chen Daqi, "Zhenli shishenmo" (What is truth?), *BDRK*, 2(1) (1923), 1–12.

23. Chen Daqi, "Renshide lunlide yiyi" (The logical perspective of knowledge), *BDRK*, 2(4) (1924), 489–496.

24. Chen Daqi, "Biranpanduan yushiranpanduan" (Assertoric and apodeictic judgments) *BDRK*, 4(3–4) (1929), 1–24.

25. Chen Daqi, "Beijing gaoxiao nushengdaode yishizhidiaocha" (A survey of the moral awareness of girls in Beijing higher primary schools), *Beijing daxue yuekan*, 1. 4 (1919), 23–52.

26. Zhou, *Jingshi renshi, chenda qizhuan*; Chen Daqi, "Xiandai xinlixue" (Contemporary psychology), *BDRK* (April 18–May 9, 1918).

27. Fritz Ringer, *The Decline of the German Mandarins: The German Academic Community, 1890–1933* (Cambridge: Harvard University Press, 1969), 312–313.

28. Murray Leaf, *Mind and Science: A History of Anthropology* (New York: Columbia University Press, 1979), 127.

29. Raymond Fancher, *Pioneers of Psychology*, 2nd ed. (New York: Norton, 1990), 167.

30. Chen Daqi, *Xinlixue dagang* (Beijing: Beijing daxue, 1918).

31. Peter Manicas, *A History and Philosophy of the Social Sciences* (Cambridge, Mass.: Basil Blackwell, 1989), 190, 234–235, 261.

32. JoAnne Brown, *The Definition of a Profession: The Authority of Metaphor in the History of Intelligence Testing, 1890–1930* (Princeton: Princeton University Press, 1992), 68–72.

33. Guo Renyuan, "Yige xinlixue gemingzhe de kougong" (The testimony of a revolutionary in psychology), *Dongfang zazhi* (The Eastern Miscellany, henceforth cited as *DFZZ*), 24(5) (1927), 49–57.

34. Guo Renyuan, "Fandui benneng yundong de jingguo he wo zuijin de zhuzhang" (The movement against the instinct theory and ideas I have recently championed), *BDRK* (March 31, 1924).

35. Zhang Jingyuan, *Psychoanalysis in China: Literary Transformations, 1919–49* (Ithaca: Cornell University East Asia Program, 1992), 28.

36. Gao Zhuo, "Yi xingweizhuyi de guandian jiangmeng" (A behaviorist interpretation of dreams), *DFZZ*, 25(10) (1928), 57–64.

37. Fan Jichang, "Xingweipai de sixiangguan" (The outlook of the behaviorists), in Shu Xincheng, ed., *Xinli zazhi xuancun* (Selected papers from psychological journals) (Shanghai: Zhonghua shuju, 1932), 17–22.

38. Gao Juefu, "Gaojuefu zizhuan" (Autobiography of Gao Juefu), in *Zhongguo xiandai shehui kexuejia zhuanlue* (Taiyuan: Shanxi renmin chubanshe, 1983), 4: 309.

39. Brown, *The Definition of a Profession*, 68–73.

40. Zhao Zonghua, ed., "MaCall yu litingfang xiansheng tan jiaoyu xinli ceyan zhi shixin fangfa" (A record of the interview of W.A. McCall by Liu Tingfang on the implementation of educational psychological testing), *Educational Review* 15(2) (1923): 22697–22716.

41. Chen, "The Chinese Scholars and the Modern University," 110–111.

42. *Jiaoyu zazhi* (Educational Review), 23(9) (1933), 135.

43. Tao Xisheng, "Zhongguo xuexiaojiaoyushi deguancha" (An observation of the history of Chinese education), *Educational Review*, 22(5) (1930), 34761–34768.

44. Jiang Wenyu (Hengyuan), "Muqian Zhongguo jiaoyu yingquzhi fangzhen ji zhiye jiaoyu shishi zhi biaozhun" (Policies current Chinese education should adopt and criteria governing professional education), *Educational Review*, 24(1) (1934), 17–24.

45. Xiao Encheng, *Ertong xinlixue* (Child psychology) (Beijing: Peking University Press, 1934).

46. Wu Junsheng (Ou Tsuin-chen), professor of education at Peking University (1931–36). A Jiangsu native, Wu obtained a bachelor's degree in education from National Southeastern University. After 1925, he started teaching at the high school attached to Southeastern University before leaving for the University of Paris in 1928 to study education. He received his Ph.D. in education in 1931 and,having received an invitation from Peking University, came to teach at the Education Department the same year. Wu Junsheng (Ou Tsuin-chen), *Jiaoyu shengya yizhoujia* (My sixty years of teaching) (Taibei: Zhuanji wenxue, 1976), 1–15.

47. Wu Junsheng, "Zhongguo jiaoyu xuyao yizhong zhexue" (We need a philosophy to guide Chinese education), in *Jiaoyu luncong* (Collection of essays on education) (Taibei: Zhonghua shuju, 1957), 36–47.

48. Wu Junsheng (Ou Tsuin-chen), *Jiaoyu zhexue dagang* (An outline of educational philosophy), 7th ed. (1934, reprinted Taibei: Shangwu, 1965).

49. Ibid.

50. Wu Junsheng, "Zhongguo jiaoyujie yingyouzhi zijue" (The self-awareness that we in the Chinese educational community ought to have), in idem, *Jiaoyu luncong*, 59–66.

51. While a student at Southwestern University, Wu doubted Dewey's educational theories, which was one reason he found the theories on society by Durkheim more

attractive, and studied at the University of Paris under Paul Façonnet, a student of Durkheim's. Eventually, though, Wu did write his dissertation on Dewey, "The Educational Theories of John Dewey" (La doctrine pédagogique de John Dewey), in 1931. Wu, *Jiaoyu shengya yizhoujia*, 16–17, 43–47.

52. "Jiaoyuxue benxuenian kechengbiao" (Curriculum of the Department of Education in 1930), *BDRK*, October 21, 1930, 1–2.

53. "Jiaoyuxi jiaoshouhui qishi" (Notice by the Professors' Conference of the Department of Education), *BDRK*, September 17, 1931, 3–4.

54. Jiang Yongjing et al., *Yangliangong xiansheng nianpu* (Chronology of Mr. Yang Lianggong) (Taibei: Lianjing chuban, 1988), 177, 179–180, 189–201.

55. "1931–1932 jiaoyu xuexi kecheng zhidaoshu" (Bulletin of the curriculum of the Department of Education in 1931–32) (Peking University Archive); "1932–1933 jiaoyuxi kecheng shoumingshu" (Bulletin of the curriculum of the Department of Education in 1932–33) (Peking University Archive); "1935 nian wenxueyuan jiaoyuxuexi kecheng yilan) (Bulletin of the curriculum of the Department of Education, College of the Arts, in 1935) (Peking University Archive).

56. Qiu Chun, *Xuezhi* (Educational Systems) (Shanghai: Shangwu, 1934).

57. "Xinlixuexi kecheng zhidaoshu, 1930–31" (Bulletin of the curriculum of the Department of Psychology, 1930–31), *BDRK*, October 24, 1930, 2–3; "Ershi niandu xinlixi kecheng dagang" (Bulletin of the curriculum of the Department of Psychology, 1931–32), *BDRK*, September 10, 1931, 4.

58. *Beiping chenbao*, May 18, 1934 (Peking University Archive).

59. Suzanne Pepper, *Radicalism and Educational Reform in Twentieth-Century China: The Search for an Ideal Development Model* (New York and London: Cambridge University Press, 1996), 72.

60. Julia Strauss, "Symbol and Reflection of the Reconstituting State: The Examination Yuan in the 1930s," *Modern China*, 20(2) (1994), 212–216.

61. Liu Tingfang, "Jinri Zhongguo zhibu jingqi yu pochanzhi quxiang" (China's dim present and its prospect of bankruptcy), *Dagongbao* (The Great Justice Daily), March 12, 1934, 11.

62. Xia Qian, "Guanyu zhongxue xunyuwenti yingyoude renshi" (What people should know about middle school political/moral education), *Dagongbao*, March 12, 1934, 11.

63. Zhang Huai, "Xunyulilunde jiantao" (An examination of political/moral educational theories), in ibid.

64. Xia Qian, "Zhongxue jiaoyumubiao yuzhongxuejiaoyu degaijin" (Educational goal for middle schools and how to improve middle school education), *Dagongbao*, August 27, 1934; idem, "Zhongxue xunyu zaiminzu fuxing mubiaoxia suoying zhuyi de

yige wenti" (A question middle school politics classes should pay attention to under the goal of national revival), *Dagongbao*, April 29, 1935; idem, "Xiuzheng houzhi zhongxue kecheng" (The revised middle school curricula), *Dagongbao*, December 16, 1935.

65. Zhang Huai, "Pingge jiaoyu" (Character education), *Dagongbao*, February 15, 22; March 1, 8, 1937.

66. See Charles Hayford, *Going to the People, James Yen and the Dingxian Experiment* (New York: Columbia University Press, 1987), and Alitto, *The Last Confucian*.

## Chapter 8

1. Liu Yingrui, *Zhongguo renshi zhidu xinlun* (A new thesis on the Chinese personnel system) (Taibei, publisher NA, 1972), 370–371.

2. Tao Xisheng, "Cai xiansheng ren beida xiaozhang dui jindai Zhongguo fasheng de juda yingxiang" (The tremendous influence Mr. Cai had on modern China during his chancellorship at Peking University), *Zhuangji wenxue*, 31(2) (1977), 21–22; Cai Yuanpei, "Wozai jiaoyujie de jingyan" (My experience in the educational community), *Zhuanji wenxue*, 10(1) (1967), 119–122.

3. Xiao Chaoran et al., *Beijing daxue zhengzhixue yu xingzheng guanlixi xishi, 1898–1998* (History of the Department of Political Science and Administration Management, 1898–1998) (Beijing: Peking University Department of Political Science and Administration Management, 1998), 14.

4. *BDRK*, October 17, 1921.

5. Cai, "Wozai jiaoyujie de jingyan," 119–122.

6. *BDRK*, May 8, 1922.

7. *BDRK*, June 16, 1923.

8. *BDRK*, September 19, 1923; July 19, 1924; September 24, 1924; September 25, 1924.

9. *BDRK*, September 21, 1923; September 17, 1924; October 5, 1925.

10. Chen Ruiyun, *Xiandai Zhongguo zhengfu* (Contemporary Chinese governments) (Changchun: Jilin wenshi, 1988), 63–65; Wang Shijie, "Zhongguo xianxing faling yu geren ziyou" (Present Chinese laws and individual freedom), *Beijing daxue shehui kexue jikan* (hereafter cited as *BDSKJK*) (Peking University Social Sciences Quarterly), 1(2) (1923), 222; idem, "Jinglu yu falu" (Police law and civil law), *Xiandai pinglun* (Contemporary Review, hereafter cited as *XDPL*), 21 (1925).

11. Yan Shutang, "Sifar zhongzhanyouguandian zhiliangda zhengdian" (Two controversial points regarding possession in civil law) *BDSKJK*, 1. 3(1923): 491–506.

12. Yan Shutang, "Guojifa yu guonei fashang zhengzhi fan wenti" (The issue of political prisoners in international and domestic law), *BDSKJK*, 1(4) (1923), 45–57.

13. Yan Shutang, "Xingshi zeren wenti" (Criteria for criminal punishment), *BDSKJK*, 1(4) (1923), 607–617.

14. Yan Shutang, "Quanli zhiguannian" (The concept of rights), *BDSKJK*, 1(1) (1922), 63–78.

15. Yan Shutang, "Yingmeizhi peishen zhidu" (The jury system in Britain and the United States), *BDSKJK*, 3(1) (1924), 91–104.

16. Yan Shutang, "Falu zhizhicai" (Legal punishment), *BDSKJK*, 2(2) (1924), 215–227.

17. "Wang Shijie xiansheng xingshu" (An account of the life and work of Mr. Wang Shijie), in *Guoshiguan xiancang mingguo renwu zhuanji* (Biographies of people in Republican China currently available at the National History Bureau), 40; Howard Boorman, *Biographical Dictionary of Republican China*, (New York: Columbia Unuversity Press, 1967–1979), 3: 395a–397a.

18. Boorman, *Biographical Dictionary of Republican China*, 3:395a–397a; *XDPL*, 1924–28.

19. Wang Shijie, "Zhongguo xianxing faling yurenshenziyou" (Current Chinese legal codes and personal freedom), *BDSKJK*, 1(2) (1923), 217–241.

20. My colleague the late Rhiman Rotz first alerted me to the use of state prosecutors in grand jury indictments. Famous trials of recent years such as that of O.J. Simpson and Andrea Yates certainly bore this out. Peter Zarrow kindly points out that in the United States today, it is always prosecutors who bring cases to grand juries for formal indictments. And in England, there is a very rare procedure whereby private individuals can begin criminal legal proceedings against someone.

21. Wang Shijie, "Guojia dui renmin de peichang zeren" (The state's responsibility for compensation), *BDSKJK*, 1(4) (1923), 585–606.

22. Wang Shijie, "Junren de renshen ziyou yenlun ziyou yu zhengzhiquan" (Freedom of speech and person of the soldier and his political rights), *DFZZ*, 22(3) (1925), 13–20.

23. Wang Shijie, "Zhe jizhong faling haibu fei zhima?" (Isn't it high time to void these laws?), *XDPL*, 61 (1926), 4–7.

24. Wang Shijie, "Lun lianbangzhi zhi jixing yu paibie" (On the basic characteristics and a classification of federal governments), *BDSKJK*, 1(3) (1923), 383–406; Wang Shijie, Lianbangxianfa yu fayuan" (The federal constitution and the courts), in ibid., 2(2) (1924), 171–196; idem, "Xingzheng he yizhi" (On the merger between the executive and the legislative), in ibid., 3(1) (1924), 49–82.

25. Wang Shijie, "Demokelaxi yu daiyizhi" (Democracy and the system of representation), *DFZZ*, 18(14) (1921), 122–125; idem, "Pingzhengfu tichu de guomin daibiao huiyi tiaoli" (On the state proposed procedures for the convocation of a national people's conference), *XDPL*, 9 (1925), 4–6.

26. Wang Shijie, "Caichanquan xingzhizhixinyi" (New views on the nature of private property), *BDSKJK*, 2(1) (1923), 25–43.

27. Wang Shijie, *Bijiao xianfa* (Comparative constitutional laws), 5th ed. (Shanghai: Shangwu, 1937), 15–18, 207–208, 212–215.

28. Wang Shijie, "Feichang guohui de xiaoxi" (News of the convocation of an extraordinary parliament), *XDPL*, 5 (1925), 2–3.

29. Wang Shijie, "Gonghui tiaoli wenti" (The issue of stipulations on the establishment of trade unions), *XDPL*, 40 (1925), 5–8; idem, "Zhongguo gonghuifa wenti" (The issue of trade union laws in China), *DFZZ*, 24(3) (1927), 5–16.

30. Cao Jie, "Lingshi caipanquan zhi duzhi shangyang ji woguo chexiao cizhi zhi fangfa" (The overuse of the extraterritoriality clause and method for our country to abolish it), *BDRK*, 1(8) (1921), 41–45.

31. Chen Hansheng, *Sige shida de wo* (My life in four historical eras) (Beijing: Zhongguo wenshi, 1988), 35–36; Zhou Gengsheng, "Shanghai zujie de xingzhiji zuzhi" (The nature and organization of Shanghai foreign concessions), *XDPL*, 27 (1925), 4–7; idem, "Zhengfu dui huande waijiao," in ibid., 28 (1925), 5–7; Wang Shijie, "Hu hanan jian de jiejue tiaojian" (Conditions for settling the Shanghai and Hankou incidents), in ibid., 29 (1925), 4–6; idem, "Women duiyu hanan de guancha" (Our observations on the Hankou incident settlement), in ibid., 110 (1927), 2–3.

32. Xiao et al., *Beijing daxue zhengzhixue yu xingzhengguanlixi xishi*, 13.

33. Gao Yihan, *Zhongguo yushi zhidu de yange* (The development of the Chinese censorial system) (Shanghai: Shangwu, 1930); Gao Yihan, *Zhongguo neige zhidu de yange* (A history of the cabinet system in China) (Shanghai: Shangwu, 1930).

34. Tang Hualong, preface to Gao Yihan, *Geguo difang zhidu gangyao* (Outline of the local institutions of various countries) (Beijing: Translation Bureau, Ministry of the Interior, 1917).

35. Gao Yihan, *Zhengzhixue gangyao* (Outline of a study of politics) (Shanghai: Shenzhou guoguangshe, 1930), 1.

36. Gao Yihan, "Fei junshi zhuyi" (On not having the ruler also serve as the teacher), *Xin qingnian*, 5(6) (1918), 583–588.

37. Gao, *Zhengzhixue gangyao*, 2–3, 61–111.

38. Gao Yihan, "Du liang rengong geming xianxu zhiyuanlilun" (On Liang Qichao's theory on the continuation of revolution), *Xin qingnian*, 1(4), 295.

39. Gao Yihan, "Gongheguo yu qingnianzhi zijue" (The republic and the spontaneous behavior expected of the youth), *Xin qingnian*, 1(2) (1915), 123.

40. Gao Yihan, "Minyue yu bangben," *Xin qingnian*, 1(3) (1915), 205–210.

41. Gao Yihan, "Lelizhuyi yurensheng" (Utilitarianism and life), *Xin qingnian*, 2(1) (1916), 29–34.

42. Gao Yihan, "Du mier de ziyoulun" (On reading Mill's *On Liberty*), *Xin qingnian*, 4(3) (1917), 233–237.

43. Gao Yihan, "Lianbang jianguozhi" (A federal government for China), *DFZZ*, 22(1) (1925), 34–44; idem, "Keerde guojia xingzhi xinlun" (New formulations of the nature of the state by G.D.H. Cole), *BDSKJK*, 1(2) (1923), 205–217; idem, "Fubing shehuizhuyi pai de fangfa he lilun" (The methods and theories of Fabian socialism), in ibid., 2(2) (1924), 131–145.

44. Zhang Weici, *Zhengzhi zhidu qianshuo* (A brief account of political systems) (Shanghai: Shenzhou guoguangshe, 1931), 49–53, 189–191, 253–261.

45. Ibid., 33–34.

46. Zhang Weici, "Erguo geming qianhou shehui jieji zhuangquang" (The conditions of the social classes before and after the Russian Revolution), *DFZZ*, 23(4) (1926), 5–16.

47. Zhang Weici, "Zhanhou de Ouzhou zhongdeng jieji" (The European middle class after World War I), *DFZZ*, 23(23) (1926), 13–24.

48. Zhang Weici, "Ouzhou de xinxianfa" (The new constitutions in Europe), *DFZZ*, 19(22) (1922), np; idem, "Bolan zhi huifu jiqi zuijin de zhengzhi zhuangquang" (The recovery of Poland and its recent political situation), *DFZZ*, 24(2) (1927), 1–12; idem, "Bolodihaiyanan de jige guojia" (The Baltic countries), in ibid., 13–19.

49. Zhang Weici, *Zhengzhixue dagang* (An outline of political science) (Shanghai, Shangwa, 1932), 24; idem, "Meiguo laodong yundong ji zuzhi" (The labor movements and organizations in America), *Xin qingnian*, 7(6) (1919), 917–931.

50. Zhang Weici, "Meiguo chengshi zizhi de yuezhang zhidu" (The Municipal home rule charter system in the United States),*Xin qingnian*, 7(2) (1919), 183–195.

51. I owe this observation of "good government" politics to Peter Zarrow.

52. "Faxueyuan falu xuexi kecheng yilan" (Bulletin of the curriculum of the Department of Law in the College of Law) (1935) (Peking University Archive).

53. Chen Qixiu, "Zhengzhixi kecheng siyi" (My personal views on the curriculum of the Department of Political Science), *BDRK*, December 16, 1930, 3–4.

54. "Faxueyuan yuanzhang bugao," *BDRK*, September 22, 1931, 2.

55. "Faxueyuan zhengzhi xuexi kecheng yilan."

56. *Beiping chenbao*, September 20, 1935 (Peking University Archive).

57. *Beida xunkan*, nos. 2–4, April 10, 1936.

58. Xiao et al., *Beijing daxue zhengzhixue yu xingzheng guanlixi xishi*, 11–12.

59. Chen Qixiu, "Guojia gaizhi yu shijie gaizhi" (The political transformation of a state and the political transformation of the world), *Beijing daxue yuekan* , 1(1) (1919), 13–24; idem, "Shumin zhuyi zhi yanjiu" (The study of the democracy) in ibid., 25–32;

idem, "Hufaji nongfa zhi falixuede yiyi" (The legal implications of defending or manipulating the law), in ibid., 1(2) (1919), 17–26; idem, "Guojia zhi benzhi jiqi cunzai zhiliyou" (The nature of the state and the rationale for its existence), in ibid., 1(6) (1920), 1–10; idem, "He weifa?" (What is the meaning of law?), in ibid., 11–17; idem, "Xiandai zhi jingji sichao ji jingji xuepai" (Contemporary economic schools of thought), in ibid., 29–34; idem, "Guomin jingji zhi yiyi" (The meaning of national economy), in ibid., 35–40; idem, "Guominquan zhi zhonglei qi cunzai liyou jiqi dengci" (The types of citizens' rights, their rationale, and degree of authority), *BDSKJK*, 1(2) (1923), 461–489;idem, "Zhongguo gaizao he tade jingji beijing" (The reconstruction of China and the economic background), *BDSKJK*, 1(2) (1923), 273–285.

60. Chen, *Sige shida de wo*, 1–29, 32–43.

61. For a detailed analysis of the background surrounding Chen Hansheng's turn to empirical research, see Yung-chen Chiang, *Social Engineering and the Social Sciences in China, 1919–1949* (Cambridge and New York: Cambridge University Press, 2001), chap.7.

62. Chen Hansheng, "Zhongguo nongcun jingji yanjiuzhi faren" (The beginning of Chinese rural economic research), in *Guoli zhongyang yanjiuyuan shehui kexue yanjiusuo shehui xuezu 1920–30 nian gongzuo baogao* (Report of the Sociology Group, Social Sciences Research Institute, Academia Sinica, 1929–30), reprinted in Wang Xi and Yang Xiaofo, eds., *Chen Hansheng wenji* (Selected Papers of Chen Hansheng) (Shanghai: Fudan daxue chubanshe, 1985), 31–42.

63. Chen, *Sigeshida de wo*, 45,

64. Chiang, *Social Engineering and the Social Sciences in China*, 184–198.

65. Chen, *Sige shida de wo*, 45–48; idem, "Zhongguo nongmin danfu de fushui" (The taxation on Chinese peasants), in Wang and Yang, ed., *Chen Hansheng wenji*, 1–30; idem, "Xiandai Zhongguo de tudi wenti" (The current land ownership system in China), in ibid., 47–73.

66. See also Chiang, *Social Engineering and the Social Sciences in China*, chap. 8, for a detailed discussion of Lenin's influence on Chen.

67. Chen Hansheng, "Gongye ziben yu Zhongguo nongmin" (Industrial capital and Chinese peasants), in *Chen Hansheng wenji*, 110–123; idem, *Sige shida de wo*, 48–50.

68. Zhou Rusong, "Zhong Gengsheng xiansheng zhuanlue" (A biography of Mr. Zhou Gengsheng), in *Zhongguo dngdai shehui kexuejia xiaozhuan* (Taiyuan: Taiyuan renmin chubanshe, 1982), 15: 153–155.

69. Zhou Gengsheng, "Women suoyao de yige shanhou huiyi" (The kind of settlement conference that we would like to have), *XDPL*, 1(2) (1924), 5–7; idem, "Yuefa wenti de jiejue" (How to solve the problem of the authority of the invalidated constitutional laws), *XDPL*, 1(3) (1924), 4–7; idem, "Duan zhengfu de zhengce ruci" (So that was the kind of policies of the Duan Qirui government), *XDPL*, 1(7) (1925), 3–5; idem, "Shiju de weiji" (The imminence of the present situation), in ibid., 1(13) (1925), 4–6.

70. Zhou, "Zhong Gengsheng xiansheng zhuanlue," 158.

71. Zhou Gengsheng, "Zujie de falu de xingzhi" (The legal status of foreign concessions in China), *BDSKJK*, 2(1) (1923), 67–85; idem, "Lieqiang zai hua shili fanwei tiaoyue de genju" (The basis of treaties certifying foreign powers' concessions in China), in ibid., 4(1–2) (1925–26), 105–132.

72. Zhou Gengsheng, "Shanghai zujie de xingzhi jizuzhi" (The nature and organization of Shanghai's foreign concessions), *XDPL*, 2(27) (1925), 4–7; idem, "Zhengfu duihuan de waijiao" (Chinese government's diplomacy over the Shanghai incident), *XDPL*, 2(28) (1925), 5–7; idem, "Huan jiaoshe de buzhou" (Steps toward solving the Shanghai incident), *XDPL*, 2(31) (1925), 3–5.

73. Zhou Gengsheng, "Changren guoji caipan fayuan zuzhi fapingyi" (Comments on the organization laws of the permanent international arbitration court), *BDSKJK*, 1(1) (1922), 79–103; idem, "Diyuequan zhi xianzhi" (Limits on state power over treaties with foreign countries), *BDSKJK*, 1(2) (1923), 181–204; idem, "Yingshu zhi mindi de guoji diwei" (The international status of British colonies), *BDSKJK*, 2(4) (1924), 441–471; idem, "Guoji zhongcai yu Rineiwa yidingshu" (International arbitration and the Geneva Protocol for the Pacific Settlement of International Disputes), *BDSKJK*, 3(2) (1925), 159–180; idem, "Guoji lianmeng yu guojifa" (The League of Nations and international law), *BDSKJK*, 3(3) (1925), 329–349.

74. Zhou Gengsheng, "Guojitiaoyue chenglizhi tiaojian," *BDSKJK*, 1(3) (1923), 407–428.

## Conclusion

1. For a more detailed discussion of life at Xinanlianda, see John Israel, *Lianda: A Chinese University in War and Revolution* (Stanford: Stanford University Press, 1998).

2. Chen Yi'ai, *Zhongguo xiandai xuesh uyanjiu jigou de xingqi, yi beijing daxue yanjiusuo guoxuemen wei zhongxin de tantao, 1922–1927* (The rise of modern academic research institutions in China, a case study of the Peking University Research Institute of Chinese Studies, 1922–27) (Taibei: Guoli zhengzhi daxue lishixuexi, 1999).

3. Cf., Wang, "Cong wenhua lunzhan daokexuan lunzhan, kexuepuxi de xiandai fenhua yu dongxi wenhua wenti," 171–175.

4. Luo Zhitian, "Xinsongxue yu minchukaoju shixue" (Neo-Song Confucianism and textual exegesis in early Republican China), *Jindaishi yanjiu*, 1 (1998), 1–36.

5. Joseph Levenson, *Confucian China and Its Modern Fate, a Trilogy* (Berkeley: University of California Press, 1968).

# Bibliography

## Newspapers and Journals


Beida Zhoukan
Beiping Chenbao
Beiping zhoubao
Beijing daxue rikan
Beijing daxue shehui kexue jikan
Beijing daxue yanjiusuo guoxuemen yuekan
Beijing daxue yuekan
Chenbao
Dagongbao
Dongfang zazhi
Furen xuezhi
Guoli zhongyang yanjiuyuan lishi yuyan yanjiusuo jikan
Guoxue jikan
Jiaoyu zazhi
Meizhou pinglun
Nuli zhoubao
Xiandai pinglun
Xinchao
Xin qingnian


## Archival Sources


Faxueyuan falu xuexi kecheng yilan (Bulletin of the curriculum of the Department of Law in the College of Law), 1935. Peking University Archive.

Guoli beijing daxue zhexuexi kecheng yilan (Bulletin of the Department of Philosphy of the College of Arts), 1931–1932, 1935. Peking University Archive.

Jiaoyu xuexi kecheng zhidaoshu (Bulletin of the curriculum of the Department of Education), 1931–1932, 1932–1933, 1935. Peking University Archive.

Tu, Ji. "Jingshi daxuetang zhongguoshi jiangyi." (Lecture notes on Chinese history) Peking University Library, 1903.

Unokichi, Hattori. "Jingshidaxuetang xinlixue jiangyi." (Lecture notes on psychology at the Imperial Peking University.) Peking University Library, 1903.

Wang, Zhouyao. "Jingshike jiangyi," (Lecture notes in the field of Confucian classics) Peking University Library, 1903.

Wenxueyuan kecheng yilan, zhexuexi kecheng (Bulletin of the curriculum of the College of Arts: the Department of Philosophy), 1932–1933. Peking University Archive.

## Other Sources

Alitto, Guy. *The Last Confucian*. Berkeley: University of California Press, 1979

Angle, Stephen. *Human Rights and Chinese Thought: A Cross-Cultural Inquiry*. Cambridge: Cambridge University Press, 2002.

Ankersmit, F.R. *Narrative Logic: A Semantic Analysis of the Historian's Language*. The Hague, Boston, and London: Martinus Nijhoff, 1983.

Ayers, William. *Chang Chih-tung and Educational Reform in China*. Cambridge: Harvard University Press, 1971.

Chen Hansheng. *Sige shidai de wo* (I in four historical eras). Beijing: Zhongguo wenshi chubanshe, 1988.

Chen Pingyuan. *Beida jinshen ji qita* (The spirit of Peking University, etc.). Shanghai: Shanghai wenyi chubanshe, 2000.

———. *Lao Beida de gushi* (Story of old Beida). Nanjing: Jiangsu wenyi chubanshe, 1998.

———. *Zhongguo xiandai xueshu zhijianli* (The establishment of modern scholarship in China). Beijing: Peking University Press, 1998.

Chen, Xiaoqing Diana. "The Chinese Scholars and the Modern University: The Appropriation of Foreign Educational Models, 1900–30." In *History of Higher Education Annual*, 1993: 99–116.

Chen Yi-ai. *Zhongguo xiandai xueshu yanjiu jigou de xingqi, yi Beijing daxue yanjiusuo guoxuemen wei zhongxin de tantao, 1922–1927* (The rise of modern academic research institutions in China, a case study of the Peking University Research Institute of Chinese Studies, 1922–27). Taibei: Guoli zhengzhi daxue lishi xuexi, 1999.

Chiang, Yung-chen. *Social Engineering and the Social Sciences in China, 1919–1949*. Cambridge and New York: Cambridge University Press, 2001.

Chow, Kai-wing. *The Rise of Confucian Ritualism in Late Imperial China: Ethics, Classics, and Lineage Discourse*. Stanford: Stanford University Press, 1994.

Dong Zuobin. "Yingxu yange" (History of the Yin Xu site). *Guoli zhongyang yanjiuyuan lishi yuyan yanjiusuo jikan* (Academia Sinica Bulletin of the National Research Institute of History and Philology), 2, pt. 2 (1930), 224–240.

———. "Wudengjue zaiyingshang" (The five titles of the feudal system in the Shang Dynasty). *Guoli zhongyang yanjiuyuan lishi yuyan yanjiusuo jikan* (Academia Sinica Bulletin of the National Research Institute of History and Philology), 6, pt. 3 (1936), 413–430.

Duara, Prasenjit. *Rescuing History from the Nation: Questioning Narratives of Modern China*. Chicago: University of Chicago Press, 1995.

Duiker, William. *Cai Yuanpei, Educator and Reformer.* University Park: Pennsylvania State University Press, 1977.

Fu Sinian. "Lunsowei wudengjue" (On the five titles of the feudal system of the Zhou Dynasty). *Guoli zhongyang yanjiuyuan lishi yuyan yanjiusuo jikan* (Academia Sinica Bulletin of the National Research Institute of History and Philology), 2, pt. 1 (1930), 110–129.

Gao Pingshu. *Cai Yuanpei nianpu changbian* (A detailed chronology of Cai Yuanpei). 3 vols. Beijing: Renmin jiaoyu chubanshe, 1996.

Gilbert, Katherine Everett, and Helmet Kuhn. *A History of Aesthetics*. New York: Macmillan, 1939.

Grieder, Jerome. *Intellectuals and the State in Modern China*. Cambridge: Harvard University Press, 1980.

Guo Jianrong et al., eds. *Beijing daxue shiliao*, 1898–1911 (Historical documents of Peking University, 1898–1911). Vol. 1. Beijing: Peking University Press, 1993.

Hao Chunwen. "Dunhuang wenxian he lishi yanjiu de huigu he zhanwang" (A retrospect and prospect of the excavation and historical study of Dunhuang documents). *Lishi yanjiu* (Historical Research), 1 (1998), 112–136.

Hardy, Grant. *Worlds of Bronze and Bamboo: Sima Qian's Conquest of History*. New York: Columbia University Press, 1999.

Hayford, Charles. *To the People: James Yen and Village China*. New York: Columbia University Press, 1990.

Hayhoe, Ruth. *China's Universities 1895–1995: A Century of Cultural Conflict*. New York and London: Garland, 1996.

Henderson, John. *Scripture, Canon, and Commentary: A Comparison of Confucian and Western Exegesis*. Princeton: Princeton University Press, 1991.

Hu Shi. "Shuo ru" (On the origin of the "ru" and their relationship to Lao Zi and Confucius). *Guoli zhongyang yanjiuyuan lishi yuyan yanjiusuo jikan* (Academia Sinica Bulletin of the National Research Institute of History and Philology), 4, pt. 3 (1934), 233–284.

Huters, Theodore. "A New Way of Writing, the Possibilities for Literature in Late Qing China, 1895–1908." *Modern China*, 14(3) (1988), 249–254.

Israel, John. *Lianda, A Chinese University in War and Revolution*. Stanford: Stanford University Press, 1998.

Karl, Rebecca, and Peter Zarrow, eds. *Rethinking the 1898 Reform Period, Political and Cultural Change in Late Qing China*. Cambridge: Harvard University Asia Center, Harvard University Press, 2002.

Keenan, Barry. *The Dewey Experiment in China: Educational Reform and Political Power in the Early Republic*. Cambridge: Harvard University Press, 1977.

Lao Gan. "Zhongguo dansha zhiyingyong jiqi tuiyan" (The original and applied uses of red sand in Chinese history). *Guoli zhongyang yanjiuyuan lishi yuyan yanjiusuo jikan* (Academia Sinica Bulletin of the National Research Institute of History and Philology), 7, pt. 4 (1938), 519–531.

Lin, Xiaoqing C. "Social Science and Social Control: The Case of Peking University, 1910s–1920s." *Chinese Science*, 14 (1997), 71–89.

———. "Historicizing Subjective Reality: Rewriting History in Early Republican China." *Modern China*, 25(1) (1999), 3–41.

———. "Yongshengming ziran fazhan de guandian lai jianli ershi shiji xinlixing: xifang meixue yu Cai Yuanpei sixiang" (The Establishment of a New Rational Man, Western Aesthetics and Cai Yuanpei, Chancellor of Peking University). In Ding Shisun et al., eds., *Cai Yuanpei yanjiu ji* (Proceedings of the International Conference on Cai Yuanpei, 1868–1998), 212–221. Beijing: Peking University Press, 1999.

Liu Longxin. *Xue shu yu zhi du : xue ke ti zhi yu xian dai Zhongguo shi xue de jian li* (Academy and institution: The disciplinary process and the foundation of modern Chinese historiography). Taibei: Yuanliu, 2002.

Liu Yingrui. *Zhongguo renshi zhidu xinbian* (A new history of Chinese bureaucratic development). Taibei: author, 1972.

Lund, Renville. "The Imperial University of Peking." Ph.D. diss., University of Washington, 1956.

Luo Zhitian. "Xinsongxue yu minchu kaoju shixue" (Neo-Song Dynasty learning and textual exegesis in early republican China). *Jindaishi yanjiu*, 1 (1998), 1–36.

———. "Xueshu yu guojia, guocui, guogu yu guoxue de sixiang lungzheng." (Scholarship and the state, the intellectual debate between national essence, national past, and national learning). *Ershiyi shiji*, 8 (2001), 102–110.

Ma Xulun. *Wo zai liushisui yiqian* (Before I turned sixty). Shanghai: Shenghuo, 1947.

———. *Ma Xulun xueshu lunwenji* (Collections of Ma Xulun's scholarly papers). Shanghai: Kexue, 1958.

Ma Yue. *Beijing daxue zhongwenxi jianshi, 1910–1998* (A brief history of the Department of Chinese Languages and Literature at Peking University, 1910–1998). Beijing: Peking University Press, 1998.

Maritain, Jacques. *Bergsonian Philosophy and Thomism*. New York: Philosophical Library, 1955.

Meng Sen. "Qingshigao zhong jianzhouwei kaobian" ("Jianzhouwei" in "Qingshikao"). *Guoli zhongyang yanjiuyuan lishi yuyan yanjiusuo jikan* (Academia Sinica Bulletin of the National Research Institute of History and Philology), 3, pt. 3 (1932), 331–344.

Metzger, Thomas. *Escape from Predicament: Neo-Confucianism and China's Evolving Political Culture*. New York: Columbia University Press, 1977.

Min, Tu-ki. *National Polity and Local Power: the Transformation of Late Imperial China*. Cambridge: Harvard University, Council on East Asian Studies, 1989.

Paulsen, Friedrich. *Lunlixue yuanli* (A system of ethics), tr. Cai Yuanpei. Taipei: Heluo tushu chubanshe, 1974.

Qu Shipei. *Zhongguo daxue jiaoyu fazhanshi* (A history of university development in China). Taiyuan: Shanxi jiaoyu chubanshe, 1993.

Sang Bing. "Boxihe yujindai zhongguo xueshujie" (Paul Pelliot and modern Chinese scholarly community). *Lishi yanjiu*, 5 (1997), 115–138.

———. "Wanqing minguo shiqi de guoxue yanjiu yuxixue" (Chinese studies and Western learning in late Qing and Republican China). *Lishi yanjiu*, 5 (1996), 30–45.

Schwarcz, Vera. *The Chinese Enlightenment: Intellectuals and the Legacy of the May Fourth Movement of 1919*. Berkeley: University of California Press, 1986.

Schwartz, Benjamin. "History in Chinese Culture: Some Comparative Reflections." *History and Theory*, 35(4) (December 1996): 32–33.

Sun, Changwei. *Cai Yuanpei xiansheng nianpu zhuanji* (Biographical chronology of Cai Yuanpei). Vol. 1. Taipei: Guoshiguan, 1985.

Sun, Lungkee. *The Chinese National Character: From Nationhood to Individuality*. Armonk, NY: M.E. Sharpe, 2002.

———. "The Presence of the Fin-de-Siècle in the May Fourth Era." In Gail Hershatter et al., eds., *Remapping China: Fissures in Historical Terrain*, 194–209. Stanford: Stanford University Press, 1996.

Tang Yijie, ed. *Beida xiaozhang yu Zhongguo wenhua* (Peking University presidents and Chinese culture). Beijing: Peking University Press, 1998.

Wang, Fan-sen. *Fu Ssu-nien, A Life in Chinese History and Politics*. Cambridge: Cambridge University Press, 2000.

Wang Hui. "Sai Xiansheng zai Zhongguo de mingyun" (The fate of Mr. Science in China). *Xueren*, 1 (1991), 49–123.

Wang, Q. Edward. *Inventing China Through History: The May Fourth Approach to Historiography*. Albany: SUNY Press, 2001.

Wang, Shiru. *Cai Yuanpei xiansheng nianpu* (Chronology of Cai Yuanpei). 2 vols. Beijing: Peking University Press, 1998.

Wang Shiru and Wen Di, eds. *Wo yu beida* (Beida and I). Beijing: Peking University Press, 1998.

Wei, Jiangong. "Guyin xueshang de dabianlun—gegeyuyu mogu dukao yinqi de wenti" (A big debate on ancient phonetics, caused by the article on the ancient pronunciation of ge, ge yu, yu). *Beijing daxue yanjiusuo guoxuemen yuekan* (Monthly of the Institute of Sinology of Peking University), 1(1) (1926), 49–108.

Weston, Timothy. *The Power of Position: Beijing University, Intellectuals, and Chinese Political Culture, 1898–1929*. Berkeley: University of California, Berkeley, 2004.

White, Hayden. *The Content of the Form: Narrative Discourse and Historical Representation*. Baltimore and London: Johns Hopkins University Press, 1987.

Wu, H.H. "Qian Xuantong yu guoyu yundong" (Qian Xuantong and the national vernacular movement). In Wu, *Minguo renwu liezhuan* (A history of various people in Republican China), 117–128. Taibei: Zhuanji wenxue, 1986.

Xiao Chaoran, ed. *Weiwei shangxiang, bainian xingchen, mingren yu beida* (Stars of the past hundred years—famous people and Peking University). Beijing: Peking University Press, 1998.

Xiao Chaoran et al. *Beijing daxue zhengzhixue yu xingzheng guanlixi xishi 1898–1998* (History of the Political Science and Administration Management Department, 1898–1998). Beijing: Beijing daxue zhengzhixue yu xingzheng guanlixi, 1998.

Yang Cuihua. "Jiang Menglin yu Beijing daxue, 1930–37" (Jiang Menglin and Peking University). *Zhongyang yanjiuyuan jindaishi yanjiusuo jikan* (Collection of the Modern History Institute of Academia Sinica), 17 (December 1988), 261–305.

Yang Jialuo, ed. *Zhongguo jindaishi wenxian huibian, wuxu bianfa wenxian huibian* (Collected documents of modern Chinese history: The Hundred Days Reform, I). Vol. 1. Taipei: Dingwen Press, 1973.

Yeh, Wen-hsin. *The Alienated Academy: Culture and Politics in Republican China, 1919–1937*. Cambridge: Council on East Asian Studies, Harvard University, 1990.

Zhang Heling. "Xiushen lunli jiaoyu zashuo jiangyi" (Lecture notes on a miscellaneous treatment of self-cultivation, ethics, and education). Peking University Library, 1903.

Zhao, Yuanren. "Liu Bannong xiansheng" (Mr. Liu Bannong). *Guoli zhongyang yanjiuyuan lishi yuyan yanjiusuo jikan* (Academia Sinica Bulletin of the National Research Institute of History and Philology), 4, pt. 4 (1934), 489–490.

Zheng Shiqu. *Wanqing guocuipai wenhua sixiang yanjiu* (A study of the culture and ideas of the late Qing National Essence champions). Beijing: Beijing shifan daxue, 1997.

Zhu Fenghan. "Jinbai nianlai de yinxujia guwen yanjiu" (On the research on the tortoise shell engravings from the Ying Shang Dynasty ruins in the past hundred years). *Lishi yanjiu*, 1 (1997), 115–139.

# Index